The Adamantine Songs

(*Vajragīti*)

By Saraha

The American Institute of Buddhist Studies (AIBS), in affiliation with the Columbia University Center for Buddhist Studies and Tibet House US, has established the Treasury of the Buddhist Sciences series to provide authoritative English translations, studies, and editions of the texts of the Tibetan Tengyur (*bstan 'gyur*) and its associated literature. The Tibetan Tengyur is a vast collection of over 3,600 classical Indian Buddhist scientific treatises (*śāstra*) written in Sanskrit by over 700 authors from the first millennium CE, now preserved mainly in systematic 7th–12th century Tibetan translation. Its topics span all of India's "outer" arts and sciences, including linguistics, medicine, astronomy, socio-political theory, ethics, art, and so on, as well as all of her "inner" arts and sciences such as philosophy, psychology ("mind science"), meditation, and yoga.

Volumes in this series are numbered with catalogue numbers corresponding to both the "Comparative" (*dpe bsdur ma*) Kangyur and Tengyur ("CK" and "CT," respectively) and Derge (Tohoku numbers) recensions of the Tibetan Tripiṭaka.

THE DALAI LAMA

Letter of Support

The foremost scholars of the holy land of India were based for many centuries at Nālandā Monastic University. Their deep and vast study and practice explored the creative potential of the human mind with the aim of eliminating suffering and making life truly joyful and worthwhile. They composed numerous excellent and meaningful texts. I regularly recollect the kindness of these immaculate scholars and aspire to follow them with unflinching faith. At the present time, when there is great emphasis on scientific and technological progress, it is extremely important that those of us who follow the Buddha should rely on a sound understanding of his teaching, for which the great works of the renowned Nālandā scholars provide an indispensable basis.

In their outward conduct the great scholars of Nālandā observed ethical discipline that followed the Pāli tradition, in their internal practice they emphasized the awakening mind of *bodhichitta*, enlightened altruism, and in secret they practised tantra. The Buddhist culture that flourished in Tibet can rightly be seen to derive from the pure tradition of Nālandā, which comprises the most complete presentation of the Buddhist teachings. As for me personally, I consider myself a practitioner of the Nālandā tradition of wisdom. Masters of Nālandā such as Nāgārjuna, Āryadeva, Āryāsaṅga, Dharmakīrti, Candrakīrti, and Śāntideva wrote the scriptures that we Tibetan Buddhists study and practice. They are all my gurus. When I read their books and reflect upon their names, I feel a connection with them.

The works of these Nālandā masters are presently preserved in the collection of their writings that in Tibetan translation we call the Tengyur (*bstan 'gyur*). It took teams of Indian masters and great Tibetan translators over four centuries to accomplish the historic task of translating them into Tibetan. Most of these books were later lost in their Sanskrit originals, and relatively few were translated into Chinese. Therefore, the Tengyur is truly one of Tibet's most precious treasures, a mine of understanding that we have preserved in Tibet for the benefit of the whole world.

Keeping all this in mind I am very happy to encourage a long-term project of the American Institute of Buddhist Studies, originally established by the late Venerable Mongolian Geshe Wangyal and now at the Columbia University Center for Buddhist Studies, and Tibet House US, to translate the Tengyur into English and other modern languages, and to publish the many works in a collection called *The Treasury of the Buddhist Sciences*. When I recently visited Columbia University, I joked that it would take those currently working at the Institute at least three "reincarnations" to complete the task; it surely will require the intelligent and creative efforts of generations of translators from every tradition of Tibetan Buddhism, in the spirit of the scholars of Nālandā, although we may hope that using computers may help complete the work more quickly. As it grows, the *Treasury* series will serve as an invaluable reference library of the Buddhist Sciences and Arts. This collection of literature has been of immeasurable benefit to us Tibetans over the centuries, so we are very happy to share it with all the people of the world. As someone who has been personally inspired by the works it contains, I firmly believe that the methods for cultivating wisdom and compassion originally developed in India and described in these books preserved in Tibetan translation will be of great benefit to many scholars, philosophers, and scientists, as well as ordinary people.

I wish the American Institute of Buddhist Studies at the Columbia Center for Buddhist Studies and Tibet House US every success and pray that this ambitious and far-reaching project to create *The Treasury of the Buddhist Sciences* will be accomplished according to plan. I also request others, who may be interested, to extend whatever assistance they can, financial or otherwise, to help ensure the success of this historic project.

May 15, 2007

The Adamantine Songs

(*Vajragīti*)

By Saraha

Study, Translation,
and Tibetan Critical Edition

By
Lara Braitstein

Treasury of the Buddhist Sciences series
Tengyur Translation Initiative
CT 1179, 1180, 1181 (Toh. 2269, 2270, 2271)

Published by
The American Institute of Buddhist Studies
at Columbia University in New York

Co-published with
Columbia University's Center for Buddhist Studies
and Tibet House US

New York
2014

Treasury of the Buddhist Sciences series
Tengyur Translation Initiative
A refereed series published by:

American Institute of Buddhist Studies
Columbia University
80 Claremont Avenue, room 303
New York, NY 10027

http://www.aibs.columbia.edu

Co-published with Columbia University's Center for Buddhist Studies and Tibet House US

Distributed by Columbia University Press

Printed in the United States of America on acid-free paper.

24 23 22 21 20 19 18 17 16 15 14 5 4 3 2 1

ISBN 978-1-935011-17-0 (cloth)

Library of Congress Cataloging-in-Publication Data

Braitstein, Lara, 1971- author, translator.
The adamantine songs (Vajragiti) / by Saraha ; study, translation, and Tibetan critical edition by Lara Braitstein.
pages cm. -- (Treasury of the Buddhist sciences series ; CT 1179–1181)
Includes bibliographical references and index.
ISBN 978-1-935011-17-0 (cloth : alk. paper)
1. Mahamudra (Tantric rite) 2. Sarahapada, active 8th century. I. Sarahapada, active 8th century. Songs. Selections. English. II. Sarahapada, active 8th century. Songs. Selections. Tibetan. III. Title.
BQ7699.M34B73 2014
294.3'85--dc23

2014029906

Contents

Series Editor's Preface

I am delighted to welcome to our Treasury of the Buddhist Sciences series Professor Lara Braitstein's excellent study, translation, and critical edition of the Tibetan translation of the *Adamantine Songs* of the great adept of the Unexcelled Yoga Tantras, the glorious Saraha. The previous studies of these "enlightenment" or "adamantine" songs have been relatively few in the past, since the cryptic utterances of the great adepts are rightly considered hard to understand. At first glance, they seem on the surface to be the spontaneous poetic outbursts of unconventional yogi masters, avoiding the excessive technical terminologies of the highly sophisticated Indic philosophers or the Tantric yogic adepts, usually considered by scholars to be mutually exclusive types of practitioners. Yet, like some of the great poetry of other cultures, the adepts' verses are often cryptic and elliptical. Even worse, in their wealth of allusions and even in their critiques of others, they seem to presuppose—even in their ways of praising the nonconceptual, the nondual, the trans-intellectual—that their listeners themselves are familiar with the complex conceptualities of the Indic psychological sciences. Therefore, with a few notable exceptions, scholars have been hesitant to venture into this area of adamantine songs, songs that emerge from the adamantine reality of the clear light of the void, the deepest level, sub-quantum, infinite energy that makes life in the universe possible and actually enjoyable.

In our multi-generational, mammoth project to excavate and translate the entire set of classical Indic Buddhist works from their translations preserved in the Tibetan Tengyur ("Treatise Translation") collection, Saraha's *Adamantine Songs* text is a pleasant departure from the more technical philosophy or inner-science-manual types of works that constitute the majority of the treatises therein translated. For the great Saraha is concerned only with the great bliss experience of the freedom of the void, the supreme bliss that seems to well up from human beings' deepest experience of reality. I am particularly intrigued with Braitstein's apt treatment of such "mystical" experience with her innovative terms "decognition" (Tib. *dran med*, Skt. *asmṛti*), as opposed to "recognition" (Tib. *dran pa*, Skt. *smṛti*), the former being the trans-mindful, nonconceptual mental state that is the subtle subjectivity that can blissfully melt ("de-cognize") into the initial experience of selflessness or emptiness as a disappearance into a void space of luminosity, only to once again flow around and throughout the ongoing latter mindful, conceptual functioning of "recognition," until in the "Great Seal" communion experience of nondual reality the two are decognized-recognized as the single-taste immersion of buddhahood. As Braitstein translates from Saraha:[1]

> Therefore, the Great Seal is the highest union:
> Recognition, decognition and the unborn are united.
> Decognition, which is the nature of nonconceptuality, and
> Recognition, which is dependently arisen and adventitious,
> These two have one taste in the unborn nature.
> The arisen and arising are beyond the intellect.
>
> The union of emptiness and clear light etc.,
> ...Compassion and emptiness, indivisible and unborn.

As for her eloquent explanation of the great bliss that is the special province of the great adepts and the Tantric depth psychologies that they master and teach, I was partiucularly truck by her explantion of what is perhaps the most central concept of all:[2]

> "The innate" appears at important junctures in the *Adamantine Songs*, although it does not appear with the same frequency as the term "Great Seal," for example. It is synonymous with the Great Seal and also carries with it the connotation of great bliss. I will discuss in particular the implications of nonduality inherent in the term as it appears not only in the *Adamantine Songs* but in the *Dohā Trilogy* as well. Where it appears in the songs it always points to the inseparability of self and other, experience and phenomena, and crucially and ultimately to saṁsāra and nirvāṇa. An analysis of the term will clarify. The Sanskrit *sahaja* is derived from *jati*—to be born—and *saha*, which means "together with." It connotes a sense

---

[1] Cf. below, pp. 116, 140.

[2] Cf. below., p. 28.

> of things coming into being simultaneously with each other. This sense is equally present in the Tibetan term. *Skye pa* means "born" or "arisen," and *lhan gcig* means "together with," or "spontaneously." What those things are that are simultaneously arising are appearance and emptiness; saṁsāra and nirvāṇa. In other words, everything is completely pervaded by every other thing, and for one like Saraha who is awakened, the experience of that indivisibility is great bliss.

In the present moment of our contemporary culture, people are waking up to the possibility of freedom from the high level of stress, dissatisfaction, and frenetic busy-ness that is even disruptive to health as well as the harmonious functioning of society; they are waking up to the idea that the "innate" energy within living reality is great bliss, a natural happiness not derived from conventional causes (such as success, fame, wealth, relationships, etc.), and that therefore happiness is something to be enjoyed rather than merely to be pursued. Some austerely spiritual personalities (including even some Buddhists) may confuse those motivated in this direction with people who are selfishly hedonistic in the pursuit of conventional pleasures. In such a climate, it is a relief to have a solid scholar like Braitstein put forward such teachings from a great adept as eminent as Saraha and defend its straighforward interpretation. The realization that what is most innate in life is in fact bliss is of course utterly consonant with the fundamental teaching of Shākyamuni Buddha, who declared that enlightenment is the discovery by intuitive wisdom that real reality, true reality, ultimate reality, is ("innately") nirvana, blissful freedom from suffering, in contrast with which ignorance-driven life is bound to be frustrating, inadequate, and unremitting suffering.

As ever, we have many people to thank. First of all the Tibetan and Mongolian scholar-lamas who opened the treasury of the Sutras, Tantras, and their associated literature of scientific and literary treatises: the late Venerable Geshe Ngawang Wangyal; the late Kyabjey Lingtsang Rinpochey; His Holiness the Dalai Lama; the late Venerable Tara Tulku Rinpochey; the late Eminence, Serkhong Tsenshab Rinpochey; the late Professor Masatoshi Nagatomi; Dr. Lozang Jamspal. I proudly and heartily thank the present author, Professor Lara Braitstein, for her patient, sustained, and insightful labor of love in researching, introducing, translating, editing, and annotating these extremely important texts of the Great Adept Saraha.

Lastly, among the many generous benefactors of the American Institute of Buddhist Studies over forty years, I must especially thank the anonymous benefactor of the Jey Tsong Khapa Endowment of the Columbia University Department of Religion's Center for Buddhist Studies; the Infinity Foundation; the Conanima Foundation; the Sacharuna Foundation; Mr. Marc Benioff and Mrs. Lynne Benioff for their generous, world-changing support; Mr. Pierre and Mrs. Pamela Omidyar for their generous and insightful support of such works; and Mr. William T. Kistler, Mrs. Eileen Kistler, and Mr. Brian Kistler of the Kistler Foundation for their visionary recognition that amid the many crises and catastrophes afflicting the multitudes of suffering beings around the world, the research and translation needed to open the door for the modern mind to the inner or spiritual science of the Buddhist tradition remains a high priority for the awakening of humanity—such awakening to the immediate possibility of the true happiness being perhaps essential to empower us to rise to the challenges we all face together at this critical planetary moment.

Robert A.F. Thurman (Ari Genyen Tenzin Choetrak)

Jey Tsong Khapa Professor of Indo-Tibetan Buddhist Studies, Columbia University;
President, American Institute of Buddhist Studies;
Director, Columbia Center for Buddhist Studies;
President, Tibet House US.

Ganden Dekyi Ling
Woodstock, New York
November 10, 2013 CE
Tibetan Royal Year 2140, Year of the Water Snake

Author's Preface

I first became aware of the existence of these poems early in 2000 when I was scouring the footnotes in Herbert Guenther's *Ecstatic Spontaneity*. I don't remember what I was looking for at that time, but I do remember the thrill that ran through me when I imagined what treasures I might find in the as-yet untranslated cycle of three Mahāmudrā songs by Saraha. My curiosity and excitement drove me to begin translating them, though my failure to find even a single commentary on them made the work slow and cautious. As I was to discover, Saraha's *Vajragīti* had not only been neglected by modern scholarship, but by the Tibetan traditions that had preserved them as well. I consulted Lamas, Khenpos, Geshes, and university-trained scholars—most had not heard of these poems, or if they had, they were familiar with the titles only. Mention Saraha's name and the works that immediately come to everyone's mind are his *dohās*. As the years wore on and I continued in my struggle to work through the poems, I remember very clearly the cold dread that gripped me when one fine day I considered the possibility that these songs had perhaps been neglected in favour of Saraha's *dohās* for a very good reason. I prefer not to dwell on that thought. But since that solitary day with Dr. Guenther's footnotes I have successfully dragged many more people into a relationship with these poems, and I feel deeply grateful to every one of you who has taken time along your busy way to help me shape both this translation and analysis. This work is the product of many minds, and is—I hope—merely a step along the way in what I wish will be a long relationship with Saraha's *Adamantine Songs*. To all of you who share in my enthusiasm to read and ponder these newly accessible poems by the Great Brahmin, this is for you. I believe that works of religiously inspired literature are like Bodhisattvas: they exist only insofar as they are performing a function, touching and transforming minds and hearts. So let's be the audience that brings these songs to life.

It is my pleasure to thank many people here, but there is one in particular without whose brilliance, patience, and care this work would have never seen the light of day: my extraordinary teacher and supervisor, Thupten Jinpa Langri. However in this world I met with the right conditions to be able to work with Dr. Jinpa I will never understand, but I will always be grateful. Week after week and year after year you shared your wisdom, experience, and insight. You have taught me so much and continue to give me the greatest example to emulate as I strive to become a better scholar and teacher myself.

For worldly beings like myself, very little is possible without material support. I sincerely thank the Social Sciences and Humanities Research Council of Canada (SSHRC), the Fonds Québecois de la Recherche sur la Société et la Culture (FQRSC), the Shastri Indo-Canadian Institute, and McGill University for making my formation and this project possible.

Richard Hayes, thank you for so many wonderful years of Sanskrit, *pramāṇa* theory, meditation, coffee, and friendship. Your support and training over the years means the world to me. Victor Hori, you were a marvelous teacher and now are a marvelous colleague and example to me. Davesh Soneji, I have so much to thank you for, but I want to thank you in particular for introducing me to the magnificent, vibrant world of the Tamil *cittars*. Roger Jackson, I will always be so grateful for the time and care you have taken to help me develop this translation. Your guidance and support has contributed so much. Tanisha Ramachandran, thank you for opening so many important doors on theory for me. Thank you to Andrew Quintman, Kurtis Schaeffer and the members and guests of the AAR seminar on "Religion and the Literary in Tibet" who so patiently wrestled with these *rdo rje'i glu* at two consecutive sessions: Pema Bhum, Ben Bogin, José Cabezón, Brian Cuevas, Jacob Dalton, Brandon Dotson, Holly Gayley, Frances Garrett, Jonathan Gold, Janet Gyatso, Lauren Hartley, Sarah Jacoby, Nancy Lin, Jann Ronis, Antonio Terrone, Leonard van der Kuijp, Nicole Willock, and Carl Yamamoto. Thank you to the wonderful students who took my seminars on Buddhist Poetry at McGill University and gave me so much helpful, honest feedback—with a special mention to Julia Stenzel. Thank you to three exceptionally kind and inspiring people who helped me so much but passed away before this project was completed: Leslie Kawamura, Hannah Nydahl, and Khenpo Tsultrim Sangpo. Thank you to the late Ellen Aitken, to Mathieu Boisvert, Sempa Dorje, David Germano, Matthew Kapstein, B. Barry Levy, Layne Little, Donald S. Lopez Jr., Lobsang Shastri, and the late E. Gene Smith. For their friendship, intellectual stimulation and lots of laughter during some tough years, I wish to thank Barbra Clayton and Martin Adam. Thank you to Carol Gerhardt and Jay Landman for your beautiful friendship, generosity, and never-ending encouragement; to Ed and Hueiling

Worthy for always opening your doors to me (especially that first time!) and for all the encouragement and support you have given me; to all my kind friends in Virginia who treated me so gently as I returned year after year during that seemingly endless writing process. Thank you Robert A.F. Thurman, and Thomas F. Yarnall for your confidence in my work and for guiding this book to its completion. And thank you, Annie Bien, for being such a thorough yet consistently kind editor.

Friendship is so precious. Without it I would not be the person that I am, and certainly would not have finished a Ph.D. or embarked on an academic career with so much light and joy in my life. Shahin Parhami, Wilson Jacob, Meera Kachroo, Khalid Medani, Rowshan Nemazee, Maureen Jones, Gaby Tordjman, Neeraj Khatri Chettri, Vanessa Sasson, Shital Sharma, Andy Ivaska, Cinthia Font, Sonia Kundu, Eva Ottmer, Elena Razlogova, Richard Walker—thank you, each of you, for being exactly who you are and for being part of my life. At different stages along this long path and in a variety of ways each of you has helped me significantly. A special mention needs to go to my dear friend Karen Fernandes, who passed away on June 13, 2013.

With my deepest gratitude and love for my mother Dianne who passed away in 1993. It was too soon and she was too young, but she had enough time to instill in me a passion for literature and faith in its transformative powers. For my father Marcel, my sister Paula, my cousin-sister Elisa Shenkier, and my husband Tsering Wangchuk Lama, for so much I cannot begin to list.

I would never have undertaken the translation of this esoteric work without the approval and guidance of my *rtsa ba'i bla ma*, His Holiness, the Fourteenth Shamar Rinpoche. And I would never have completed it without the hours and days that stretched across years and continents that he so generously shared with me. Your kindness, Rinpoche, is something I will never be able to repay. May you return quickly to benefit limitless sentient beings.

And of course my deepest gratitude goes to Saraha, King of the Mahāsiddhas, for sharing his realized mind with us all, across the boundaries of time, space, and language.

None of us would have access to this or countless other literary treasures were it not for the Tibetan cultures that sustained and developed the practice lineages and intellectual/artistic traditions that the Kangyur and Tengyur both embody and represent. May the cultures, practices, and languages of Tibet be recognized as the jewels that they are, and may they flourish unobstructed long into the future.

Whatever benefit accrues from this work, I sincerely dedicate to the welfare of all beings:

> May all beings have happiness and the cause of happiness;
> May they be free from suffering and the cause of
> suffering;
> May they not be separated from the supreme happiness
> that is untouched by suffering;
> May they rest in great equanimity, free from attachment
> and aversion to those near and far.

Lara Braitstein
Montreal, Quebec
Saga Dawa, 2014

PART ONE

INTRODUCTION

Introduction

Saraha's *Adamantine Songs* have curiously little life outside of their inclusion in lists of works attributed to Saraha in Tibetan sources. There are no commentaries on them, they are not cited or referenced in *sādhanas*, biographies, or practice manuals, and they have never been substantially treated or translated in full in modern scholarship. They are, nonetheless, an intriguing set of poems. They abound in direct descriptions of the nature of mind as awakening, explicitly describing it as the Great Seal (*mahāmudrā*); they situate the Great Seal in the context of a system of four seals; they use the language of the three bodies of the Buddha (*trikāya*); and they consistently deploy terms that are key to commentaries on his well-known Trilogy of *dohā*s.

It is impossible to determine with any certainty if they are a window onto a particular period in Indian Buddhist history (circa ninth century CE), direct instructions for recognizing the nature of mind as the goal of the Great Seal, a set of texts that established a framework of key terms and concepts that would come to guide the reception and interpretation of Saraha's more accessible works, a random hodge-podge of verses, or all of the above. Readers will not find answers to those questions here. What will be evident is that although the public life of these poems begins with the publication of this book, there is much to learned from, said about, and drawn from these works. After a hibernation of some 1100 years, a slumber disrupted only once for the transmission and translation of the songs from "the Indian language" to Tibetan, Saraha's *Adamantine Songs* may now stir to life in the minds of their readers.

What follows below is an introduction to Saraha, both as a historical figure and as a vibrant presence within the Tibetan Buddhist tradition. That is followed by a discussion of how Saraha fits in with the pan South-Asian siddha movement, including a treatment of the Indian literary genres associated with mahāsiddhas, and the Tibetan literary genres associated with them after the transmission of their work and practice to that new context. Finally, after a discussion of my methodology as a translator and how it is grounded in both post-structuralist and Tibetan translation theory, I introduce the *Adamantine Songs*.

Saraha: Pasts and Presence

> Although the historicity of Saraha cannot be doubted, the elusiveness of the man is matched by that of his teaching.[3]

> Saraha has been definitively dated by modern scholarship to somewhere between the third century BCE and the twelfth century CE, and located in East, North, or South India—though curiously never West.[4]

There is little about Saraha that can be said for certain despite his importance to the Indo-Tibetan traditions of Buddhism. But we can begin with a treatment of what is known about him, beginning with his name. He is most commonly known as Saraha or Sarahapā, meaning "the one who has shot the arrow." This is an explicit reference to an incident in many versions of his biography when he studied with a ḍākinī disguised as a low-caste arrowsmith. Metaphorically, it refers to one who has shot the arrow of nonduality into the heart of duality. He is also often referred to as "The Great Brahmin,"[5] at times Rāhulabhadra, and in Tibetan he is also often referred to as "The Arrow Shooter."[6]

Some claim that he was the first of the Eighty-four mahāsiddhas, as do sources in the Karma Kagyu tradition and some scholarly accounts, such as the work of Benoytosh Bhattacharyya[7] and Sankrtyayan.[8] Sumpa Yeshe Peljor (gsum pa ye shes dpal 'byor; 1704–1788), in his *Auspicious Wish-Fulfilling Tree: A Dharma History*[9], also lists Saraha as the first.[10]

---

[3] Guenther 1969, 12–13.

[4] Schaeffer 2005, 13.

[5] *bram ze chen po*.

[6] *mda' snun*. Drakpa Dorje Pel Sangpo (*grags pa rdo rje dpal bzang po*; b. circa 1444) even argues in his *History of the Three Ordination Lineages (mkhan rgyud rnam gsum byon tshul gyi rnam thar)* that *mda' snun* is an incorrect translation, and that *mda' 'dzin* (Arrow Handler) is more appropriate (quoted in Schaeffer 2000, 106ff.).

[7] Chakravarti 1999, 236.

[8] Sankrtyayan 1984, 121.

[9] *chos 'byung dpag bsam ljon bzang*.

[10] Sumpa Yeshe Peljor, 238.

Abhayadatta's late eleventh/early twelfth century *Lives of the Eighty-four Mahāsiddhas*[11] places Saraha as number six. Other accounts prioritize the lineage of specific Tantras as they have been passed along through a line of great adepts. According to some accounts, the lineage of the *Cakrasaṁvara Tantra* begins with Saraha.[12] Depending on the function and context of the particular list being cited, the order of names will almost always differ. Per Kvaerne sums it up well when he writes: "It is futile to attempt to establish historically the existence of a 'first Siddha.' The various schools and lineages inevitably regarded their founder as a 'first Siddha.'"[13] Indeed, "history" as a record of "facts" that stand outside of their function in a particular context is not relevant to every facet of the study of Saraha or any of the siddhas. It will suffice for our purposes to note that Saraha is inevitably included in the lists of Eighty-four mahāsiddhas and in some contexts he is listed as the first.

Little is actually known about when he lived. We can loosely place him in a range of about 1300 years. Earliest claims place him in the fourth century BCE as a direct disciple of Buddha's son,[14] most emic accounts hold that he was the preceptor of Nāgārjuna (circa second century CE) and a number of estimates place him in the eleventh century.[15] Since Saraha already had international status as an authority by the early eleventh century—evidenced by references to him in the biography of Nāropā (1016–1100 CE) and the active transmission of his work into Tibet during that same century[16]—I am satisfied that the latest estimate is untenable. Combining the fact that there are a number of commentaries on the *Buddhakapāla Tantra*[17] attributed to him, and that the language he

---

[11] *Caturaśītisiddhapravṛtti, grub thob brgyad cu rtsa bzhi'i lo rgyus*

[12] Chakravarti 1999, 236; Gray 2007, 35 n107; Gö 2003, 460.

[13] Kvaerne 1986, 6.

[14] Pema Karpo (*pad ma dkar po;* 1527–1592) in his *The Conqueror's Storehouse: A Discourse of Key Instructions on the Great Seal (phyag rgya chen po'i man ngag gi bshad sbyar rgyal ba'i gan mdzod)* claims that Saraha was born only thirty years after the Buddha's death (p. 108).

[15] Shahidullah 1928; Kvaerne 1986; Nakamura 1989.

[16] Roerich 1988, 72; Schaeffer 2000.

[17] According to Davidson (2002, 247–48) the *Buddhakapāla Tantra* is "a ninth-century or later work." He also discusses Saraha's commentary on the Buddhakapāla (250ff.).

most likely composed his works in is Apabhraṁśa,[18] leads me to conclude that the most plausible range appears to be the ninth to tenth centuries CE.

There is in fact no consensus in what language he composed his works. The two possibilities that have been discussed in secondary literature to date are Sanskrit and Apabhraṁśa, though since Apabhraṁśa is also a literary language and Saraha's work is traditionally believed to have been "composed" orally, this may indicate the language of composition was *neither* Sanskrit nor Apabhraṁśa.[19] His complete works are extant in Tibetan translation only, and only fragments exist in Apabhraṁśa. Particularly exciting is a recently discovered Apabhraṁśa manuscript of his most famous work, the *Treasury of Dohā*,[20] and this discovery has led many to believe that this was the language in which he originally composed his work: "After some initial uncertainties, the language of the *Dohākośas* has been identified as an eastern dialect of Apabhraṁśa (sometimes called Avahaṭṭha)."[21] Jackson's discussion of the genealogy of the Apabhraṁśa version of Saraha's *Dohākośa* immediately preceding this conclusion, however, hints that there remain some doubts:[22]

> The "standard" Apabhraṃśa version, discovered in a Nepalese royal library in 1907 and published in 1916 by Haraprasad Sastri, then worked and reworked by Muhammad Shahidullah and Prabodh Chandra Bagchi, never has been found as an independent manuscript but rather has been extracted from a later (eleventh-century?) commentary, in Sanskrit, the *Dohākoṣa-Pañjikā* of Advayavajra—who may be the same as the Indian tantric theorist Maitripa. In 1929, Bagchi found in Nepal

[18] If this is the case, we can narrow down his dates to somewhere in the range of seventh to tenth century, since that is the approximate period of the ascendancy of that language where the dates of his life are believable.

[19] See Jackson 2004, 9.

[20] *Dohākośa*.

[21] Jackson 2004, 9.

[22] Jackson 2004, 7–8.

> a fragment of still another Apabhraṃśa version that coincides with the other editions not at all. Yet another version of the Apabhraṃśa of Saraha's text was discovered by Rahula Saṃkṛtyāyana at Sakya monastery in Tibet in 1934 and published in 1957; it only replicates about half the verses in the "standard" edition. Furthermore, the Tibetan translation contains both common and unique verses, adding further evidence, as if it were needed, of the complexity and fragmentation of the textual tradition surrounding Saraha's signal work.

Schaeffer acknowledges the same sketchy history of the Apabhraṁśa texts at the same time that he affirms, "The *Dohākośa*...is one of a handful of these late Indian Buddhist poetic works initially composed in the Apabhraṃśa dialect."[23] While this conveys some sense of the certainty that Saraha worked in Apabhramśa, the matter is vexed both by the possible folk-origins of the meters used in Saraha's poems that are explored below, and the assertion by some scholars that Saraha wrote in Sanskrit. Herbert Guenther is one academic writer who refutes at least the certainty that Apabhraṁśa was Saraha's "original" language of composition:[24]

> It has been argued that the language in which Saraha expressed his ideas is a late Apabhraṃśa form pointing to Bengal.... [I]t remains a strange fact, reflecting rather unfavorably on the scholarliness of those who have dealt with the "People Dohās," that none of them noted that the Tibetan translation, apart from being larger than the alleged original, does not tally with the Apabhraṃśa version. The latter studiously avoids all the technical terms characteristic of Saraha's line of thought.

Tibetans devised and maintained a rigorous and accurate system of translating texts and the multiple versions of Saraha's texts that exist in the diverse editions of the Tengyur (*bstan 'gyur*) more or less agree with each

[23] Schaeffer 2000, 5.

[24] Guenther 1969, 8–9.

other. Therefore, because the Tibetan version is longer necessarily means that the "Indian" language version[25] was not the Apabhraṁśa text—at least not the one scholars are working with today. Traditional accounts, accounts of Saraha's life and teachings given by Tibetan Buddhist Lamas and scholars who have been trained principally in monastic settings, tell us that Saraha taught in Sanskrit. During an interview conducted in February, 2000, Professor Sempa Dorje informed me he believes Saraha was one of very few mahāsiddhas who actually used Sanskrit. Given that he is renowned in both Indian and Tibetan traditions as "The Great Brahmin," it seems a plausible scenario.

Unsurprisingly, Saraha's location is also uncertain. Abhayadatta's *Lives of the Eighty-four Mahāsiddhas*, stated that he came from a village called Rajñī in the land of Roli, somewhere in Eastern India.[26] According to Pema Karpo's *The Conqueror's Storehouse: A Discourse of Key Instructions on the Great Seal*,[27] Saraha was born in Varanasi.[28] Pawo Tsukla Trengwa (*dpa' bo tsug lag phreng ba*; 1504–1566) and Karma Trinlepa (*kar ma 'phrin las pa*; 1456–1539) concur that Saraha was from Beta, or Baidharbha (Vidarbha) in Southern India.[29] Also, an episode from Marpa's biography locates Saraha in the south when the famous translator encounters Saraha in a dream vision in Śrī Parvata.

Having established uncertainty with respect to Saraha's dates and language, it is an appropriate time to present some traditions of his biography. While the multiple and diverse accounts of his life and times have been compiled in detail by Schaeffer, it is worth at least reviewing in brief the most common versions of his biography. In its tamest form, Saraha's life is recorded in the *Lives of the Eighty-four Mahāsiddhas*:[30]

---

[25] The Tibetan translations always prefaces the "original" title as being in *gya gar skad du*—meaning, "in the Indian language"—without ever specifying what that language was.

[26] *Yul rgya gar shar phyogs kyi grong khyer ra'dznyi' zhes bya ba'i bye brag saroli zhes bya ba yin*. (Abhayadatta 1998, 29)

[27] *phyag rgya chen po'i man ngag gi bshad sbyar rgyal ba'i gan mdzod*.

[28] Pema Karpo 1973, 108.

[29] Schaeffer 2000, 15.

[30] Translation my own. Tibetan text from Sempa Dorje's 1998 bilingual Tibetan/Hindi edition of Abhayadatta's text (Abhayadatta 29–33).

Saraha was born into the Brahmin caste in Roli, part of a town named Rajñī in Eastern India. Because he was the son of a *ḍākinī*, he was a *ḍāka* himself. Although he was a Brahmin, he believed in the Buddhadharma. He listened to the Dharma of innumerable teachers and had faith in the way of secret mantra (i.e. Tantra). He maintained the duties of both a Brahmin and a Buddhist. During the day he practiced the Brahmanical religion. At night he practiced the religion of the Buddhists.

When he was discovered drinking beer by his fellow Brahmins, they all gathered together in order to banish him. They said to King Ratnapāla: "You are King. Tell us, is it right that in your land one is confusing customs? This Saraha is master of 15,000 in the village of Roli. Since he is drinking alcohol and breaking with what is correct, you should expel him!"

The King thought: "Since he governs 15,000, it is not desirable to banish him," and said as he approached Saraha: "You are a Brahmin, this beer drinking is not good."

Saraha said: "I don't drink beer. Gather all the Brahmins and all the people together and I will take an oath." Everyone gathered. Saraha said, "If I drink beer, my hand will burn; if I don't drink, it will not burn." He then placed his hand in boiling ghee and it did not burn.

The King asked the crowd, "Is it true that he drinks?"

The Brahmins said, "It's true, we say he drinks."

Speaking as before, Saraha drank molten copper and was not burned. And again they said, "He drinks." Saraha said, "Well then, let's enter the water, and whoever sinks, drinks; whoever doesn't sink, doesn't drink." When he entered the water together with another Brahmin, Saraha did not sink. The other one sank, and Saraha said, "I don't drink."

Saraha commanded them to weigh him on a scale: "Whoever is heavier does not drink, and whoever is lighter drinks," he said. Weighing him against another man, Saraha was heavier, and said, "I don't drink." They put a man together with three pieces of steel of equal weight on the scale. Still Saraha was heavier, and when Saraha was heavier than even six pieces of steel, the King said, "If he has powers like that and he wants to drink beer, let him drink!"

All the Brahmins and the King prostrated and asked for instruction. Since he sang a song for the King, Queen, and people, it is known as the "Cycle of Three *Dohās*" (*dohā skor gsum*). The Brahmins abandoned their own religion and accepted the teachings of the Buddha; and the King and his retinue also attained *siddhi*.

Then Saraha took a fifteen year-old girl with him and together they went to another land. Staying in an isolated place, Saraha devoted himself to practice and the girl prepared and delivered him food. Once Saraha asked her for cooked radishes. She prepared radishes and buffalo curd and arrived before him. Since he had entered *samādhi*, she left without giving him the food. Saraha did not arise from that *samādhi* for twelve years.

When he arose, and said to her, "Where are my radishes?"

She said, "You didn't arise from *samādhi* for twelve years, so now where are the radishes? It's Spring there aren't any."

Saraha said to her, "I will go to practice on the mountain."

She said, "Physical solitude is not solitude. Solitude from dualistic mind and conceptual thought—that is the highest solitude. Although you abided in meditation for twelve years, you could not even sever the thought of radishes. What good will it do you to go to the mountain?"

> Saraha realized the truth in that [statement]. He abandoned dualistic mind and conceptual thought. He achieved the essential meaning, the highest *siddhi* which is the Great Seal, and he achieved the limitless welfare of beings. Together with the girl he went to the celestial realm.

A more exciting version of his biography is attributed to the Kagyupa Lama Karma Trinlepa.[31] The youngest of five sons, Saraha and his brothers were famous for their knowledge of the Vedas. His four older brothers were seduced one day by four ḍākinīs disguised as Brahmin girls who had been sent by Hayagrīva (*rta mgrin*, a protective deity). Somehow this motivated him to become a Buddhist monk, and with the King's permission (King Mahāpāla) he did so. He became a noted scholar and spiritual master. One day, he was approached in a park by four ḍākinīs disguised as Brahmin girls, who offered him four cups of beer. Succumbing to their begging, he drank the cups of beer and felt four extremely pleasant sensations (the four kinds of joy or bliss).[32] He met the Bodhisattva Sukhanātha face to face, who told him to go seek "a mysterious arrowsmith woman who is making a four-piece arrow."[33] He found, in the marketplace, a woman of low-caste who was making her four-piece arrow with intense concentration. He asked her if she was an arrowsmith and she replied, "My dear young man, the Buddha's meaning can be known through symbols and actions, not through words and books."[34] She explained the symbolic meaning of the arrow to him[35] and

---

[31] See Schaeffer (2005, 22) for a problematization of the text translated by Guenther 1969.

[32] Joy, Highest Joy, Free of Joy, Innate Joy (*dga' ba*, *mchog dga'*, *dga' bral*, *lhan cig skyes pa'i dga' ba*). These are stages of psycho-spiritual experience, felt and established as states by *yogins* and *yoginīs* engaging in union practices—whether with an actual consort, by means of visualization of a consort, or taking place as processes within the subtle body.

[33] Guenther 1969, 5.

[34] Ibid.

[35] "The reed is the symbol for the uncreated; the three joints, that of the necessity to realize the three existential norms (*kāyas*); the straightening of the shaft, that of straightening the path of spiritual growth; cutting the shaft at the bottom, that of the necessity to uproot Samsāra, and at the top, that of eradicating a belief in a self or an essence; the splitting of

(cont'd)

he recognized her as a teacher, abandoned his studies and monastic vows, and moved to a cremation ground with her to practice.

A well-respected Brahmin man turned Buddhist monk, who appears one day in a charnel ground openly drinking alcohol and living as the student and consort of a low-caste woman, does attract attention. Soon word got out to the King, and the story ends in much the same way as the first one I cited does.

Schaeffer points out that the theme of a "female figure without whom Saraha would not have achieved realization"[36] pervades all the narratives about Saraha. Whether that female figure is the "radish girl" or the "fletcheress" changes from narrative tradition to narrative tradition, however, the arrow itself is consistently iconographically related to Saraha. He is usually recognizable in religious art by the downward or horizontally pointing arrow in his hands, his shorts, his meditation belt, and his long yogin's hair tied up in one topknot.

There are also numerous accounts of his life that attribute a phase of life as a Buddhist monastic to him. As mentioned above, he is taken by many to have been the preceptor of Nāgārjuna. Pawo Tsukla Trengwa has an account of Saraha's life in his work *The Scholar's Banquet*[37] in which he takes ordination from Rāhula (Buddha's son?) and "became perfect in ethical conduct and was an incomparable scholar."[38] According to Drikung Chöje Kunga Rinchen's account (1475–1527) in *Golden Rosary of Kagyu Masters*,[39] Saraha not only took ordination, but became

---

the bottom into four sections, that of memory (*dran pa*), nonmemory (*dran med*), unorigination, and transcendence; inserting the arrowhead, that of the necessity to use one's intelligence; tying it with a tendon, that of being fixed by the seal of unity; splitting the upper end into two, that of action and intelligence; inserting four feathers, that of looking, attending to the seen, acting on the basis of what has been seen and attended to, and their combination of fruition; opening one eye and closing the other, that of shutting the eye of discursiveness and opening that of a priori awareness; the posture of aiming at a target, that of the necessity to shoot the arrow of nonduality into the heart of the belief in duality." (Guenther 1969, 5–6)

[36] Schaeffer 2000, 8.

[37] *mkhas pa'i dga' ston.*

[38] Schaeffer 2000, 40.

[39] *bka' rgyud bla ma rnams kyi rnam thar rin chen gser phreng.*

the abbot of Vikramaśīla Monastery.[40] Karma Trinlepa also relays the ordination part of the story. In all Kagyu iterations of Saraha's story, he becomes a yogin *after* his ordination, abandoning the monastic life. In contrast, as recounted in Schaeffer's work, the Tibetan historian Drakpa Dorje Pel Sangpo places Saraha in a monastic ordination lineage. Since as a member of such a lineage, it would be most unseemly for him to have abandoned the monastic life in favour of such radical practices as the imbibing of alcohol and sexual yogas, his story is reworked such that his ordination takes place *after* his career as a yogin.

The Kagyu school attributes to him the very foundation of the Great Seal that crowns the lineage to this day. The Great Seal is "simultaneously the climax of *Vajrayāna* and the thread running through the entire Kagyu path."[41] That it is inextricably tied to Saraha is of course not a coincidence. While in some iterations of the Great Seal lineage, the name of Ratnamati falls between Vajradhara (as the enlightened source of the teachings) and Saraha, when the direct transmission of the Great Seal occurs, it comes directly from Saraha. Ratnamati is in any case a curious character, as it remains ambiguous whether he is understood to have been a human being or a kind of intermediary bodhisattva. There exists no biography or detailed record of Ratnamati, and as Saraha's is the (human) name associated most closely with the birth of the Great Seal lineage, I will allow Ratnamati to maintain his obscurity. In Gö Lotsawa Shönupel's (*'gos lo tsa ba gzhon nu dpal*; 1392–1481) *Blue Annals*,[42] it is written: "With respect to this teaching of the Conqueror Śākyamuni called the Mahāmudrā, it was Saraha the Great Brahmin who favored it as the path to be taught above all."[43]

Shākya Chokden (*shAkya mchog ldan*; 1428–1507), a master of the Sakya tradition attributes the founding of Madhyamaka philosophy to

---

[40] Schaeffer 2000, 43.

[41] Thinley 1980, 34.

[42] *deb ther sngon po*. The full title is: *The Blue Annals, the Stages of the Appearance of the Doctrine and Preachers in the Land of Tibet (bod kyi yul du chos dang chos smra ba ji ltar byung ba'i rim pa deb ther sngon po).*

[43] Gö, 984–5.

Saraha. In *Wish Fulfilling Meru: A Discourse Explaining the Origination of Madhyamaka*,[44] he writes:[45]

> As it was said: "Four hundred years after my nirvana..." etc,[46] it is generally accepted that initially the tradition of Madhyamaka treatises was pioneered by the Protector Nāgārjuna. Nevertheless, besides him, a short time before, the Great Brahmin, the Glorious Saraha, in a form of singing a song, composed a Madhyamaka treatise whose topic was the mind-vajra free from [conceptual] analysis.

Thus, for this Sakya writer, Saraha not only precedes Nāgārjuna's articulation of Madhyamaka philosophy but encompasses and surpasses it as well. Karma Trinlepa writes the following in his homage to Saraha which appears in his *Middle Commentary on the Three Cycles of Dohā*:[47]

> To the illustrious arrowsmith Saraha I bow down.
>
> Though he has known and seen suchness before the Buddha,
>
> Out of compassion for living beings he acted in this realm of becoming with the drama of illusion.
>
> For his descendants, the famous Karmapas, the black-hatted scholars who point out the mirage of becoming and quiescence,
>
> Saraha himself is the very foundation of non-referential reverence.

---

[44] *dbu ma'i byung tshul rnam par bshad pa'i gtam yid bzhin lhun po*.

[45] Chokden 2000, 9. The translator's footnote to this passage is worth quoting in full: "Saraha actually was Nāgārjuna's guru and the person from whom he received monastic ordination. When we say that Nāgārjuna pioneered the Madhyamaka tradition, we usually mean pioneering Madhyamaka of Sūtras. But Saraha can be said to have pioneered the Madhyamakas of both Sūtras and Tantras." (Chokden 2000, 66 n54)

[46] This is a reference to a prophecy from the *Mañjuśrīmūlatantra* which predicts the appearance and Madhyamaka teachings of Nāgārjuna.

[47] *do ha skor gsum gyi ti ka 'bring po*. Schaeffer 2005, 36.

What is remarkable here, and certainly worth drawing attention to, is that Saraha is lauded as an awakened master whose accomplishment of the ultimate goal *precedes* that of the historical Buddha, Śākyamuni.

The task of locating Saraha is a complex one, one that necessitates engaging not only with tales of his life, but with tales of people's encounters with him in their own lives. Because we cannot definitively access historical data about Saraha as he *was,* any search for the elusive author of the poems contained in this volume must also look at who he *is*. Over the past one thousand years, he has defied the boundaries of time and space to make his actual presence known and felt. One of the most famous examples of this occurred in the eleventh century CE. During his first of three journeys to India, Marpa Lotsawa (Marpa the Translator), traveling by foot across the Himalayas to meet his guru Nāropā, was delayed in a town on the Nepalese border on his way back to Tibet:[48]

> His last night there, he had a dream in which dakinīs lifted him up in a palanquin and carried him to Śrī Parvata in the South. There Marpa met the Great Brahman Saraha, who blessed his body, speech, and mind. Saraha gave him the signs and the meanings of the dharma of the essential truth, mahāmudrā. Undefiled bliss dawned in his body, and unperverted realization dawned in his mind, so that Marpa's dream was filled with immeasurable delight. Even after he awoke, he did not forget what Saraha had said.

Despite the fact that there is no attempt made in his biography to link him to Saraha in what a contemporary audience would understand as "real" terms (i.e. a face to face, physical encounter), this dream-vision nonetheless constitutes a very real encounter as far as the tradition is concerned. There is no question that Marpa was a legitimate, direct recipient of Saraha's teachings and blessings.

This type of direct encounter with Saraha in dreams or meditative visions pervades Tibetan traditions, and constitutes a legitimate manner of receiving his direct transmission. Another vivid example can be drawn

---

[48] Tsang 1995, 42.

from the life of the second Karmapa, Karma Pakshi (1204–1283). Karma Pakshi clearly experienced Saraha as present:[49]

> The eternal presence of Saraha was a concrete phenomenon for the second hierarch of the Karma Kagyu school, Karma Pakshi (1204–1283), who in his autobiography relates visions of Saraha and all the other Eighty-Four Adepts. He rejoices at having received their blessings as they wove magical illusions and danced throughout the Mongolian lands and regions north of Tibet.

Therefore we can talk about two distinct connections between Saraha and the much later development of Tibetan Buddhism in the later translation (*gsar ma*) period: one is historical, relating to the past, describing the relationship of specific lineages of teachings to Saraha via an unbroken chain of individuals; the other is ahistorical, relating not only to the present but to the *presence* of Saraha as figure who disrupts time and space freely in order to directly teach and inspire.

A useful illustration of these two forms of connection with Saraha occurs in the shape of the Karmapas, the reincarnate heads of the Karma Kagyu school. On the one hand, they are considered to be the inheritors of Saraha's tradition, his "descendents"; and on the other, they are also seen as reincarnations of Saraha himself. In other words, the Karmapas are both devoted to, and identical with, Saraha. Here I will make an example of the third Karmapa, Rangjung Dorje (rang 'byung rdo rje; 1284–1339), whose relationship to Saraha embodies the very complexity of the Great Brahmin. Saraha is revered as the principal master of the Great Seal, but his distance—both temporally and geographically—is no obstacle for the third Karmapa:[50]

> When [I], the yogi Rangjung Dorje was staying at Tashi Sarma, in a dream one night myself and two friends went to Śrī Parvata Mountain to search for the Great Brahmin, Master [Saraha]. My two friends went south of the mountain, and I [went] east. There signs arose on a

[49] Schaeffer 2005, 41.

[50] Schaeffer 2005, 41–2.

> panoramic and euphoric high plain, and an unfathomable rain of flowers fell. We then arranged a border [with the flowers] and when we were sitting equiposed within their ring a small melodious voice sounded from the sky:
>
> Listen you noble sons,
> The master, the Great Brahmin
> is mind itself,
> And to search elsewhere is, alas, a mistake!
>
> As that was proclaimed, so this did I speak:
>
> The Master, the Great Brahmin
> Is our own minds,
> And in this circle where manifold [experiences are of]
> a single taste,
> Free of what searches and what is searched for,
> My two friends are done with searching;
> We stay together as one.
> Rejoice, the symbolic teaching of the Great Brahmin
> Are indeed wondrous.
>
> Because I so spoke, the voice of the Great Brahmin resounded from the sky... [Saraha sang his song, and] the border [of flowers] which we arranged, all the earth, stones and animals transformed into the nature of the Great Brahmin, and remained. And when the meaning of what is real, free of becoming, cessation and abiding, uninterrupted and impartial, continuous and overflowing, was in our minds, there was no difference between waking and sleeping.

Rangjung Dorje, devoted to Saraha as the unsurpassed originary master of the Great Seal, supplicated and received direct teachings from Saraha (who also clearly has become identified with primordial awakening) centuries after his death. This is complicated even more by the fact that in his own lifetime, Rangjung Dorje was seen as an embodiment of Saraha.[51]

---

[51] Thinley 1980, 55.

Clearly Saraha constitutes a polysemic presence in Karmapa Rangjung Dorje's entire being.

Saraha's presence isn't only reserved for the highest masters of the lineage, however. He pervades even the most basic practices for Kagyupas, not only in their devotion to the Karmapas, but in private practice as well. A recent version of the Refuge Tree (*tshogs zhing*, literally "accumulation field") illustrates this well. The Refuge Tree is an elaborate visual depiction of the Buddhist refuge. It includes not only the Three Jewels, but also what are referred to as the Three Roots (*rtsa ba gsum*): the spiritual master or guru (*guru*, *bla ma*), meditational deities (*iṣṭadevatā*, *yi dam*) and Dharma protectors (*dharmapāla*, *chos skyong*). The central character on the refuge tree is the guru, often depicted as Vajradhara (*rdo rje 'chang*), a primordial Buddha. Vajradhara is understood by practitioners to not only represent the guru, but to actually *be* the guru's mind. The *yi dam* and protectors represent transformed mental states and the activity of the guru. While devotion to one's main teacher (*rtsa ba'i bla ma*) is foundational to any Tantric practitioner,[52] the extent to which that devotion is meant to be personal is limited. Picturing the Root Lama as Vajradhara can function as an antidote to the clinging that can arise if one's visualization of the guru has become too personal. Additionally, having Vajradhara as generically representing the guru's mind on a *thangka* or any other representation of the Refuge Tree, allows any number of practitioners to use the same image as an aid for practice, even if some opt to visualize a form of their guru in Vajradhara's stead. While some Refuge Trees have a specific guru depicted in the center—Karmapa for Kagyupas, Padmasambhava for Nyingmapas, or Tsongkhapa for Gelukpas—all show that central figure surrounded by the founders and lineage holders of the school the Tree represents. The Refuge Tree is

---

[52] An incident from the biography of Marpa illustrates well the centrality of the guru. The following details the last night and morning spent together of Marpa and his guru Nāropā: "That night they slept near each other and at dawn Mahāpaṇḍita Nāropā manifested the maṇḍala of Hevajra with the nine deities, bright and vivid in the sky. He said, 'Son, teacher Marpa Chökyi Lodrö, don't sleep, get up! Your personal yidam Hevajra with the nine emanation devis has arrived in the sky before you. Will you prostrate to me or to the yidam?' Marpa prostrated to the bright and vivd mandala of the yidam. Nāropa said, 'As it is said: Before any guru existed/ Even the name of the Buddha was not heard. / All the buddhas of a thousand kalpas / Only come about because of the guru." (Tsang 1995, 92)

important because it is the focus of one of the most basic practices of all practitioners of Tibetan Buddhism: prostrations. While visualizing this elaborate tree and its denizens (usually with a representation before oneself) a practitioner must perform over one hundred thousand full prostrations, while repeating the refuge formula. This is the first of four practices that together constitute the Preliminary Practices (*sngon 'gro*) and the prostrations alone can take years to complete. Given that, the details of the tree become rather important, and ingrain at many levels what one's refuge consists of. In one particular stream of Karma Kagyu Buddhism, practitioners under the guidance of the Fourteenth Shamar (zhwa dmar) Rinpoche, Mipham Chökyi Lodrö (mi pham chos kyi blo gros), are instructed to visualize Saraha as that central Lama. While a typical Kagyu *sādhana* for accomplishing the Preliminary Practices may read:[53]

> In front of me, in the center of a lake, is a wish-fulfilling tree.
> It has one root, one trunk, and four main branches.
> At the central fork is lion throne, on which rests a lotus, sun, and moon.
> On this sits my root guru as Vajradhara,
> Surrounded by all the Kagyu gurus.

Compare this to the Preliminary Practice *sādhana* composed by the Fourteenth Shamar Rinpoche, Mipham Chökyi Lodrö:[54]

> In the middle of a lake in front of me is a wish-fulfilling tree with one trunk and four branches. At the crown of the central trunk is Saraha, the master of the *mahāmudrā* teachings, manifesting in the form of Vajradhara. He is seated on a lion throne, on a lotus and moon disc, and is surrounded by all the *mahāmudrā* siddhas.

---

[53] *mdun du mtsho dbus dpag bsam ljon shing gi / sdong po rtsa bag cig la yal ga lngar / gyes pa'i dbus mar seng khri pad ma dang / nyi zla'i steng du rtsa ba'i bla ma ni / rdo rje 'chang la bka' brgyud bla mas bskor*. (Chökyi Wangchuk 9–10)

[54] *mdun du mtsho dbus dpag bsam ljon shing gi / sdong po rtsa ba gcig la yal ga lngar / gyes pa'i dbus mar seng khri pad zla'i steng / phyag chen bstan pa'i bdag po sa ra ha / rham pa rdo rje 'chang gi skur sprul bzhugs / de la phyag chen grub pa yongs kyis bskor*. (Mipham Chökyi Lodrö, 3a–b)

Though one would be hard pressed to find someone who identifies Saraha directly as her Lama, the direct transmission is in theory still possible to attain, and in the context of the Great Seal, the transmission one receives from one's teacher is understood to be that of Saraha.

Saraha has also left his traces on other lineages as well. For example, an association between Saraha and the Palyul Nyingma was established in the nineteenth century by the famous Treasure Revealer (*gter ston*) Düdjom Lingpa Rinpoche (bdud 'joms gling pa; 1835–1904) who not only claimed to have received teachings from Saraha (among others) in dream visions, but also claimed to be part of a line of incarnated awakened masters, among whom Saraha was the third and to which he was heir (a line of reincarnated teachers still in existence).

The Sakya school also has a connection to Saraha, predominantly highlighted by Shākya Chokden, mentioned above in the course of discussing Saraha's role in the founding of Madhyamaka philosophy. Shākya Chokden composed a lengthy homage to Saraha:[55]

> From the prince Rāhula,
> First-born son of the King of the Śākyas,
> You took ordination, Brahmin Rāhula.
> ....
> You were Nāgārjuna's master.
> ....
> Then, in the realm of immortal nectar,
> You dwelt on the Great Seal ground.
> ....
> Glorious Saraha,
> I hold you in my eyes and in my mind.
> Acting out straightening arrow and reed,
> You saw that there's nothing
> Other than your own primordial awareness.
> ....
> Fearless Saraha, you swiftly
> Opened the three doors,
> And saw that all things are empty of essence,

[55] Schaeffer 2005, 175–77.

> Without cause,
> Without result, but rather
> Your own face—primordial awareness.
> ....
> The ocean, where primordial awareness frolics without
> grasping,
> A single taste you showed to be, Glorious Saraha.

The Geluk school is no exception to the trend of revering Saraha. The First Panchen Lama, Losang Chökyi Gyeltsen (blo bsang chos kyi rgyal mtshan; 1570–1662), is renowned for having evoked Saraha in the opening passage of his treatise on *mahāmudrā*, the *Path of the Conqueror: Root of the Mahāmudrā of the Precious Geluk-Kagyü*.[56] Of particular interest in the relationship of the first Panchen Lama to Saraha, is an episode from his biography where he embarks on a number of projects to build stūpas and retreat centers that would please Saraha so that he would actually appear:[57]

> Following the retreat, with renewed energy, he once again undertook great construction projects. He had new stupas built and completely refurbished the retreat dwellings surrounding Tashilunpo, making their appearance so excellent as to invite the actual coming again of such great meditators as the great yogi Chokyi Dorje and the great siddha Saraha.

Thus, while Saraha is strongly associated with the Kagyu traditions, his link with the Great Seal in its various forms carries his inspiration and presence well beyond the confines of any one school. It indeed appears that Saraha functions as a kind of wishfulfilling spring for all who call on him—as root guru, teacher, preceptor, or philosopher. Saraha is something for (and in some cases *as*) everyone.

---

[56] *dge ldan bka' brgyud rin po che'i phyag chen rtsa ba rgyal ba'i gzhung lam.*

[57] Willis 1995, 93.

Defining Siddhas

The term siddha is derived from the Sanskrit verbal root √*sidh*, which means to accomplish or perfect. A siddha is therefore one who has accomplished, or perfected—in other words, an adept. I will be using the terms "adept" and siddha interchangeably.

The Buddhist adepts tend to be associated roughly with the Pāla period (eighth to twelfth centuries CE) in modern-day Bengal and Bihar, though the siddhas as a class of religious practitioner span all the major religious traditions that are or have been present in South Asia. The earliest saint adepts date back to the first centuries before the common era,[58] but by the early medieval period (c. 500–1200 CE) there were siddha saints who were Jains, Vaiṣṇavas, Śaivas, Śāktas, Nāthas, and of course Buddhists, who had communities and individuals striving against their respective normative structures, and together constituting an antinomian tradition which—despite the major differences between the orthodox/orthoprax versions of their religions—coheres together in some rather striking ways. They emphasize the potential for individuals to attain spiritual goals without having to participate in institutionalized religion, as well as the rejection of social norms and values, "going naked along their own paths, devoted solely to their own subjective experiences."[59] The adepts are renowned for their shocking behavior, unconventional and often extreme teaching styles, and Buddhist great adepts in particular, for their accomplishment in a single lifetime of the ultimate *siddhi*: awakening.[60]

At the start of the eighth century CE, when the Buddhist siddhas began to make their presence felt, institutional South Asian Buddhism was peaking: the great monasteries (such as Nālandā, Vikramaśīla, etc.) housed monastics numbering collectively in the thousands, royal and popular patronage was being successfully solicited, and monastic Buddhism

---

[58] Davidson 2005, 32.

[59] Davidson 2002, 169.

[60] A number of relevant sources have been published since the completion this work a number of years ago that would have helped to shape this discussion but could not, for practical reasons, be incorporated into my analysis. In particular, I mention here Christian Wedemeyer's *Making Sense of Tantric Buddhism* (2012) and Andrew Quintman's *The Yogin and the Madman* (2013).

—serving the lay population's needs and its own—was flourishing. It was also at this point in time that many forms of Tantric Buddhism were flourishing. From as-yet undetermined beginnings (it began to gain popularity in the sixth century CE) it had become a highly complex and highly ritualized mode of striving for Buddhist enlightenment and had been largely integrated into monastic curricula. Complex and refined so as to be almost totally inaccessible to most people, it had principally come to entail level upon level of initiation, a comprehension of complicated ideas, rituals, and visual depictions. Dasgupta writes:[61]

> Though Tāntricism condemned orthodoxy in the strongest possible terms, it developed within its province the most elaborate form of practices. In formalism, ceremonialism, ritualism, magic, sorcery and in the most complicated system of worship accompanied by the muttering of innumerable Mantras Tāntricism superseded all the other orthodox systems.

Although his characterization of Tantra as an orthodox system which superseded all the others is perhaps a little strong, his point is well-taken. By the time the great adepts emerged as a Buddhist phenomenon to be reckoned with, the complex of rituals and practices that characterize Tantra—their uses of maṇḍala, intricate rituals and mantras—had been incorporated into monastic practice and had thus become what Ronald Davidson refers to as institutionalized esoterism.[62] As often happens, what started as an alternative movement eventually became exclusive and intensely rarified itself.

Ronald Davidson also situates the emergence of the Buddhist adepts between two poles. He writes, "In their public personas, siddhas occupied a space between institutional esoterism and the larger world of Śaiva and Śākta personalities."[63] The siddhas, therefore, brought the radical language of their non-Buddhist counterparts into the arena of their interactions with Buddhist monasticism: "Buddhist siddhas' language

---

[61] Dasgupta 1962, 76.

[62] Davidson 2002, 170.

[63] Ibid.

and literature were inherently destabilizing, for they challenged the ideological bond of Buddhist institutions."[64] Not only were their language and literature destabilizing, but their life-style, their example, their teachings and followers must have been dreadfully so as well.[65]

It is into this atmosphere—postured against monasticism and institutional esoteric or Tantric practice—that the great adepts emerged. The great adepts were initially individuals whose method of liberation and subsequent lifestyle situated them on the periphery of all the systems they coexisted with:[66]

> The development of the siddha as a new form of Buddhist saint ultimately relied on the synthesis of a number of disparate factors: the perceived need for a new variety of saint, the encounter with tribal peoples and outcaste groups, the appropriation of Śaiva and Śākta practices and textual materials, the dislocation of populations from the great trading centers that had sustained Buddhism before and continued to sustain institutional esoteric Buddhism, and the integration into local or tribal-based emerging feudal systems, to name but a few.

The mahāsiddhas constituted a movement on the periphery of all the systems with which it coexisted. Though some mahāsiddhas began their careers as monastics, and all were—in terms of their practice and its underlying system—tāntrikas, still, the great adepts were notoriously opposed to anything institutionalized (within and without Buddhist tradition) and often went to great lengths to impress the force of their disdain upon the populace at large. As it is Saraha's best-known work, it is appropriate to cite an excerpt from the "People Dohā" poem, third of the three works that together comprise his *Dohā Trilogy*. The opening stanzas demonstrate well Saraha's disdain of all traditions: [67]

---

[64] Davidson 2002, 196.

[65] While Davidson's argument is *not* principally centered on the siddhas' public personas, mine is. For the reason I am not engaging with them in the same way, my treatment of Davidson here is cursory.

[66] Davidson 2005, 33.

[67] Jackson 2004, 53–59.

Bah! Brahmins—
They don't know what's what:
In vain they incant
their four Vedas.
They incant, holding earth
And water and kuśa grass,
And sit at home
Making offerings to fire.
Their oblations
are pointless—
the acrid smoke
just stings their eyes.

With staff or trident,
Dressed like lords,
They pose as sages,
Imparting ascetic advice.
They're fakes—
Their error deceives the world;
They don't know right
Any more than wrong.

These 'saints'
Smear their bodies with ashes,
And wear their matted locks piled on their heads.
....
Fixing his gaze,
Bound in a posture,
He whispers in to the ears
Of rich folk...
He grants a consecration—
For a fee.

The long-nailed yogin
Looks filthy,
Goes naked,
Pulls out his hair by the roots.
Jains mock the path by the way they look;
They deceive themselves in teaching freedom.

If going naked means release,
Then the god and the jackal must have it.
If baldness is perfection,
Then a young girl's bottom must have it.

Self-proclaimed
Novices, monks, and elders,
These dress-up
Friars and ascetics!
Some sit writing comments
On the sutras,
Others seek
To dry up intellect.
Others run around
In the Great Way,
Where scripture turns to sophistry
And word play.
Some contemplate the mandala circle…
….
You may give up the innate
And fancy nirvāṇa,
But not an ounce of the ultimate
Will you gain.

The first poem of the *Adamantine Song* trilogy, the *Body Treasury*, begins in the same manner:[68]

Hey! Wearing matted-locks, grasping at self and agent,
Brahmins, Jains, hedonists,
Materialists accepting a real basis for things
Claim omniscience but don't even know themselves.
They are deluded and far from the path of liberation.

Vaibhāṣikas and Sautrāntikas,
Yogācārins and Mādhyamikas, etc.
Criticize each other and argue;

---

[68] *Body Treasury,* verses 1–2.

Ignorant of the space-like equality of appearance and
emptiness itself,
They turn their backs on the innate.

As must be obvious from the above two excerpts, Saraha likes to begin his work with a sound thrashing of all the traditions surrounding him, including Buddhism.[69] Jackson comments that "these thoroughgoing social and religious critiques...do not seem to conform with the ecumenical spirit typified by so many Buddhists today."[70] He adds that "satire, caricature, and scorn, along with pointed philosophical criticism, have been part of the Buddhist rhetorical arsenal for a very long time."[71] Indeed, that critical spirit is something that pervades siddha literature and doctrine in general. It is not enough to say that what the Buddhist siddhas have in common is a love of flouting social conventions. If that were the case, there would be no distinction between the revered adepts and the average teenager. What distinguishes them? What informs their rebellious behavior that makes it different from that of "regular" rebels? Their principal distinguishing feature is their insight into the nature of reality. The great adepts are understood to have been awakened masters. As explained above, Saraha is understood by his devotees to be identical with enlightened mind itself. The awakening of the siddhas is generally associated with a few key terms and concepts. The principal one I translate as "the innate" (*sahaja*, *lhan cig skye pa*),[72] which has a connotation of that which is natural or spontaneous, particularly so in the context of the siddhas. Per Kvaerne writes, "*Sahaja* is an ontological category; it is the true nature of 'the world,' of that which can be experienced. However, it is also, and basically, an experience, a psychological category."[73] The

---

[69] It is of particular interest to me to note how he dismisses the Mādhyamikas, whose tradition he is later credited with founding!

[70] Jackson 2004, 19.

[71] Jackson 2004, 20.

[72] Jackson's list of various translations of *sahaja/lhan cig skye pa* is worth citing: "'the Together-born,' 'the Simultaneously-arisen,' 'the Spontaneous,' 'Coemergence,' 'Connate,' 'Complementarity-in-Spontaneity,' and 'Being.'" (Jackson, 2004, 21)

[73] Kvaerne 1986, 62. Kvaerne's description is accurate for the siddha context. See Davidson (2002) for a detailed treatment of its meanings and contexts.

term "innate" appears relatively frequently in the *Adamantine Songs*[74] (just over a dozen times in the *Body Treasury*, and three times in each of the *Speech* and *Mind* treasuries), and pervades his famous *Dohā Trilogy*. "The innate" appears at important junctures in the *Adamantine Songs*, although it does not appear with the same frequency as the term "Great Seal," for example. It is synonymous with the Great Seal and also carries with it the connotation of great bliss. I will discuss in particular the implications of nonduality inherent in the term as it appears not only in the *Adamantine Songs* but in the *Dohā Trilogy* as well. Where it appears in the songs it always points to the inseparability of self and other, experience and phenomena, and crucially and ultimately to saṁsāra and nirvāṇa. An analysis of the term will clarify. The Sanskrit *sahaja* is derived from *jati*—to be born—and *saha*, which means "together with."[75] It connotes a sense of things coming into being simultaneously with each other. This sense is equally present in the Tibetan term. *Skye pa* means "born" or "arisen," and *lhan gcig* means "together with," or "spontaneously." What those things are that are simultaneously arising are appearance and emptiness; saṁsāra and nirvāṇa. In other words, everything is completely pervaded by every other thing, and for one like Saraha who is awakened, the experience of that indivisibility is great bliss. In the *Body Treasury*, Saraha writes of the ignorant: "Ignorant of the space-like equality of appearance and emptiness itself, / They turn their backs on the innate."[76] We may even draw a parallel between the innate and the Buddha-nature as in the following passage where he writes that "It abides as the innate nature within sentient beings."[77] The *Mind Treasury* begins with a reference to the innate: "Hey! The pristine wisdom is the innate nature."[78] In the *People Dohā*, we find the following: "You may abandon the innate and / cultivate nirvāṇa, / But although you may be rent with joy, / You

---

[74] In Saraha's *Adamantine Songs*, "the innate" is synonymous with the Great Seal as it functions as basis and fruition, as well as the great bliss.

[75] *saha jāyate iti sahajaḥ*; *saha*: with, together with; *jāyate*: born, that which is born.

[76] Verse 2.

[77] Verse 14.

[78] Verse 1.

won't accomplish even the first step toward the ultimate."[79] Further he writes of experiencing the innate when all attachment has ceased: "When thoughts will stop / and the fetters of the body will be cut, / Where the innate and one-taste are experienced, / Then there is no more low-born caste and no more Brahmin."[80] Realization, nonduality, and the one taste of bliss are what all references to the innate have in common.

In truth, any discussion of siddhas necessitates an explicit discussion of "the innate," as it is so central to their teachings and hagiographies that there are a number of scholars[81] who identify siddhas across the gamut of religious traditions they emerged in as *sahajiyās*. Defining themselves "against the formalities of life and religion,"[82] the *sahajiyās* are understood to be linked by their goal of directly realizing the ultimate nature of self and all dharmas. From the *sahajiyā* point of view, maintaining an outwardly disciplined life (i.e., monasticism) demonstrates nothing of inner realization (the opposite, one must assume, must also be true: maintaining an outwardly radical life may equally demonstrate nothing of inner realization). If one has really understood nonduality, then the idea of a "religious" or "nonreligious," "disciplined" or "nondisciplined" lifestyle is meaningless. These are all conventional dualities. Spontaneity and authenticity are key concepts in characterizing the behavior of the great adepts—indeed all those who are considered to have penetrated the innate.

Though employing esoteric yogic practices developed in Tantric or Vajrayāna Buddhism, they sought to relieve their movement of all ritualistic and philosophical accretions. Bhattacharyya cites a description of the main principles of the *sahaja* movement:[83]

---

[79] *lhan cig skyes bral gzhan gang gis / mya ngan 'das gang sgom byed pa / de dga' gas kyang don dam ni / cig shos 'grub par mi 'gyur ro /* (verse 13)

[80] *gang tshe yid ni nye bar 'gags gyur na / lus kyi 'ching ba rnam par 'chad par 'gyur / gang tshe lhan cig skyes dang ro mnyam pa / de tshe dman pa'i rigs dang bram ze med //* (verse 46)

[81] Most notable are Mircea Eliade's *Yoga: Immortality and Freedom* (1958); N. N. Bhattacharyya's *History of the Tantric Religion* (1982); and Shashibhusan Dasgupta's *Obscure Religious Cults* (1946).

[82] Dasgupta 1962, 51.

[83] Bhattacaryya 1999, 297.

> Negatively speaking, these were (a) sharp criticism and rejection of all external formalities in regard to religious practices and spiritual quests; and (b) protest against and rejection of priestly and scriptural authority, celibacy, penances, austerities, and the like. Positively, the most important elements were (a) recognition of the guru as essential for any spiritual exercise and quest, (b) recognition of the human body as the seat and habitat of all religious and spiritual experience, indeed, of the Truth or Ultimate Reality and finally (c) recognition of the experience of the ultimate Reality as one of inexpressible happiness and ineffable radiance, waveless equipoise, absolute peace and tranquility, and of absolute nonduality or complete unity.

Interestingly, though I have found no evidence of anyone claiming that the above is not true of the Buddhist siddhas, many scholars entirely dismiss the notion of a *sahajiyā* cult, or *sahajayāna*, including Per Kvaerne and Roger Jackson. Though clearly the idea of the mahāsiddhas belonging simply to a movement one may term *sahajiyā* has passed out of vogue, to my knowledge no comprehensive study has explored the reasons for it (although Kvaerne's rather short comment, putting the identification of the Buddhist siddhas as *sahajiyā*s down to "confusion with the term sahajiya used in the connection with the Vaiṣṇava Sahajiyā movement in Bengal"[84] may touch on something like a truth). Perhaps the blatant sectarianism present in the works of individual siddhas from an assortment of traditions has led to the discarding of that idea; there is, in any case, no denying the centrality of the notion of *sahaja/lhan cig skyes pa* to the mahāsiddhas in general and to Saraha in particular.

The importance of the innate to siddha Buddhism brings us back to the connection between the siddhas and Tantra. As mentioned above, the siddhas constituted a movement that resisted the rarification and ritualization of Tantric practice that took shape in monastic contexts. At their outset, both movements may be considered to have been elite. They were not so in the sense of being the preserve of a certain social or economic

---

[84] Kvaerne 1986, 61.

class, but rather in the sense that as movements which prescribe transgressive behavior, disciples and gurus both had to be selected with great care, as the potential for all-out debauchery was rather high. If we may at least provisionally accept Ronald Davidson's hypothesis that in the medieval period, Buddhist Tantra actually became mainstream as it attracted royal patronage, it may also be possible to assert that the siddhas were actually also rebelling against the growing popularity of Tantric doctrine and especially practice.[85] The underlying doctrine of the siddhas is the same as that propagated by the Tantras as a general class of literature, and most specifically by the highest Tantras, the Mother Tantras belonging to the so-called *Anuttarayoga* Tantras.[86] These *Anuttarayoga* Tantras are traditionally divided into two categories: "Father Tantra," whose synonyms are listed by Panchen Sonam Drakpa (bsod nams grags pa) in his sixteenth century work *Overview of Buddhist Tantra* as Yogi Tantra, "Method Tantra" and Ḍāka Tantra; and Mother Tantra, also known as Yoginī Tantra, "Wisdom Tantra" and Ḍākinī Tantra (Sonam 43).[87] Khedrup Je (mkhas grub rje), in his fifteenth century work *Introduction to the Buddhist Tantric Systems*[88] adds to this list the appellation *Mahāyoga* Tantra for the Father Tantras. The principal text representing the Father Tantras is, according to Alex Wayman, the *Guhyasamāja*, though Panchen Sonam Drakpa further lists the *Kṛṣṇayamāri* and the *Mahātantrarājānāma*; while chief among the Mother Tantras (still according to Wayman) is the *Cakrasaṁvara,* though includes such important and influential works as the *Kālacakra* and the *Hevajra*. Wayman summarizes Khedrup Je's explanation of the difference between the two classes of *Anuttarayoga* Tantra:[89]

---

[85] David Gordon White's *Kiss of the Yoginī* (2003) supports that hypothesis in a pan-South Asian—though predominantly Hindu—context.

[86] I say so-called, as Elizabeth English presents a rather convincing argument in *Vajrayoginī: Her Visualizations, Rituals and Forms* that the Sanskrit term *anuttarayoga* never existed as such in the Indian Buddhist Tantric context, but rather is a translation of the indigenously created Tibetan term for the category, *rnal 'byor bla na med pa'i rgyud.*

[87] In Vajrayāna systems, *prajñā / ye shes* and *upāya / thabs* are a pair that must be united in perfect harmony in order for full Buddhahood to occur. Traditionally they are associated with "male" and "female" aspects and qualities (*yab-yum*—"father-mother"), and are depicted iconographically by deities in union.

[88] *rgyud sde spyi'i rnam par gzhag pa rgyas par brjod.*

[89] Wayman 1977, 61.

> [A] Father Tantra emphasizes the "means" side of the "means-insight" union, and so deals especially with the topics so prominent in the present work [*Guhyasamāja Tantra*] of evoking the three lights and the Clear Light.... A Mother Tantra puts emphasis on the "insight" side of the "means-insight" union, and so treats the indissoluble bliss and void.

Khedrup Je explains there is a difference between the understanding of skillful means ("means": *upāya*, *thabs*) and wisdom ("insight": *prajñā*, *yeshe*) in their proper context, understood as individual terms, and as the appellations associated with the two divisions of the *Anuttarayoga* Tantras. On its own, "skillful means" refers to "the Knowledge born together with (*sahaja*) Great Beatitude (*mahāsukha*)";[90] and "wisdom" refers to "the knowledge which fully comprehends that all natures (*sarvadharmaḥ*) are devoid of intrinsic reality (*niḥsvabhāva*)."[91] In other words: bliss and emptiness. He contrasts this with their meanings in their contexts as names for the divisions for the Highest Tantras:[92]

> A Mother Tantra is established as follows: It is any Tantra which emphasizes the subject matter of the Knowledge of indissolubility of Beatitude [bliss] and Void [emptiness] in the part of "Insight" [wisdom] on the Void side, while not especially emphasizing such things as the method of accomplishing the Illusory Body in the part of 'Means' on the phenomenal side.

In other words, a Mother Tantra is one which deals with insight into the union of bliss (*mahāsukha*) and emptiness (*śūnyatā*; *niḥsvabhāva*). He explains the Father Tantra as consisting more in practices, "those which teach elaborately the coming forth with skill in the method of accomplishing the illusory body from the five rays of wind riding on the four voids in the part of the 'Means.'"[93]

---

[90] Khedrup Je 1998, 261.

[91] Ibid.

[92] Ibid., 265.

[93] Ibid.

I focus primarily on the Mother Tantras, as it is specifically within this class that we find a worldview and system of developmental stages consistent with what is found in the works of the mahāsiddhas. Indeed, in the introduction to the index (*dkar chag*) of the Derge Tengyur (*sde dge bstan 'gyur*), Shuchen Tsultrim Rinchen (zhu chen tshul khrims rin chen; 1697–1774) explicitly states that the teachings of (and those associated with) the *dohā*s refer to the Mother Tantras;[94] and additionally Saraha's work comes after the section of the Tengyur dedicated to the *Cakrasaṁvara Tantra* indicating that they belong together thematically.

The Mother Tantras emerge in written form sometime around the eighth century CE, and represent one of the latest bodies of Indian Buddhist literature. Roger R. Jackson provides a useful summary of characteristic traits of the Mother Tantras, as he asserts that the *dohā* treasuries of Saraha (as well as those of his fellow mahāsiddhas Tilopa and Kāṇha) "each presents clear evidence that its author was familiar with, and probably a practitioner of, the Yoginī tantras."[95] In common with most South Asian yogic traditions, the Mother Tantras base themselves on a "saṁsāra-nirvāṇa" cosmology, which describes at a general level the state and goal of all sentient beings. In specifically Buddhist terms, sentient beings are propelled from one life to the next by the force of their karma or past actions, words, and thoughts, and because of their affliction by basic ignorance do not easily change the bad habits which perpetuate the suffering experienced throughout their endless existences. Following the *bodhisattva* path, all sentient beings must strive to attain full awakening —Buddhahood—which is achieved by some particular means, in the Tantric context. Central to any understanding of Tantra is the relationship of body to universe. "Body" here does not refer to merely the physical body, or imply a body-mind duality. In the Tantric context, "body" refers to the subtle body (*sūkṣma śarīra*), which is neither distinct from nor identical to the gross physical body or "mind" as it's conceived of, and which consists of a network of channels (*nāḍi*, *rtsa*), winds (*prāṇa*, *rlung*) and drops (*biṇḍu*, *thig le*). The subtle body is the locus of all spiritual work, transformation, and eventual awakening. Its relationship to the

94 Shuchen Tsultrim Rinchen 1985, 698.

95 Jackson 2004, 10–11.

universe or cosmos at large, is one of identity. Transformations effected at the micro-level of the subtle body influence the experience at the macro-level that is the cosmos. Conversely, practices that engage with the gross, physical world effect transformations at the level of the subtle body. The universe as a sacred realm is mapped onto the subtle body, and *vice versa*. In conceiving the outer world as a sacred realm, the yogin conceives him/herself as the principal deity inhabiting that realm, thus experiencing everything as a maṇḍala. Particular to the practices associated with the Mother Tantras, is the elaboration of a set of "seals" (*mudrā*, *phyags rgya*) which refer at once to a type of practice and a level of attainment, the highest of which is the Great Seal (to be discussed further below). Also particular to the Mother Tantras are the four blisses[96] that build on each other and culminate in the "great bliss" (*mahāsukha*, *bde ba chen po* / *bde chen*) which is held to be synonymous with both *sahaja*, the innate, and the Great Seal.[97] In the *Hevajra Tantra* it is written in a discussion of the four blisses, "*caturthaṁ sahajaṁ smṛtam*": "the fourth is known as the Innate."[98]

Another key concept is that of "one taste" (*samarasa*, *ro gcig* / *ro snyoms*), which characterizes the "flavor" of all experiences and phenomena.[99] It entails not only the one blissful flavor of all experiences, but points as well to the nature of all phenomena and the indivisibility of experiences and phenomena. The innate great bliss is the true nature of everything, and so everything should be experienced with the same joy. Learning to experience the diversity of life's experiences as being uniformly blissful expressions of awakening is not a simple process, and

[96] Bliss, highest bliss, free of bliss, innate bliss (*dga' ba*, *mchog dga'*, *dga' bral*, *lhan cig skyes pa'i dga' ba*). These are stages of psycho-spiritual experience, felt and established as states by *yogins* and *yoginīs* engaging in union practices—whether with an actual consort, by means of visualization of a consort, or taking place as processes within the subtle body.

[97] Jackson 2004, 12–15.

[98] Farrow 1992, 124.

[99] While it doesn't appear very frequently in the *Adamantine Songs*, where it does appear it is significant, as when used to describe the "flavor" of *Dharmatā*: "*Dharmatā* has one taste, the same as flowers for bees. / The faults and virtues are themselves equal in the indivisible nature." (*Body Treasury*, verse 21)

necessitates difficult and intense training. This notion underlies the theory of the higher Buddhist Tantras in general:[100]

> The work of transformation requires overcoming dualistic aversion to notions of pure and impure, a willingness on occasion to transgress conventional moral norms, and skillful manipulation of one's mind and energies.... In order to harness one's energies, one must be willing on occasion to ingest 'impure' substances such as alcohol, semen, and blood, and engage in sexual yoga practices.... The result of controlling one's energies is the production —or revelation—within the central channel of a blissful, enlightened gnosis.

The relationship of subtle body to cosmos, the four seals and four blisses, the innate and "one taste" are indeed all central to both the Mother Tantras and to the teachings of the mahāsiddhas. Another important aspect is the importance of the guru. Interestingly, though Saraha is not understood to have had a human guru, his work is nonetheless permeated by exhortations to revere the guru above all. In the *Body Treasury* he writes: "In your reverence to the Guru, the discipline of the secret vehicle is complete."[101] Further, he ends the second song of the trilogy, the *Speech Treasury*, with the following statement: "Pleasing the Guru is basis of all *siddhi*s. / Not abandoning the precious Guru, the awakened qualities arise."[102] As a narrative example about the importance of the Guru, drawn from the biography of two of the mahāsiddhas whose stories are told together as they are sisters, I particularly enjoy the story of Mekhalā and Kanakhalā. Mekhalā and Kanakhalā were born into the family of a householder in Devīkoṭṭa. Though their behavior is irreproachable, the townspeople gossip about them maliciously, moving them to

---

[100] Jackson 2004, 13. For a discussion of the history of ingesting these ritually impure substances and their various functions in a number of contexts, I refer readers again to David Gordon White's *Kiss of the Yoginī*.

[101] Verse 34.

[102] Verse 48.

seek refuge in something other than worldly life. Kāṇha[103] comes to town and when the sisters witness his numerous, impressive *siddhi*s, they beg him to be their guru. He accepts, instructs them in a practice on Adamantine Sow (*Vajravārāhī*, *rdo rje'i phag mo*), and they retreat to practice for twelve years. After that time, they went back to Kāṇha to present him with offerings. After a brief exchange, Kāṇha demands his fee: their heads. Without hesitation they lop off their own heads (with wisdom swords that emerge spontaneously from their own mouths) and present them to their guru. The guru restores their severed heads and they go on to achieve full awakening and the benefit of many sentient beings.[104] The biographies of the mahāsiddhas are full of stories like this one, detailing

---

[103] Another aspect of this particular story which seems quite appropriate to this chapter is the fact that their guru is Kāṇha, another mahāsiddha who, like Saraha, is renowned for his songs. For translations of his work see Jackson (2004) and Shahidullah (1928).

[104] *Gu ru mekhalaa'i lo rgyus ni / yul dewiikota na khyim bdag cig la bu mo gnyis yod pa la / ded dpon zhig la yang bu gnyis yod pa gnyen du byas pa dang / bu mo de gnyis la thams cad kha zer bar byed pa la / de gynis kyis ngan pa byas pa ni ci yang med do // de'i tshe nu mo na re / rgyu mtshan med pa la kha zer ba 'di 'dra las / gzhan du 'khyams dgos zer / phu mo na re / gang du phyin kyang tshogs ma bsags pas 'di dang khyad mi 'ong bas 'di rang du bsdad dgos zer ba'i tshe bla ma kanhapaa bya be der byon / de ni rnal 'byor pho mo bdun brgyas bskor ba / ma reg pa'i gdugs dbu la 'khor ba / daamaru'i sgra ma dkrol bar 'khrol ba la sogs pa'i yon tan dpag tu med pa dang ldan par grags pas / spun gnyis kyis 'o skol gnyis la yul mi dang khyos kyang kha zer bas / bla ma 'di la gdams pa zhus nas sgrub pa byed dgos byas nas de'i can du phyin nas / sngar gyi lo rgyus bsnyad cing gdams pa zhus pas / des kyang gnang ste / dbang bskur nas lta ba sgom pa spyod pa 'bras bu zung 'jug phag mo'i gdams pa gnang ngo // de gnyis kyis brtson pas bsgrubs pas lo bcu gnyis nas grub pa thob ste / bla ma can du phyin nas phyag dang mchod pa byas / bka' drin gyis khyab pa'i gtam btang bas / khyed gang pa yin / ngas ma shes gsungs pas / sngar gyi lo rgyus bsnyad do / 'o na nga la yon 'bul dgos gsungs pas / bla ma ci bzhed pa 'bul zhus pas / 'o na nga la khyed gnyis kyi mgo bo byin cig gsungs pas des kyang bla ma bzhed na 'bul zer nas / de gnyis kyis rang gi khan as ye shes kyi ral gri rno ngar dang ldan pa re phyung nas yan lag gi dam pa mgo bcad nas pul te / bdag cag gnyis po bla ma'i bka' drin gyis // bskyed rdzogs zung 'jug 'khor 'das spros pa bcad // lta spyod zung 'jug spang blang spros pa bcad // dbyings rig zung 'jug bdag bzhan spros pa bcad // sbros med brda yi tshul du 'di 'bul lo //* (1) *zhes gsungs gzhin dbu bcad de gar mdzad pas / kanhapa'i zhal nas / e ma rnal 'byor chen mo gnyis // yon tan mchog thob dge ba ste // rang nyid zhi bde dman pas na // 'gro ba'i don phyir gnas par mdzod // (2) ces gsungs pas / mgo bo slar gsos te rma med par gyur pas / thams cad ngo mtshar skyes nas dbu bcad ma spun gnyis su grags / Kanhapaa'i zhabs 'bring byas nas phyag rgya chen po'i dngos grub thob / lo mang du 'gro don mdzad nas rtogs pa brjod pa la sogs pa mdzad / de nas mkha' spyod du gshegs so //* (Abhayadatta 228–231)

the devotion of the disciples to their guru. Among the numerous other crucial factors derived in large part from the Mother Tantras in the practice and theory of the Buddhist siddhas, the teacher is also a factor of high importance.

Non-Buddhist South Asian Siddha Traditions

As I mentioned above, most religious traditions that have flourished in South Asia at one time or another have witnessed the flowering of a siddha tradition. While there are of course differences between them, some important commonalities may be found. One feature strongly shared by all is that the goal is achieved within and incorporating the living body of the practitioner. David Gordon White opens an essay on the "microcosmology" of the medieval siddhas with the following statement: "The goal common to all Tantric practice, in very general terms, is to embody the divine, to incorporate it into oneself and have an embodied experience of the deity."[105] While in specifically Buddhist terms, the idea of a deity engages a particularly Buddhist ontology, this is nonetheless a fair statement to make. All siddha traditions are "Tantric" in the sense that they conceive of the locus of practice and transformation to be the body. While the number and name of such features as channels, winds, drops, and energy centers (cakras) of the subtle body change from tradition to tradition (and sometimes within traditions—the number of cakras for example varies from one Buddhist Tantra to the next), the basis of transformation and its relationship to the universe at large is consistent. In his comparison of siddha traditions (including Tamil siddhas, Nātha *yogīs*, Vaiṣṇava sahajiyās and Bāuls), Peter Heehs writes:[106]

> First, all of them were unorthodox and opposed to mechanical devotion and ritualism. Though associated with the Śaiva or Vaiṣṇava traditions, they did not view the Supreme as an object of worship but as a living presence within. Instead of scriptures, they relied on human gurus

---

[105] "Le but commun de toutes les pratiques tantriques, dit en termes très généraux, est d'incarner le divin, de l'incorporer en soi et d'obtenir ainsi une experience corporelle de la divinité." Translation mine. (White 2002, 189)

[106] Heehs 2003, 282.

> or the inner guide; instead of ritual or worship, they emphasized practices that opened the way to mystical experience. Since they viewed the Godhead as a principle within them, they gave a good deal of importance to the body, which they regarded both as a vessel of divinity and a means for its attainment.

Interestingly, one of the sites where the cross-fertilization of siddha cultures makes itself evident is in lists of adepts' names as they are presented by the various traditions. The amazing proliferation of names common to many different lists is painstakingly detailed by David Gordon White in *The Alchemical Body*. I will not repeat his work here, but will rather draw out one comparison to illustrate my point. There are reputed to be nine Nāth siddhas who are traditionally looked to as the basis of the Nāth movement. First on the list is generally Matsyendranāth, whose name some conflate with both Minanāth (also known as Minapa) and Luipa,[107] two of the Eighty-Four mahāsiddhas whose biographies are recounted in the *Lives of the Eighty-Four Mahāsiddhas*. Second on the Nāth's list is Gorakhnāth, or Gorakṣa, another siddha also claimed by the Buddhists in their famous list of eighty-four. In fact, both Matsyendranāth and Gorakhnāth appear on siddha lists belonging to numerous traditions, frequently alongside such names as Nāgārjuna.[108] For example, Matsyendranāth and Gorakhnāth are appropriated as two of the eighteen Tamil siddhas (*cittar*s) as Gōrakkar and Maccamuṉi.[109]

A consideration of the poetry of the siddhas across traditions helps to highlight the striking similarities in a way that no discussion can. Śivavākkiyar, a Tamil saint who lived at approximately the same time as Saraha (circa ninth century CE) writes:[110]

> In the Four Eternal Vedas,
> In the study and reading of scripts,

[107] White 1996, 91.

[108] For a detailed account of the "cross-indexing" between siddha lists, see Chapter 4 in White's *The Alchemical Body* (78–122).

[109] Little 2006, 28, n28.

[110] Heehs 2003, 288; Zvelebil's translation.

In sacred ashes and in Holy Writs
And muttering of prayers
You will not find the Lord!
Melt with the Heart Inside
And proclaim the Truth.

Most striking here is that Śivavākkiyar opens his song (*pāṭal*) with a dismissal of the Four Vedas—precisely where Saraha begins his critique in his famous *Dohākośa*:[111]

Bah! Brahmins—
They don't know what's what:
In vain they incant
Their four Vedas.

I am not suggesting that there was necessarily any poetic borrowing going on; indeed it is hard to say anything about this for certain except that these two siddhas were critiquing a common milieu. Akappēy *cittar* (dates unknown) describes the path and goal in purely negative terms, providing a striking parallel to the language of Saraha's *Adamantine Songs*:[112]

I do not exist
The Lord does not exist
The Self does not exist
The Teacher does not exist

Mantras do not exist
Experience does not exist
Tantras do not exist
Doctrines have been destroyed

Rites are just devil's play
Knowledge—a hollow stable
The Lord is but an illusion
Everything is like that

---

[111] Jackson 2004, 53.

[112] Heehs 2003, 288; Zvelebil's translation.

Why and what for to study?
Why and what for to act?
All set rules and all forms
Have been burnt and annulled

All manifested actions
You see are only Void
Those which in fact do not appear
Will appear in Pure Nothingness

—Akappēy *cittar*

Compare this to the following lines from the *Body Treasury Adamantine Song*: "Don't think of saṁsāra, don't be concerned with nirvāṇa.... / No effort in anything, no views, nothing to accept and reject";[113] or:

The practice of meditation and recitation of mantras are
 but one's mind,
Even meditational deities are one's own mind.
Due to that, ḍākinīs, making prophecies, etc., are one's
 own mind:
Mind displays itself in whatever thoughts appear.
Where there is no recognition, no*thing* can be observed.[114]

The last example I will cite is by Lalla, a fourteenth century CE poet-saint who is claimed by both Kashmiri Śaivas and Sufis. The reader should note that her poem iterates a strong sense of anti-ritualism and a clear familiarity with Tantric worldview (how the body and cosmos are not separate, and when awakened both reflect pervasive perfection) and techniques of practice:[115]

I took the reins of the mind-horse
Through practice, I learned breath control

---

[113] Verse 16.

[114] Verses 55–56.

[115] Heehs 2003, 294–**95**. Sun and moon in Tantric terms refer to specific yogic techniques involving the subtle body.

Then only the orb of moon melted and flowed down into
my body
Nothingness merged with nothingness.

Cold changes water into ice or snow
Discernment shows the three states though different are
not really different
When the sun of consciousness shines,
The plurality is dissolved into oneness
Then the universe appears throughout permeated with
Shiva.

When teachings disappear, the mantra remains
When the mantra disappears, nothing remains
Nothingness merges with nothingness.

Easy to read but difficult to follow
Attaining self-knowledge is subtle and difficult
Absorbed in practice, I forgot the scriptures
Consciousness-bliss I realized.

I am struck by many features of Lalla's work, including her use of the relationship of water and ice as an analogy to describe the single nature (one taste?) of what appears as multiplicity. Saraha uses precisely the same analogy in the *Body Treasury Adamantine Song*:[116]

In the direct encounter with just that, the experience of the
unborn,
The empty nature of appearance dawns as great bliss.
Just as melted ice can be drunk as water,
So, whatever appears, does so richly as unborn great bliss.

Equanimity is free of recognition although
conceptualization is not obstructed;
By being beyond the intellect, it is free of deluded
meditation.
When one rests in that, the experience of great bliss
occurs.

---

[116] Verses 100–103.

First the experience of appearance and emptiness occurs,
Like recognizing water even when it appears as ice.

Second, without obstructing the appearance of recognition,
Emptiness and bliss arise undifferentiated.
Just as ice melts into water,
Recognition and decognition dissolve in the unborn.

Since everything is undifferentiated, it is one in the great
bliss.
This is like ice melting into water.
If one knows whatever is encountered to be the nature of
everything,
One will not be held by bondage and freedom and will not
chase after recognition.

Another area where we may tentatively suggest that there is evidence of influence is between the lives and traditions of the great adepts of Buddhism and the lives and traditions associated with bhakti saints. In his work, Davidson squarely associates the Śaiva and Śākta personalities whose influence on the Buddhist siddhas is clear exclusively with ascetic siddha movements such as the *pāśupata* and *aghora* traditions. He characterizes them as discrete from bhakti, which as a social and religious revolution had been sweeping across South Asia from the fifth century CE onward. I am inclined to not make such a strong distinction, as my examination of the hagiographies and poetry associated with early Tamil bhakti—whether Śaiva or Vaiṣṇava—reveals cross-fertilization among poetic and hagiographic traditions as clearly as that between ascetic traditions.

The Tamil bhaktas emerged slightly earlier than the Buddhist siddhas (circa fifth century CE) and continued to flourish until the twelfth century CE. This makes them both predecessors and contemporaries of the Buddhist siddhas, and therefore an interesting point of comparison with them. Their hagiographies have some parallels with those of the Buddhist siddhas, including humble origins, transgressive behavior that leads to alienation from mainstream/orthodox society, tales of converting nonbelievers, and teaching through spontaneously uttered songs and poems. Like the Buddhist siddhas, the bhaktas' legacy is preserved in a text that consists of hagiographies and poems. Here I summarize the story of Kaṇṇappaṉ as an illustration. Kaṇṇappaṉ, one of the sixty-three Nāyaṉārs (Tamil Śaiva saints), was from a tribal background and lived as a hunter. One day he came upon an image of Śiva in the forest and deep devotion was aroused in his heart:[117]

> Sighs he heaved for a long time; the hair
> On his body stood erect as he felt thrilled
> In every pore of his; his eyes rained tears.
> "Ha! I, the servitor, have here found my Lord!"
> It was as though peerless love assumed his form.

He would bring offerings, including water that he would carry in and pour onto the image from his mouth, and flesh from animals that he had hunted sometimes even pre-chewed. Śiva accepted his devotee's offerings because they were gestures of pure devotion, made in innocence of how transgressive they were. One day a Brahmin priest came upon the remains of bone and flesh that Kaṇṇappaṉ had offered. Outraged by what he perceived as a pollution of a sacred site, he cleaned the area and conducted purifying rituals. A regular pattern ensued of Kaṇṇappaṉ offering meat to Śiva and the priest cleansing the site. Finally the priest, at his wit's end, supplicated Śiva to put an end to the pollution. Śiva came to him in a dream and told him not to worry, that the hunter existed only to love him (Śiva). He also told the priest to conceal himself the next day to watch a test of Kaṇṇappaṉ's love planned by the Lord himself. The next day when Kaṇṇappaṉ arrived Śiva caused one eye on the image to start bleeding. In response, Kaṇṇappaṉ gouged out one of his own eyes and placed it carefully in the bleeding eye socket of the image. Śiva then caused the other eye to start bleeding. Kaṇṇappaṉ, worried that he wouldn't know where to place his second eye after he plucked it out (because he would be blind), placed the big toe of his left foot on the bleeding spot on the image, then prepared to gouge out his other eye. Śiva was overcome with emotion and stayed Kaṇṇappaṉ's hand saying, "Stop! Oh Kaṇṇapa!"[118]

---

[117] Cēkkiḻār, 162.

[118] Cēkkiḻār, 172. Iconographically, Kaṇṇappaṉ is often imaged standing with one foot pressed against a *liṅgaṁ*.

The hagiographies and poetry of the sixty-three Nāyaṉārs, together with those of the twelve Āḻvārs (Tamil Vaiṣṇava saints), are filled with stories of extreme acts of devotion expressed in deeply unconventional ways, abandonment of the norms of society leading at first to rejection and even persecution, followed by eventually being recognized as a saint (sometimes posthumously), and miraculous happenings that rupture the constraints of time and space that characterize most living beings' experience of reality. For example, one may note that there is a clear parallel in the fact that the outrageous and violent behavior of the Eighty-four Buddhist mahāsiddhas and that of the sixty-three Nāyaṉārs, bear positive results. The Saints are inevitably vindicated when, by miraculous means, their transgressive behavior is revealed as a proof of their superior devotion or insight. There are critical differences as well. For example, whereas in the case of the mahāsiddhas there is a strong sense that the siddha who is committing a particular act is doing so on the basis that ultimately the nature of all things is śūnya, or empty, and the display of seemingly immoral behavior is a kind of *upāya* or skillful means employed to help others attain some insight; in the case of the Nāyaṉārs the transgressive behavior is rooted in profound, devotional love (*aṉpu*) for Śiva and bears fruit according to how Śiva is moved.[119] My object is not to demonstrate identity between these traditions, but to point to meaningful similarities.[120]

---

119 For that reason, I see more of a parallel between the Nāyaṉārs antinomianism and that which takes place in the Guru/disciple context in Indian and Tibetan Buddhist hagiographies/biographies (see *Life of Nāropā, Life of Marpa the Translator*, or the *Life of Milarepa* for good examples of this), where there is a relationship between two agents based on love and devotion. For a discussion of Nāyaṉārs and *aṉpu* see D. Dennis Hudson's (1989) "Violent and Fanatical Devotion Among the Nayanars: A Study in the *Periya Purāṇam* of Cekkilar."

120 Among important distinctions to be made between adepts is the goal of the transformation sought by the siddhas. The mundane *siddhi*s, or "accomplishments," are more or less consistent between schools—from the power of flight, to being able to enlarge, shrink, or multiply one's physical form, to invisibility to the power to transfer one's consciousness to the body of any recently deceased sentient being, there is a seemingly endless list of possibilities. As far as the "ultimate" aim goes, however, differences begin to emerge. For Buddhist siddhas, there is only one ultimate *siddhi*: full awakening. For many other South Asian siddha movements, however, achieving immortality (*jīvanmukti*) is the ultimate goal. The *rasa* siddhas are a good example of this. See White (1996).

Another important shared feature between the Buddhist and Tamil Śaiva and Vaiṣṇava adepts is the textual vehicle of their preservation and transmission. Much has already been said of Abhayadatta's *Lives of the Eighty-four Mahāsiddhas*, but it is important to remember that it is part of a larger corpus of work related to the siddhas, a collection of biographies, songs, and commentaries that were translated into Tibetan in the late eleventh or early twelfth century.[121] In the twelfth century in a different region of the sub-continent, another collection of hagiographies and songs was compiled, one that would become so important to Śaivas that it is included in the Śaiva canon and is known as the Fifth Veda. It is called the *Periya Purāṇam* or *The Great Epic* and it contains the hagiographies and poems of the sixty-three Nāyaṉārs. It is a mix of material compiled and composed by Cēkkiḻār (himself later included in the canon). He wrote an epic poetic formulation of their hagiographies based on the sources he had access to, and compiled the poems of the sixty-three Nāyaṉārs as well.[122] While it is clearly a more important text to Śaivas than the *Lives of the Eighty-four Mahāsiddhas* is to Buddhists, it is fascinating to consider that these two traditions of poetry-uttering heterodox saints were rendered as startling similar literary traditions during the same century.

Literary Context: South Asia

Saraha's transmission does not consist merely in his presence—past and present—but also in the corpus of his work. As befits a mahāsiddha, his method of teaching was spontaneous, inspired, and challenging. Saraha is said to have uttered collections of esoteric verses designed to directly point to the nature of mind and reality. Despite the size of the corpus (there are twenty-four works attributed to him in the Tengyur alone),[123] the only ones that have received any serious attention to date are his *Dohā*

[121] See Kapstein (2001) for a discussion of some of the sources and a translation of two of the less known siddha texts.

[122] This is strongly reminiscent of the narrative we find in the *Garland of Gems,* translated by Kapstein (2001) as "King Kuñji's Banquet."

[123] Tōhoku numbers: 1652, 1655, 1656, 1657, 2224, 2263, 2264, 2266, 2267, 2269, 2270, 2271, 2272, 2273, 2274, 2275, 2276, 2345, 2351, 2440, 3164, 3165, 3171, 3427.

Trilogy (*Doha skor gsum*; *grub snying*),[124] a trilogy of songs that have eclipsed everything else attributed to the master Saraha. His "King" and "People" *dohās* have been translated numerous times into English and into other Western languages[125] and have been the subject of major studies. Saraha's *Adamantine Songs*, however, have scarcely been touched.[126] While this is to a degree a reflection of the emphasis placed on Saraha's *dohās* within Tibetan traditions themselves, it remains a curiosity to me, given both the scope of his *Adamantine Songs* and the pervasiveness of the genre in general. Adamantine, or "Diamond" Songs (as they are often called) are one of the most popular genres of spiritual poems in Tibetan Buddhist culture. From Marpa in the eleventh century to Allan Ginsberg in the twentieth, the composition, recitation, reading, and study of *Adamantine Songs* quietly pervades Tibetan Buddhist literary and religious culture, especially the Karma Kagyu.

While it is impossible to really separate the Indian and Tibetan contexts of the *Adamantine Songs*, since it is through their preservation in the Tibetan cultural sphere that we have access to them, it is nonetheless important to examine the *Adamantine Songs* and other chief genres of the Buddhist siddhas first in their South Asian context.

As mentioned above, the author of the songs I have translated is equally well known as "Saraha" and "The Great Brahmin." Much has been made of his Brahmanical youth, and it is therefore easily believable that not only was he well-trained (and very possibly composing his songs) in Sanskrit, but may also have been educated in Sanskrit poetics. As aesthetic manuals consider both Sanskrit and Apabhraṁśa to be appropriate to the task of composing literary works,[127] it is therefore also

---

[124] It is often referred to as *grub snying* or "The Heart of Accomplishment" in *The Blue Annals*.

[125] See Conze (1954); Guenther (1969, 1993); Shahidullah (1928); Schaeffer (2000); Jackson (2004); Khenchen Thrangu (2006). The "Queen" song has only been translated twice, to my knowledge (Guenther 1993; Jackson 2012).

[126] There are cursory references to it in Guenther (1993) and Schaeffer (2005), but overall they have been neglected.

[127] Daṇḍin says of the language: "What is called 'Apabhramsha' is the language of the Ābhīras and others when used in literary works; whereas in scholarly discourse anything that deviates from correct Sanskrit is so named" (cited in Pollock 2006, 91–92). On the use of Apabhraṁśa as a literary language, see Pollock (2006).

appropriate to surmise that a Brahmin composing poetry in either Sanskrit or Apabhraṁśa would be carrying the burden of the language's literary history with him. Though the fact that he is said to have spontaneously uttered his songs and that those same songs are said to have been preserved by oral tradition for a time precludes considering them as *kāvya*[128] at least during the time of their composition, and although his work cannot be said to conform to the aesthetic and structural norms described by Daṇḍin, Bhārata, and others, it is still interesting to imagine that he may have had to consciously shed that training, adding still another layer onto his already rebellious persona.

Dohā

This section discusses three forms of "yogic" songs that emerged first in the South Asian context: *dohā*, *caryāgīti* (*spyod pa'i glu*), and *vajragīti* (*rdo rje'i glu*), all of which appear to emerge from folk literary/ musical traditions. *Dohā*s are one of the best-known styles of poetry or song composed by Saraha and the other great adepts. There are two principal etymologies: first, if one takes accepts *dohā* to be a Prakrit meter,[129] the name can be broken down as "do" referring to the number, 2, and "hā" meaning, roughly, "said." *Dohā*s, then, would simply be poems composed in 2-line stanzas, or couplets. *Dohā* is difficult to describe. Each couplet will share the number of syllables and exhibit a patterned emphasis of long and short letters; each "line" (*pāda*) is divisible into three syllabic feet (*gaṇa*), and the last syllable of the two *pādas* will rhyme. Between couplets, however, there is no regularity in the number of syllables or distribution of long and short letters between couplets.[130] This may enforce the idea that the *dohā* are far removed from their Sanskrit relatives, and more closely linked to the Prakritic poetic traditions that include more flexible meters enabled by, for example, the

---

[128] "One thing that could not be *kāvya* was the purely oral… [N]ot only is *kāvya* defined practically if not explicitly by writing for us modern readers who cannot know an unwritten literary past, but it was so for the premodern actors themselves" (Pollock 2006, 3–4).

[129] Vaudeville 2005; Dundes and Vatuk 1974.

[130] See Shahidullah (1928, 60ff.) for a careful metrical study of Saraha's *People Dohā*.

mātrika system.[131] This would support the strong hypothesis that Saraha was writing or singing in Apabhraṁśa. Charlotte Vaudeville explains that "the *dohā*... appears as the most typical form of Apabhraṁśa literature"[132] and differs from earlier forms of Prakrit poetry in a number of respects, including that it is the first prosodical form to introduce rhyme.[133] From the Apabhraṁśa *dohā*s to the Old Western Rājasthāni *dūhās*, the form was popular among ascetics from all traditions.[134]

There is some suggestion that the corresponding Sanskrit meter would be *dodhakam*.[135] *Dodhakam* has 11 syllables in each quarter (*pāda*), each of which has four syllabic feet (*gaṇa*): three *bhagaṇa*s (a three syllable *gaṇa* in which first letter is long and the second two are short: - ˇˇ) and one *gaṇa* that has two *guru* (long) letters (--). This structure does not appear to be consistently borne out by the extant Apabhraṁśa *dohā* texts attributed to Saraha and other siddhas.

Alternatively, we may allow that it comes from the Sanskrit root √*duh* "to milk," "since the language of *dohā* is employed as the milking which deeply fills, it is milking the primordial awareness of one's mind which is a mind filled with primordial awareness."[136] Both the "couplet" and "milking"' definitions make sense, even bracketing the issue of prosody, which is a matter vexed by many factors. It appears that the meter of *dohā* collections of various authors, still extant in their (presumably) original language, do not maintain regularity in that respect (although rhyming *is* a consistent feature), so that no discussions of Saraha's *dohā*s has been able to focus on that particular feature. David Templeman states:[137]

> As the *dohā* was primarily a means of direct, authentic communication between master and disciples, it had to

[131] Dundes 1974, 94. *Mātrā* describes a style of regulating meter through measuring syllabic instants rather than through syllables.

[132] Vaudeville 2005, 110.

[133] Ibid., 111.

[134] Ibid.

[135] Shahidullah 1928, 62; Vaudeville 2005, 110.

[136] Schaeffer 2000, 267.

[137] Templeman 1994, 17.

> express a spiritual truth in a way which would resonate with its listeners, rather than being understood by them at a conceptual level only. It had to fit into a wide range of folk rhythms and meters, as such songs had to travel into many cultural areas among unlettered people whose most practical way of gaining the message might well have been listening to such songs.

Caryāgīti

It is difficult to present a precise definition of the genre designated by the term *caryāgīti*. The name of the genre translates to "performance songs" and so clearly, the *caryāgīti* are song-poems that are meant to be performed. The locus of their performance is at Tantric gatherings. That they are meant to be sung is evident because in most collections of them, there is a *rāga* specified for each. In the collection of *caryāgīti* translated by Kvaerne, he has noted that each of the songs also has a refrain (*dhruva-pāda*) "indicating that a chorus alternated with a soloist."[138] Beyond these specifications, even Kvaerne himself writes that "it is a general term used to designate a genre of spiritual songs."[139] They are still very much in use in vajra Buddhist traditions of Nepal,[140] and in siddha cultures throughout South Asia. Templeman points out that much of the imagery and many motifs are drawn from everyday life of simple people:[141]

> The freewheeling confidence and the ebullient language of the *caryās* perfectly complements the rustic ingenuity of the motifs. There is neither fussiness nor ceremony in these downright practical songs, but neither does their functionality make them dour or 'spiritual.'

---

[138] Kvaerne 1986, 8.

[139] Ibid., 7.

[140] David N. Gellner's (1992) *Monk, Householder, and Tantric Priest,* a study of Newar Buddhism, details some rituals in which Tantric singers are employed.

[141] Templeman 1994, 30.

Templeman also explains that *caryās* are typically short songs, "consisting mostly of five verses of two lines per verse."[142] Since the songs are typically composed as part of a cycle, or group of songs, and are performed accompanied by instruments, elaborate rituals and often dance, a Tantric song performance can take hours or even over a day to complete.[143] As might be obvious to readers at this point, the *caryāgīti* are not transmitted or performed as a genre of spontaneous song, as they are performed by trained Tāntrikas at Tantric gatherings. While some of the composers of these songs (such as Saraha) may have initially created them spontaneously, their function has not retained that aspect of them. For an example of a *caryāgīta*, I cite here in full Kvaerne's translation of song 32, attributed to Saraha:[144]

> Neither Sound nor Drop, neither Sun nor Moon—
> The Mind-King is in its own-being free
> Abandoning the straight do not take the crooked!
> Enlightenment is near—do not go to Lankā!
> The bangle is on your wrist—do take a mirror (to see it)!
> You yourself must understand your Innate Mind.
> Whoever goes on either bank certainly dies in the
> company of evil folk.
> (As for) the ditches and holes on the left and the right—
> Saraha says: oh! They have been thought to be the straight
> path.

As is abundantly evident from this typical example, the *gīti* are short, technical, and obscure, and require instruction in order to understand.[145]

---

[142] Ibid., 31.

[143] Ibid.

[144] Kvaerne 1986, 199.

[145] Kvaerne (1986) helpfully provides Munidatta's commentary as well as his own explanations: "Whoever goes on either bank certainly dies" is glossed by Munidatta as "sinks in the ocean of saṃsāra" (199); "in the company of evil folk" is glossed by "delusion, etc." (ibid.); "As for the ditches and holes on the left and the right" he adds himself "Sun and Moon" (ibid.), which is a clear reference to the left and right channels of the subtle body (*lalanā* and *rasanā*); "Saraha says: oh! they have been thought to be the straight path" is glossed by "of the avadhūtī, leading to the City of Great Bliss" (ibid.).

Vajragīti: Adamantine Songs

"*Śūnyatā vajram ucyate*"[146]

Adamantine Songs (*vajragīti*, *rdo rje'i glu*) are most easily identified on sight by the fact that their titles usually will have "adamantine (vajra) song" worked into them. They do not have a meter or mood (*rasa*) that defines them apart from other forms of verse. In a way even more pronounced than with *dohās* and *caryāgīti*, *vajragīti* do not constitute a "genre" in the way that we usually understand this term. This becomes particularly evident when one attempts to find a definition for "vajra songs." Often defined contextually according to their function as the songs that were performed at Tantric assemblies,[147] definitions also have been attempted according to the aesthetic experience of particular readers.[148] It was explained to me that the "vajra" of "vajra songs" refers primarily to the *meaning* of the songs, not the form.[149] The content, in other words, has the same qualities as a vajra is understood to have in a Buddhist context: it is pure, impossible to stain or alter, clear, unbreakable, and precious. In Tantric contexts, it is also synonymous with śūnyatā, or emptiness. A particular feature of Tantric, or Vajrayāna thought is this particular understanding of emptiness. Whereas an interpretation of emptiness that is firmly rooted in Mādhyamika philosophy will understand emptiness to be synonymous with *pratītyasamutpāda* (dependent arising),[150] in a Vajrayāna context emptiness can be additionally nuanced in a different way. The songs treated here, very much in harmony with the poetic expressions of many yogins, express emptiness in terms of having some positive qualities.[151] While there is not a fully consistent list

---

[146] "Emptiness is said to be the Adamantine." From *Advayavajrasaṁgraha*, cited in Dasgupta 1952, 26.

[147] Templeman 1994; Jackson 2004.

[148] Schaeffer 2005.

[149] Fourteenth Shamar Rinpoche, personal communication.

[150] There are numerous academic works dedicated to the Madhyamaka interpretation of emptiness, usually based on the *Mūlamadhamakakārikā* of Nāgārjuna. I refer readers Garfield (1995; 2002); Hopkins (1995); and Nagao (1991).

[151] See Nagao (1991).

of such positive qualities, one that does span all the lists is "bliss" (*mahā-sukha*). Others, including the indestructibility, inherent purity, and clarity of emptiness, also make it synonymous with vajra, as those are equally qualities of a diamond. This understanding of emptiness is, I believe, reflected fully in the "other-empty" doctrine (*gzhan stong*; held by some Tibetan philosophers and many yogins, predominantly in Kagyu and Nyingma contexts), which holds that "emptiness" is empty of all qualities not innate to it—in other words, empty of everything *other* than itself.[152] Bhattacharya writes of the definition of the Adamantine Vehicle:[153]

> It was called Vajrayāna, because *śūnya* came to be designated by the term *vajra* on account of its indestructibility. The *śūnya* of the Vajrayāna is something different from the *śūnya* of the Mādhyamikas (nihilists) or the Vijñānavādins (idealists), because it includes the three elements *śūnya* (reality) *vijñāna* (consciousness), and *mahāsukha* (great bliss).

While one may disagree with both Bhattacarya's identification of Mādhyamikas as nihilists and his characterization of Vijñānavādins (Yogācārins) as idealists, the purpose of including this citation is to draw attention to the identity of vajra and śūnya. On the subject of the transformation of South Asian Buddhism from Mahāyāna to Vajrayāna, Dasgupta writes:[154]

> In this mode of transformation the most important point is the transformation of the idea of Śūnyatā (vacuity) into the idea of Vajra, or the thunderbolt. The Śūnyatā-nature of the world is its ultimate immutable nature, as immutable as the thunderbolt, and so it is called the Vajra. It has been said in the *Advaya-vajra-samgraha*, 'Śūnyatā, which is firm, substantial, indivisible, impenetrable, incapable of being burnt and imperishable, is called the Vajra.' This transformation of Śūnyatā to Vajra will explain the

---

[152] See Hookham (1991); Khenchen Thrangu Rinpoche (1994).

[153] Bhattacharyya 1996, 95.

[154] Dasgupta 1952, 26–27.

> title Vajrayāna and in the Vajra-yāna all the gods, goddesses, articles for worship, yogic practices and elaborate rituals have been marked with the Vajra to specialize them from their originally accepted nature.

Thus it becomes clear that the term vajra denotes the ultimate nature of reality, and that reality is sealed with the qualities of a diamond. This vast and deeply significant term carries all its connotations with it when used in "Vajragīti." As songs that express something about the ultimate nature of reality, *Adamantine Songs* have a special place in the Vajrayāna. Above all, *Adamantine Songs* can be defined by their having a function, and that function is more than merely emotive.

Tibetan Poetic Genres: An Introduction

Because this book is focused on a group of songs composed initially in a South Asian language, I will introduce the Tibetan song genres which can be directly linked with the transformative tradition of siddha songs like those of Saraha.[155] Many more evolved by the twelfth and thirteenth century into their own properly Tibetan genres, but the two sets become nearly impossible to distinguish in literature composed after the twelfth/thirteenth century, because naturally development in some spheres of poetics will bleed into the literary culture as a whole. Jinpa comments:[156]

> The spontaneous and fluid songs of Milarepa and his followers, full of vernacular terms and not so far from the language of the ordinary Tibetan, gave way to a much more stylized, refined, and elaborate poetic diction. In effect, the predominantly oral poetry of the eleventh, twelfth, and thirteenth centuries was transformed into a fully fledged literary and scholarly tradition.

[155] Though Tibetan masters, even those directly influenced by Indian siddha songs like Marpa, still retained their "Tibetan-ness." For a discussion of this, see Kapstein (2003, 770ff.).

[156] Jinpa 2000, 11. What Jinpa describes here may be understood, in Pollock's terms, as the *literarization* of Tibetan.

Jinpa begins this discussion with Milarepa (1052–1135), arguably Tibet's greatest and most famous yogin and poet. There is so much material available on Milarepa that recapitulating it is unnecessary, but it should be noted that his inspiring life story permeates most of Tibetan popular religious memory, and his abundant output as a poet is read and revered to this day. Throughout his long career as a Buddhist yogin and teacher, Mila used spontaneously composed poems and songs to express just about everything—from devotion, to realization, to reprimands, to instructions. Singing a genre of song known as *gur* (*mgur*), Mila is more or less single-handedly responsible for turning that genre into a vehicle for religious songs.[157] Initially a subdivision of the older *lu* (*glu*) genre (one which today is predominantly used for secular and life-cycle songs but which, prior to the eleventh century just meant "song" and referred to all poetry) *gur* evolved as a genre of religious song "with an experiential component: they might be either reports of spiritual realization or instructions based upon such realizations, or a combination of the two."[158] Mila's *gur* were solely preserved orally for hundreds of years after his death, though the influence of his stylistic innovations was felt immediately. Jackson identifies two main influences in the style of *gur* that Mila innovated: first, the indigenous Tibetan poetic traditions of songs of "positive personal experience"; and second, the tradition of Tantric songs brought to Tibet by Marpa.[159] He further cites Döndrup Gyel's (*don grub rgyal*; 1953–1985) more contemporary work[160] which designates seven categories of *gur*, generally according to content.[161]

A form of *gur* that stands apart is the *nyam gur* (*nyams mgur*), or "Song of Experience," which may be characterized by its intense subjectivity and reflection of direct insight. Jinpa writes, "More than being

---

[157] Jackson 1996, 372.

[158] Ibid.

[159] Jackson 1996, 373.

[160] *bod kyi mgur glu byung 'phel gyi lo rgyus dang khyad chos bsdus par ston pa rig pa'i khye'u rnam par rtsen pa'i skied tshal: mgur glu'i lo rgyus dang khyad chos* (1985).

[161] There are, according to Don grub rgyal, *gur* that (1) remember the guru's kindness, (2) indicate the source of one's realizations, (3) inspire the practice of Dharma, (4) give instructions on how to practice, (5) answer disciples' questions, (6) admonish the uprooting of evil, and (7) serve as missives to gurus or disciples (Jackson 1996, 374).

merely a subgenre of poetry, the songs of spiritual experience are a profound element of meditative practice and inspiration."[162] Later he adds that: "the key themes of Tibetan experiential songs touch on the most personal aspects of the spiritual path and on the profound insights into the nature of reality that are the fruits of the path."[163] It is the *nyam gur* that retained the spontaneity and freshness of the siddha songs from the subcontinent.

Jackson divides the Tibetan genre that predates *gur*, *lu*, broadly into two categories: royal songs (*rgyal po'i glu*) and popular songs (*'bangs kyi glu*). As "songs of positive personal experience" prior to Mila's time, *gur* were one of two classifications of the royal songs, the other of which is *chi* (*mchid*), "which are 'usually songs of provocation and dispute...(which combine) vivid, sophisticated symbolic imagery with more direct insults to create sung verbal combat.'"[164] Standard verse was defined by two principal meters, one of nine syllables and the other of seven. With the accent falling on the first syllable of each foot, they look like this: --/--/--/--- and --/--/---.[165] The *gur*, in comparison, as it evolved under the influence of Mila and his colleagues, "deliberately defy this convention."[166] Jinpa lists five potential meters for the post-Mila *gur*: --/-/--, --/--/--, -/--/--/---, --/--/---/--, --/--/--/---/--. In all of these meters, the accent again falls on the first syllable of each foot.

The tradition of composing various types of *lu*, *gur*, and *nyam gur* is one that is still very much in practice in contemporary Tibetan religious culture.[167] Presenting songs that express devotion to one's lineage and guru, and one's realization are "proofs" of insight, skill, and education. While most Lamas and Tulkus must spend most of their youth submitting to the strict curriculum of a monastery, training in "spontaneity" in some sense provides a controlled break from that. Jinpa writes:[168]

---

[162] Jinpa 2000, 15.

[163] Jinpa 2000, 17.

[164] Ellison, cited in Jackson 1996, 370.

[165] Jinpa 2000, 13.

[166] Ibid.

[167] See Sujata (2004) for an extensive study of the *mgur* of the seventeenth century Tibetan siddha poet Kalden Gyatso (*skal ldan rgya mtsho*).

[168] Jinpa 2000, 15.

> Just as the continuing lineage of writing spontaneous poetry acted as a counterforce to the impact of the rigid formalization of verse writing, so in the lives of individuals the spontaneity of the experiential songs was most important counterbalance to rigorous philosophical training and analysis.

There is no denying the enormous impact of Sanskrit poetics on Tibetan literary culture; once the intricacies of *kāvya* (*snyan ngag*) became part of an educated person's knowledge base, it was impossible to avoid its influence in composition. Nonetheless, cultivated as it may be, spontaneous poetic expression is a critical part of Tibetan literary culture.

The principal Sanskrit text that has guided the development of Tibetan poetics since its introduction to Tibet in the thirteenth century is Daṇḍin's seventh century work, the *Mirror of Poetry*.[169] The *Kāvyadarśa* was first introduced into Tibet by Sakya Paṇḍita Kunga Gyaltsen, or Sapan (sa skya paṇḍita kun dga' rgyal mtshan; 1182–1251) in *Gateway for the Learned*,[170] in which he lays out the required fields of knowledge to be mastered before one can be called "learned" (*paṇḍita*, *mkhas pa*). Sapan's work made an enormous impact on the curriculum of educated Tibetans from his own time forward, making the *Kāvyadarśa* or some of the famous commentaries on it required material in any study of the science of language (*śabdavidya*, *sgra rig pa*). According to van der Kuijp, the *Kāvyadarśa* was transmitted into Tibet some seven times, beginning with Sapan in the thirteenth century and ending in the sixteenth century.[171] Among Tibetan commentaries on the work considered to be authoritative, foremost among them are those by the Fifth Dalai Lama Ngawang Losang Gyatso (ngag dbang blo bzang rgya mtsho; 1617–1682), Mipham Gelek Namgyel (mi pham dge legs rnam rgyal; b. 1618) and Khamtrul Tenpe Nyima (khams sprul bstan pa'i nyi ma; b. 1745).[172] In very general terms, Daṇḍin's *Kāvyadarśa* defines and classifies *kāvya*

---

[169] *Kāvyadarśa, snyan ngag me long.*

[170] *mkhas pa rnams la 'jug pa'i sgo.*

[171] van der Kuijp 1996, 396.

[172] Jinpa 2000, 9.

(as "a series of words characterized by agreeable sense")[173]; discusses and develops *mārga* theory (diction, or the appropriate combination of word and sense); explores fully the art of ornamentation (*alaṁkāra*); examines the qualities (*guṇa*) and defects (*dośa*) of *kāvya*; and finally the poetic figures (*ārthālaṁkāra*) among which ideal figures readers are most likely to be familiar with the concept associated with the *rasa* and *bhāva*, or sentiment/taste/mood, of which Sapan says there are nine.[174] Jinpa writes of Daṇḍin's work:[175]

> The *Kāvyadarśa* is a remarkable work of synthesis that brought together the vast array of poetic traditions in the Sanskrit language from the north and south of the Indian subcontinent. Its principal concerns were the detailed codification of all the different uses of metaphor in poetry and how they affect poetic meaning, and a lengthy discussion of the linguistic skills...involved in the mastery of rhymes, puns, and acrostics.... Each verse of the *Kāvyadarśa* consists of an exposition of a particular use of metaphor or a poetic device.

Jinpa goes on to explain how one studies the *Kāvyadarśa* in a Tibetan context:[176]

---

[173] Gupta 1970, 121.

[174] They are: *sgeg pa nyams* or "elegant"; *dpa ba'i nyams* or "majestic"; *mi sdug pa'i nyams* or "repulsive"; *bzhed gad kyi nyams* or "ironic," "humorous"; *drag shul gyi nyams* or "wrathful," "fierce"; *'jigs rung nyams* or "terrifying," "awe-inspiring"; *rnying rje'i nyams* or "compassionate," "empathetic"; *zhi ba'i nyams* or "peaceful," "pacifying"; and *rmad 'byung nyams* or "admiring" (Jinpa 2000, 5). This is Sapan's adaptation of Daṇḍin's list of eight *rasas*, which is the standard number of *rasas* in aesthetic manuals until the time of Abhinavagupta who introduced *śāntarasa* (peaceful). The eight *rasas* are: *śṛṅgāra* or "love," *vīra* or "heroic," *bībhatsa* "terrible," "disgusting," *hāsya* or "humorous"; *raudra* or "wrathful"; *bhayānika* or "terrifying"; *kāruṇya* or "compassionate," "pity"; *adbhuta* or "wonderful." This may suggest that while he emphasizes the study of Daṇḍin, Sapan himself may have also been familiar with Abhinavagupta. See Gold (2007) for a study of Sapan's adaptation of Indian scholarship to the Tibetan context. See Kapstein (2003) for a study of the Tibetan adoption of Indian literary culture.

[175] Jinpa 2000, 9.

[176] Jinpa 2000, 9–10.

> The method of study is for the teacher to explain the intricacies of the verse to be covered that day and to present sample poems by great masters illustrating how they conform to the rules of poetics set down in the *Kāvyadarśa*. Students are then expected to read the commentary and to write their own sample stanzas for each of the forms studied that day.

To cover even one book of the *Kāvyadarśa* using this method of study takes over six months. Given that this is the education in poetics and composition one would receive, in a monastic context, even "spontaneous" verses would be thoroughly imbued with the aesthetics and structural parameters set by Daṇḍin, Sapan, and others. One of the predictable outcomes, therefore, of the introduction of this sophisticated Sanskrit poetics was to make many forms of poetic composition in Tibet an activity for the elite educated members of society.[177] No longer a spontaneous outpouring in direct response to insight or confusion, the vehicles of metaphors, the style of verse, the use of *rasa* and many other features relied directly on Daṇḍin's influence. Kapstein writes:[178]

> These works left an enormous legacy in Tibet, and from the fourteenth century onwards virtually every Tibetan author of note, whether monk or layman, tried his hand at some *kāvya*. Even the exponents of yogic song, who well appreciate the power of the Tibetan song-poem (*mgur*), were not untouched by the allure of Ratnākara's metrics and Daṇḍin's classifications of ornaments.

What this has done to the concept of spontaneity is touched on here by Jinpa:[179]

> Traditionally, this transformation of Tibetan poetry has been regarded very positively. In poetry in general it is

[177] I suggest that this represents the literarization of Tibetan, following the process that Pollock (2006, 4ff.) describes.

[178] Kapstein 2003, 782–83.

[179] Jinpa 2000, 12.

> hard to see any serious defects in the impact of Sanskrit poetics. But for the poems with which this book [*Songs of Spiritual Experience*] is concerned—songs of spiritual experience and meditative realization, the kinds of songs for which Milarepa had already set a virtually supreme model by any standard—there was a price. The essence of spiritual songs is their spontaneity, their immediacy, the momentary capturing of a transformed state of mind while all the rules of meter, metaphor, and language encouraged by formalization can (and did) have the effect of hindering the natural flow of spontaneity in favor of technically refined forms. To a degree, mastery of form was emphasized at the cost of immediacy of content.

Though to be sure, not every Tibetan poet-yogin had the benefit (or hindrance, depending on one's view) of a monastic education, and therefore would have been much more influenced by indigenous literary and bardic traditions, Sapan's work in the thirteenth century wrought transformations to Tibetan literary culture that resonate to this day. He is responsible for firmly planting the idea of being a paṇḍita as an ideal in Tibetan society[180] and from his time onwards, many Tibetans have striven to meet that ideal. As he devised the theoretical framework that justifies translating sacred texts into Tibetan, Sapan provides our link to the discussion of translation below.

Methodology: Translating Saraha

While my translation is from Tibetan, Tibetan was not the original language of composition. The translation presented in this book is therefore the second (or perhaps even the third) such transformation performed on the text. Translation is never an easy task—it is never simple or straightforward. There is no escaping the fact that translation is always *at least* an interpretation. At times it is composition, and sometimes—as explored by post-colonial and translation theorists—a violation, a subjection to a particular ontology, epistemology, and historiography. This is especially an issue when the languages involved entail a particular

[180] Kapstein 2003, 782.

relationship of power between the cultures and people. It also depends enormously on the intention of the translator and of the target reader. In the process of translating the enormous corpus of Sanskrit and other Indian works into Tibetan, the underlying motivation was the transfer of an entire religious system to be absorbed and assimilated in its new context. The translation of Tibetan works into English has been performed for a variety of reasons and with an equally great variety in intention. This places a tremendous burden of responsibility on the translator to be as well-equipped as possible for the task, for, as Gayatri Spivak writes, "translation is the most intimate act of reading."[181] Engaging the language of intimacy is most appropriate here, as the relationship of the translator to text is as complex, delicate, rewarding, or destructive as any intimate relationship can be. Likewise, the subsequent relationship of translated text to its new audience is a complex and delicate one.

Approaching a translation from a non-self-reflexive point of view can place the translator squarely within what may be termed a colonialist or neocolonialist discourse. Tejaswini Niranjana writes: "Translation functions as a transparent presentation of something that already exists, although the 'original' is actually brought into being through the translation."[182] In other words, approaching a text as a static artifact of the past gives that text an identity it never had in its proper context. It is created by the translator for the translation. Schaeffer writes:[183]

> Previous attempts at editing and explicating the Treasury of Dohā Verses, as well as attempts at identifying Saraha have been aimed at eliminating what are seen to be errors and inconsistencies wrought by tradition, and uncovering the original form of the work, as well as the 'historical' Saraha. These attempts have been misguided by a methodological imperative which makes a strict division between, on the one hand, the author as the sole creative force and owner of the original, and therefore correct, literary work, and on the other hand, the subsequent

[181] Spivak 2000, 398.

[182] Niranjana 1992, 3.

[183] Schaeffer 2000, 4.

> tradition of scribes, orators, teachers, and interpreters whose activities amount only to a degeneration of the original purity of the author's intended work.

I believe this articulates well many of the difficulties faced in studies of Saraha to the present time, and Schaeffer's attempt to shift scholarly attention away from the "misguided methodological imperative" he describes is both timely and useful. Niranjana writes:[184]

> Conventionally, translation depends on the Western philosophical notions of reality, representation, and knowledge. Reality is seen as something unproblematic, 'out there'; knowledge involves a representation of this reality; and representation provides direct, unmediated access to a transparent reality.

In other words, according to Niranjana's terms, a conventional approach to translation relies on an unproblematized conception of subject and object; it additionally relies on an unproblematized conception of language, where a word is a sign that simply denotes *one thing*. That translations of Buddhist texts would challenge a rigid understanding of language and a singular definition of truth and reality should come as no surprise. Buddhism has always been a *translatable* tradition. Nothing in it depends on a single sacred language. A famous passage from the *Vinayapiṭaka* reads:[185]

> Two monks, Brahmans by birth, were troubled that other monks of various clans, tribes, and families, were corrupting the Buddha's words by repeating them each in his own dialect. They asked the Buddha, "Let us put the Buddha's words into [Vedic-Sanskrit][186] verse (*chandaso āropema*)." But the Blessed One, the Buddha, rebuked them, saying "Deluded men! This will not lead to the conversion of the unconverted...." And he commanded

---

[184] Niranjana 1992, 2.

[185] Cited in Pollock 2006, 54.

[186] Square brackets belong to the citation.

> (all) the monks: "You are not to put the Buddha's words into [Vedic Sanskrit] verse. To do this would be to commit an infraction. I authorize you, monks, to learn the Buddha's words each in his own dialect."

An injunction against using Vedic Sanskrit (or another such formal language) to formalize the Buddha's words is an injunction "against the Mīmāṁsā tenet that the relationship between word and meaning is *autpattika*, originary or natural."[187] Against this "natural" relationship of word to meaning (what Niranjana refers to as "conventional" above, though she is addressing habits of language theory particular to Western traditions, not to the Mīmāṁsā), Buddhists "typically argued for a relationship based on pure convention,"[188] where "convention" means dependent (i.e., contingent). In other words, the Buddhist approach to the relationship of word to meaning was one that did not appeal to a natural or divine order of language. This freedom allowed its teachings to be easily translatable, although I do not mean to suggest that the process of translation was easy or without standards.

The general parameters of what define a viable translation depend on a number of factors, including an appropriately trained translator and an appropriately trained reader/listener. In the days of the first transmission of Buddhism to Tibet (*snga dar*), rigorous standards of translation were ensured by a translation manual composed in the eighth or ninth century CE that standardized a lexicon for translating Buddhist texts from Indian languages to Tibetan.[189] In the second period of the transmission of Buddhism to Tibet (*phyi dar*), Sapan refined the approach to translation in terms recognizable today in approach and substance as translation theory. As discussed above, he had a tremendous impact on the course of Tibetan scholarship. He designed the curriculum that would be followed in some form or another for the whole of Tibetan monastic history following him. Most relevant to the discussion at hand, he lived at the end of the most prolific period of translation during the new translation period. Among the works of many other great Indian Buddhist masters,

---

[187] Ibid., 52.

[188] Ibid.

[189] Called either *bye brag tu rtogs par byed pa*, or *sgra sbyor bam gnyis*.

Saraha's collected works were transmitted (and therefore translated in some sense of the word) no less than seventeen times between the eleventh and thirteenth centuries.[190] The potentials and pitfalls of translation were, therefore, among the most critical concerns of great scholars like Sakya Paṇḍita during this exciting period of transmission and indigenization of the Indian Buddhist traditions. Essentially, Sakya Paṇḍita believes in the fundamental *translatability* of texts, arguing—according to Gold—that changes and losses in translation are "both inevitable and unproblematic."[191] He goes so far as to assert that "strong theories of untranslatability are non-Buddhist."[192] Gold states:[193]

> Sa-pan recognizes that shifts in phonetic qualities, grammatical relations, and etymological implications are the inevitable result of the translation process. But rather than taking this to show a decay in the dharma, Sa-pan uses the occasion to argue that linguistic meaning operates not through the words themselves, but through the speaker's intention. As long as that intention is preserved, the linguistic changes are insignificant.

This harmonizes startlingly well with both Niranjana's critique of the conventional Western approach to translation, and the early Indian Buddhist resistance to the idea of "natural" language.[194] Sapan's argument for the translatability of Buddhist texts depends on a text not being a static artifact. It depends on it being a living, changing medium of communicating a particular meaning. In other words, the translator need not be concerned with the unavoidable changes wrought by translation; what is critical is that he or she has the appropriate intellectual training and intention. That intention and training is guaranteed by lineage (one's teacher, one's teacher's teacher, etc.), and according to Sapan is as critical

---

[190] Schaeffer 2000, 121–22.

[191] Gold 2007, 37.

[192] Ibid.

[193] Ibid., 36.

[194] It is also supported by Davidson's (1990) analysis of Buddhist hermeneutics of authenticity.

a characteristic of the reader as it is of the translator.[195] In other words, translation is both possible and unproblematic, provided that both the translator and the reader are adequately qualified. He explains:[196]

> Translation changes only the context-bound, linguistic conventions. Since it is the intention, and not the word, that determines meaning, certain kinds of loss in translation are acceptable—as long as the translations preserve the speech intention (*brjod 'dod*) of the original.

That the translations of Indian texts into Tibetan was accomplished as meticulously as possible is beyond doubt. That the skills and intentions of translators of those same Tibetan works into an assortment of contemporary languages are less easily discernable is also beyond a doubt. The present context of scholarship and translation requires a serious interrogation of the unquestioned assumption that everyone who can read Tibetan is qualified to understand the text at hand, and that everyone who is drawn to the translation can understand what has been translated. The relationship between poet, text, translator, and audience is a complex one, and no element of it is simple or can be taken for granted. Approaching a text with the assumption that it has been a static object since its composition, that it constitutes an original with a meaning that inheres in it and that can be transmitted *in toto* if the quality of the translation is of sufficient quality, seriously underestimates the complexity of the relationship of text to audience, of text to time, and of language to meaning.

Here it is useful to consider Christian Novetzke's discussion of bhakti as a phenomenon that "form[s] publics of reception rather than communities that imply a single cohesive issue or idiom."[197] He discusses bhakti as a *mise en scène* rather than as a static artifact, supported as he helpfully points out the literature and practices associated with bhakti (poetry, pilgrimage, etc.) necessarily imply or entail an audience as well. Whether it is a crowd of angry Brahmins witnessing Saraha's miracles in

---

[195] Gold 2007, 38.

[196] Ibid., 38.

[197] Novetzke 2007, 255.

his hagiographies, or something as simple as the *baṇa* lines[198] in his poetry, or the way he addresses his audience with imperative verb forms, Saraha's lives and poems clearly entail layers of reception as well. His hagiographies and works, dependent as they are on a receptive audience, have of course changed over time to meet the needs and contexts of evolving publics. Novetzke points to this challenge in the context of studying bhakti when he explains that scholars who wish to study the hagiographies or poetry of bhakti *sants* "must grapple with long traditions of emendation and intercession upon the body of a bhakti text as it passes through time, as it continues to locate itself in reference to a changing stream of historical contexts."[199] This equally describes the transmission of Saraha's corpus and hagiography. I would further argue that the presencing of Saraha in the lives of later Tibetan masters suggests a particularly elegant solution to the problem posed by the seeming contradiction posed by, on the one hand, Saraha's appeal to immediacy and spontaneity, and on the other, his location in the past and his identification with texts. This additionally supports the parallel between bhakti and Saraha (as a metonym for the Buddhist adepts) as a *mise-en-scène*.

Saraha often uses the same word in multiple contexts to refer to a range of objects and concepts. Often the meaning is deliberately ambiguous, and clearly relies on the reader/listener for its fruition. It is not *meant* to be clear to everyone—what the audience brings to the text helps to *create* the text. The meeting of text and reader is the arena of possibility, of the very creation of meaning. The moment when text and reader arise in dependence on one another is the moment when a dependent meaning crystallizes. It is particular, contingent, and shifting.

As a translator, therefore, I had to allow Saraha's *Adamantine Songs* to speak to me in the present, rather than trying to seek out some "original," "authentic," static version of them from the past. This does not mean that I have given myself creative license with the text—the Tibetan text is presented alongside the English so that those who wish to do so may compare for themselves. I have made every effort to compose as faithful a translation as possible, but by attempting to respect the

---

198 The *baṇa* line is a moment in a poem when the author self-reflexively inserts him/herself into the work, with an exclamation like, "Saraha says...."

199 Novetzke 2007, 263.

intentional ambiguities and shifting, playful, and challenging way that Saraha uses language, I have not attempted to make his songs *clear* where clarity is not intended. The truly adamantine clarity depends on the *reader*. According to his biographies, the composition of his works was indeed a *mise-en-scène*, and I suggest that the present-day reading of his works is the same.

Every kind of translation has its unique challenges. A philosophical treatise, for example, requires that the translator can with some semblance of accuracy explain the philosophical context the text emerges in, and the cultural, political, and religious context the author was writing in. Once poetry gets involved, a whole new set of variables come into play—playfulness of language, literary conventions, culturally specific analogies and references, rhythm, alliteration, puns—not to mention the complexities of deliberate ambiguity, and the deliberate toying with the very limits of language. Pauses. Silence. Religious poetry, then, makes things so much the harder—as the translator's facility with the both the languages and religions is crucial. With works like Saraha's *Adamantine Songs*, where the poems are nothing short of vehicles for the transmission of realization, the burden is overwhelming.

Sources

I have grounded myself in the primary texts as much as possible, namely, the *Adamantine Songs* themselves. Since there are no extant commentaries on them, the next "layer" of information comes from Tibetan indigenous sources on the Great Seal, commentaries on Saraha's *dohās*, the history of Buddhism in Tibet and polemical texts. As the Great Seal has received relatively little scholarly attention, and as it is a thriving living tradition, I have also made use of the many teachings made available by modern teachers of that tradition, in this case principally drawn from the Karma Kagyu school which informs my own interpretation of the Great Seal.

Saraha's Adamantine Songs

While it cannot be definitively established that Saraha wrote the *Adamantine Songs*, unlike the case of the *Queen* and *King Dohās* their attribution to Saraha is uncontroversial in the Tibetan tradition. The absence of controversy is not as satisfying as positive proof, but it is not an insignificant point. Despite the fact that no fragments of the *Adamantine*

Songs have been found in any South Asian language, in my opinion the author is nonetheless most likely South Asian and not Tibetan. I base that on circumstantial evidence: these songs were transmitted by Vajrapāṇi in the same collection containing the three *Adamantine Songs* together with *Mentally Unfabricated Body, Speech, and Mind*,[200] the *Sixth Stage of Cultivation*,[201] a set of instructions on the moment of death called, *A Mahāyāna Sūtra on the Wisdom of the Moment of Death*,[202] and the *Unsullied King of Tantras*[203] together with its commentary.[204] Locating that moment of transition from the South Asian to the Tibetan cultural sphere is an important piece of the puzzle. Further, a single translator is identified for the three *Adamantine Songs* and the *Unfabricated Body, Speech, and Mind*. Schaeffer writes:[205]

> Nakpo Sherday was the last student of Vajrapāṇi to receive Saraha's teachings from the Indian scholar. According to Go Lotsawa, Nagpo [sic] traveled to eastern India to meet an aged Vajrapāṇi and was given instruction in ten *Great Seal* works, including six dohās by Saraha. Here we find the only clue to the transmission history of what can be considered Saraha's other major set of dohās, named the *Body*, *Speech* and *Mind Treasuries,* together with the *Body, Speech and Mind Treasury*.... Zhuchen Tsultrim Rinchen states that all four of these dohās were translated by the same scholar. On the basis of the meeting between Vajrapāṇi and Nakpo Sherday recounted by Go Lotsawa, I suggest that Nakpopa is in fact Nakpo Sherday, and thus that these

200 *sku gsung thugs yid la mi byed pa.*

201 *sgom rim drug pa.*

202 *'phags pa 'da' ka ye shes zhes bya ba theg pa chen po'i mdo.*

203 *rgyud kyi rgyal po rnyog pa med pa.*

204 Gö 1984, 1010.

205 Schaeffer 2005, 65. Here a minor amendment may be made to Kurtis Schaeffer's discussion of the colophons of the *Adamantine Songs* and the *Unfabricated Song*: where he states that the *Speech Treasury* alone specifies the translator, in fact it is the *Unfabricated Song* that has the only reference to a translator among the four.

> four massive but apparently unpopular dohās stem from this last period of Vajrapāṇi's tremendous efforts toward the propagation of the dohās in Tibet.

Additionally, all three songs are included in every version of the Tengyur, and in every version they are attributed to Saraha. While the evidence that the *Adamantine Songs* are of South Asian origin is scant, there is *no* evidence to the contrary. Let us say that the songs are of South Asian origin, written by a single author. And let us say that his name was Saraha.

The songs translated in this volume are *Adamantine Songs*, and constitute a root text of the Great Seal tradition in Tibetan Buddhism. Together, the songs are three long poems which are meant to be read (or heard) together as a "cycle" (*skor*). Engaging with the highest view of the Great Seal through the three doors of body, speech, and mind, their titles are, in order of appearance, "A Body Treasury[206] called the Immortal Adamantine Song";[207] "A Speech Treasury called the Gentle Voiced Adamantine Song";[208] and "A Mind Treasury called the Unborn Adamantine Song."[209]

Broadly speaking, the three *Adamantine Songs* describe in form and content the Great Seal as ground, path, and fruit. While they predominantly detail the Great Seal *view* of the innate (*sahaja*, *lhan cig skyes pa*), they also bring up aspects of practice and attainment that are discussed below.

---

206 Each is identified in its title as a *kośa* (Skt.) or *mdzod* (Tib.), which I am translating as "treasury." The term "treasury" is an ennobling one for a collection of verses, as a *kośa* can be a vessel of any kind. The verses in these collections do not fit together in a completely harmonious manner (the same may be said of the *Dohākośa*; see Jackson [2004, 10] for details), so I have toyed with the idea that since one might just as easily translate *kośa* as "grab-bag," the term might better be translated in this context as "miscellany."

207 *kāyakośāmṛta vajragīti, ku'i mdzod 'chi med rdo rje'i glu.*

208 *Vāk kośa rucira svara vajragīti, gsung gi mdzod 'jam dbyangs rdo rje'i glu.*

209 *Cittakośa aja vajragīti, thugs kyi mdzod skye med rdo rje'i glu.*

Analysis of the Adamantine Songs

> Hey! In the Great Seal are present body, speech, and mind, the nature of fruition.[210]

This analysis begins with a brief examination of the structure and construction of the three treasuries as a unit, followed by a brief analysis of the structure of each of the three Treasuries individually, and concludes with a treatment of the principal themes: (1) the Great Seal (*phyag chen*); (2) the innate (*lhan cig skyes pa / lhan skyes*); and (3) the four symbolic (*brda*) terms, including recognition (*dran pa*), decognition (*dran med*), the unborn (*skye med*), and beyond the intellect (*blo las 'das / blo 'das*). Since no commentary on the *Adamantine Songs* has ever been found, whether in Sanskrit, Apabhraṁśa, or Tibetan, to my knowledge this is the first attempt to "make sense" of these little-known works of Saraha. This attempt to lay out a kind of interpretive map for the *Adamantine Songs* is only provisional. By grouping the verses according to common themes and drawing out some of the more complicated ideas, the intention is that readers will be better armed to tackle the essential meaning on their own.

Body, Speech, and Mind

One may broadly structure the *Adamantine Songs* into three parts, based on the titles of the poems themselves: the *Body Treasury*,[211] the *Speech Treasury*,[212] and the *Mind Treasury*.[213] This immediately tells us that the *Adamantine Songs* were most likely received as a single, multipart work. Body, speech, and mind are the "three doors"; the three spheres of activity of human beings, ranging from the gross to the subtle. The range of lengths of the songs themselves reflect these levels of materiality: the *Body Treasury* weighs in at 513 lines (divided by me into 117 verses); the *Speech Treasury* at 192 or 193 lines (depending on the edition; divided into 48 verses); and the *Mind Treasury* is a slender 105

---

210 *Body Treasury*, verse 35.

211 *kāyakośa, sku'i mdzod.*

212 *vākkośa, gsungs gi mdzod.*

213 *cittakośa, thugs kyi mdzod.*

(divided into 27 verses). The tradition (and we) are therefore justified in reading the *Body Treasury* as an extensive treatment of the Great Seal, the *Speech Treasury* as a middle-length treatment, and the *Mind Treasury* as a condensed treatment. While they are principally considered as single work throughout this analysis, a brief examination of the individual structure of the poems is nonetheless a useful exercise.

The Body Treasury

Each of the three poems contains: (a) an homage to the Bodhisattva of Wisdom (either as Mañjuśrī or Mañjughoṣa), followed by (b) the main body of the poem, (c) a wishing prayer or dedication, and (d) a short colophon.

The *Body Treasury* is broadly divisible into sections or groupings of stanzas that either address a particular subject or take a particular point of view. The 117 verses of the *Body Treasury* that fill up the main text of the poem can be divided thus:

(a) Homage		
(b) Main Body of Poem		
	1–2	Broad critique of religious and philosophical systems.
	3–12	Description of the nondual nature of the innate, and the inseparability of aspects by which it is described.
	13–25	Practical instructions with an intense focus on cognizing nonduality.
	26–29	Critique of conventional meditation techniques and practice instructions on the Great Seal.
	30–37	Divisions of the Great Seal teachings: the four branches; distinguishing the Great Seal from both the Mahāyāna and Tantric paths of practice; the four symbols; and the four seals.
	38–51	Reflections on the diversity of nonduality, including precise instructions on mind-only understanding of phenomena.
	52–65	Descriptions of and instructions on nonduality of the Great Seal.
	66–70	Presentation through metaphors.
	71–87	Praise and instructions on Great Seal practice.
	88–99	Critique of the conventional path, contrasted with instructions on the Great Seal.
	100–109	Presentation through metaphors.
	110–116	Instructions on recognizing the Great Seal with an emphasis on the path of equanimity.
(c)	117	Final wishing prayer.
(d) Colophon		

The Speech Treasury

The *Speech Treasury* has a more dialectical form, reminiscent of philosophical literature. A more condensed poem than the *Body Treasury*, the *Speech Treasury* begins by listing the positions that Saraha will refute. The rest of the poem is his response. Like the *Body Treasury*, it focuses on treating the Great Seal as direct cognition of the nature of mind, avoiding the Mahāyāna and Tantric paths of practice:

(a) Homage		
(b) Main Body of Poem		
	1	A condensed summary of the *Body Treasury*.
	2–4	Importance of compassion to realization of the Great Seal.
	5–6	Reliance on the Guru in order to accomplish the Great Seal.
	7–10	The voice of the opponent who advocates formal initiation and Tantric practice as the path.
	11–47	Saraha's response, instructions on nonduality, refutation of conventional practice.
(c)	48	Great Seal as direct cognition and final wishing prayer.
(d) Colophon		

The Mind Treasury

The *Mind Treasury* is still more condensed than the first two poems. Like the first two, it begins with an homage to Mañjuśrī and ends with a wishing prayer and short colophon. A very short collection of verses, the *Mind Treasury* is principally focused on illuminating the Great Seal as the innate:

(a) Homage		
(b) Main Body of Poem		
	1–6	Presentation of the innate through metaphors, principally through that of a lamp.
	7–14	Instructions on nonduality.
	15–23	Instructions on the Great Seal.
	24–25	Critique of dualistic Tantric practice.
(c)	26–27	Reliance on the Guru in order to accomplish the Great Seal and wishing prayer.
(d) Colophon		

The Treasury of Adamantine Songs[214]

References to the three doors are found in the *Body Treasury*. Each mention of them simultaneously refers to the three doors themselves, and intertextually to the other poems in the collection. The *Body Treasury*, with its explicit reference in the title to a sort of physicality or phenomenal presence, emphasizes the nondual union of body, speech, and mind three times. Verse 3 reads:

> Body, speech, and mind are resplendent like cotton and oil
>   in a lamp,
> Endowed with just that, they are radiant like a lamp that is
>   self-illuminating.
> Because illuminating reflexive awareness pervades all
>   beings
> Indivisibly, that is the unborn nature.

Thus just as illumination only occurs with the correct combination of cotton, oil, and vessel, the three doors must be united in just the right way for "illuminating reflexive awareness" or apperception to arise. Later in the same poem we read:[215]

> Don't think of saṁsāra, don't be concerned with nirvāṇa,
> The three times and three worlds are contained in body,
>   speech, and mind.
> No effort in anything, no views, nothing to accept and
>   reject,
> Not differentiating centre and perimeter, the middle way is
>   the straight path.

Here Saraha is saying two things: that the totality of diverse experiences and phenomena are all contained in the three doors of body, speech, and mind; and additionally that they are contained within the triad of the *Adamantine Songs*. The nonduality of that unity is, according to Saraha,

---

[214] I have treated the many points that explicitly link these three songs together as a single work in "Exploring Saraha's Treasury of *Adamantine Songs*" (2008). Some of what follows has been adapted from that article and I wish to thank to the *Tibet Journal* (Dharamsala, India) for permitting me to use portions of my article.

[215] Verse 16.

the middle path itself as it is the avoidance of all possible extremes. The last reference to the three doors in the *Body Treasury* reads:[216]

> Hey! In the Great Seal are present body, speech, and mind,
> the nature of fruition.
> The result of the Great Seal is only suitable for the
> essential meaning, but not for provisional and
> definitive.
> It is the unsurpassed secret vehicle, the essence of all.
> The essence of the heart of all path and fruition are
> distilled there,
> The authentic highest Mahāyāna and the distinctness of the
> vehicles.

Finally, in the Peking and Narthang (*snar thang*) editions of the Tengyur, the *Adamantine Songs* are preceded by a title page reading: *sku gsungs thugs 'chi med rdo rje'i mdzod kyi glu rnal 'byor gyi dbang phyug chen po sa ra ha'i zhabs kyis mdzad pa bzhugs*: "Herein is contained the Immortal Adamantine Body, Speech, and Mind Song Treasury, authored by Saraha-pāda, Lord of Yogis." In addition to the three doors as a unifying device, there are other parallels embedded in the texts indicating the unity of the work. The most evident is the three bodies of awakening (*trikāya*, *sku gsum*), reflecting levels of materiality and subtlety of the transformation body (*nirmāṇakāya*, *sprul sku*), enjoyment body (*sambhogakāya*, *longs sku*), and the truth body (*dharmakāya*, *chos sku*). For Saraha, each of the three bodies equally express the Buddha's awakening but according to the needs and capacities of beings. Saraha's commentary to the *Buddhakapāla Tantra* explaining the accessibility and appropriateness of various methods for beings of varying capacities reads: "It is everywhere: the transformation body is seen by śrāvakas, etc.; the perfect enjoyment body by bodhisattvas; likewise the truth body by Buddhas."[217] We should not be surprised, then, to find the three *Adamantine Songs* expressing the same idea. Throughout the poems the three bodies are

---

[216] Verse 35.

[217] *thams cad du ni sprul pa'i sku / nyan thos la sogs pa yis mthong / byang chub sems dpa' rdzogs longs spyod / de bzhin chos sku sangs rgyas kyis* (*dpal sangs rgyas thod pa'i rgyud kyi bka' 'grel ye shes ldan*, f. 124a).

frequently referenced as the supreme example of how things can be diverse and yet united; arising in the world of impure appearance as appearances and yet pure.

Again, in Saraha's commentary on the *Buddhakapāla Tantra* the three bodies are said to be associated with cakras located in the navel (*nirmāṇacakra*); the throat (*saṁbhogacakra*); and the heart (*dharmacakra*).[218] At the center of the physical body, the association of the navel center, the *nirmāṇakāya*, and the body is very strong. The location of the *saṁbhogakāya* cakra in the throat associates it clearly with speech, and the location of the *dharmakāya* cakra in the heart aligns it clearly with the mind. This allows one to map the three bodies onto the three *Adamantine Songs* accordingly: the *nirmāṇakāya* cakra is aligned with the *Body Treasury*, the *saṁbhogakāya* cakra with the *Mind Treasury*, and the *dharmakāya* cakra with the *Mind Treasury*.

The three bodies doctrine permeates the language of the first Adamantine Song, the *Body Treasury*, and is one of the chief indicators of the relationship of the three songs to each other through the frequent references:[219]

> There is no inner or outer, self or other.
> Knowing the object as it is, is taught as natural liberation.
> Although in the truth body the three *kāyas* are inseparable,
> If one practices, distinct results arise.

The three bodies are referenced here as ideal examples of how something can be multiple and diverse in its forms (or lack thereof) and yet still share an identical nature. While this is clearly focused on establishing the unity or single nature of phenomena from the point of view of awakening —and so points out the mistake of engaging in practice that reinforces one's dualistic experience of mind and phenomena—it is worthwhile drawing attention here to the emphasis in the above stanza on the bodies as three, where their unity is described as the truth body (*dharmakāya*)

---

[218] Ibid., 124b. A similar articulation is found in the *Hevajra Tantra*: "The four centres, comprising the three Bodies, the Essential Nature (*dharma*), Enjoyment (*sambhoga*) and Creation (*nirmana*) Bodies, and the fourth, the Centre of Great Bliss (*mahasukhacakra*), are located in the heart, throat, yoni and head, respectively." (Farrow 1992, 221)

[219] Verse 23.

and *not* as the essence body. Saraha later reinforces this assertion of the indivisibility of the three bodies through their nature, which cannot be approached with the intellect:[220]

> Like space, it is devoid of origination and cessation.
> Just as the rope that is grasped as a snake is devoid of snake,
> The truth body, enjoyment body and the transformation body are indivisible.
> The essential nature is beyond the sphere of the intellect.

Ordinary beings live in a world of phenomena upon which they mistakenly impute essences through the intellect, failing inevitably to understand the true nature of what is perceived and experienced. Just as a rope mistakenly perceived as a snake causes precisely the same anxiety as a "real" snake would in spite of the fact that there is no snake at all in the rope, so the identityless transformation body of a Buddha causes faith, devotion, etc., to appear in a deluded being just the same as if that body existed independently, in spite of the fact that the Buddha does not exist independently.

Within the *Adamantine Songs* there are numerous references to the union of the three bodies as the fourth *kāya*, the *svabhāvikakāya* or essence body. Interpreting the the three poems as the three bodies, then, allows one to see the union of the three as the *svabhāvikakāya* as the union of the three poems as a single song cycle. Finally, there is one explicit mention of the Buddha bodies in the *Speech Treasury* that nicely summarizes the theme treated above:[221]

> The result that is the accomplishment of the four *kāyas* is the realm of great bliss.
> Bodies that are the path of appearances arise;
> But possessing the power of the three *kāyas*, one is completely free of conceptualization.

---

[220] Verse 71.

[221] Verse 18.

Key Theme 1: The Great Seal

THE GREAT SEAL AS THE HIGHEST VIEW OR RESULT

In Saraha's *Adamantine Songs*, "Great Seal" (*mahāmudrā*, *phyag rgya chen po* or *phyag chen*) is variously used to describe the basis of reality, the true nature of mind, the ultimate fruition of the Buddhist path, and the ultimate nature of reality.[222] A very mundane but nonetheless telling indication of how central Mahāmudrā is to our text is how frequently the Great Seal is mentioned: it appears a total of sixty-two times in fifty-three separate verses in the three songs, over a quarter of the total 192 verses. In the *Body Treasury* it appears forty-three times (in thirty-seven of the 117 verses); in the *Speech Treasury* it appears sixteen times (in thirteen of the forty-eight verses) and in the *Mind Treasury* three times in the twenty-seven verses.

To begin with the most basic definitions: *mahā* or *chen po* means "great" in most senses of the English word, including being large in number, size, or extent; of major significance or importance; remarkable or out of the ordinary in degree, magnitude, or effect; very good; denoting someone who has achieved honour and distinction.[223] *Mudrā* or *phyag rgya* here means "seal," in the sense of something that is used to signify identity and authenticity. It is a seal in the way someone like a political or a religious authority may have a ring or stamp that is used to identify the source and authority of official documents. The Sanskrit term *mudrā*, however, has multiple meanings, ranging from anything from a ritual hand gesture, to parched grain (which functions ritually as an aphrodisiac), to an image, to a Tantric practitioner's female consort. The Tibetan term *phyag rgya* shares all those meanings, and takes on a few more, such as a bone ornament[224] and a symbolic encounter or gesture.

---

[222] In Tibetan contexts, "Great Seal" is also used to describe an elaborate curriculum of practice, and especially in the Kagyu traditions there exist a vast number of practice manuals or *khrid yig* that all purport to describe *phyag chen*—the most famous of which is probably Takpo Tashi Namgyel's (dwags po bkra shis rnam rgyal) sixteenth-century *Phyag chen zla ba'i 'od zer*.

[223] Oxford English Dictionary.

[224] Bone ornaments are symbolic of the transformative practices characteristic of Tantra. Made from human bones found in charnel grounds—traditional sites of certain forms of Tantric practice—they are part of the ritual costume of wrathful deities and mantrins.

In the *Gaganagañjaparipṛcchā Sūtra*, "seal" is further glossed as synonymous with the *tathāgata* (*de bzhin gshegs pa*), and is:[225]

> The seal of the utterly unborn, the seal of utter emptiness, the seal of utter non-compoundedness, the seal of utter desirelessness, the seal of suchness, the seal of authentic reality, the seal of the sky-treasury.

The compound term Mahāmudrā is subject to further interpretation in scriptural (Sūtra and Tantra) and *śāstric* elaborations. While they are not in all cases relevant to an understanding of Saraha, it is useful to be aware of the range of meanings the term acquired throughout the canonical and commentarial traditions in order to not confuse what one feels one already knows about Mahāmudrā with how Saraha uses the term. The *Karṇatantravajrapāda* explains: "*phyag*: the acquisition of nondual knowledge; *rgya*: bliss since saṁsāra's tangled skein is disentangled; *chen po*: authentic being (Dharmakāya), free in itself and being the shining lamp of coincidence."[226] According to the *Mahāmudrātilaka*, "*Phyag* is the wisdom of emptiness / *rgya* is liberation from saṁsāric phenomena / *chen po* is their union."[227] The *Pañcakrama* elaborates that *phyag* is "whatever is well seen, wisdom that is itself self-reflective" and *rgya* is "free of the duality of saṁsāric phenomena and imprints its seal upon all phenomena."[228]

A commentary on the *Kālacakra Tantra* entitled *Padminī* states:[229]

---

[225] Takpo 2005, 134: *shin tu ma skyes pa'i phyag rgya / shin tu stong pa nyid kyi phyag rgya / shin tu 'dus ma byas pa'i phyag rgya / 'dod chags dang bral ba'i phyag rgya / de bzhin nyid kyi phyag rgya / yang dag pa'i mtha'i phyag rgya / nam mkha'i phyag rgya*.

[226] Guenther 1971, 222. I am unfortunately restricted to Tibetan citations of these texts so am preserving the syllabic breakdown in Tibetan as I am not certain how *mudrā* is broken down in the Sanskrit texts. In examining the possibilities it seems likely that *phyag* is equivalent to *rā* (to impart, grant, bestow) and *rgya* to *mud* (joy, delight).

[227] Takpo 2005, 134: *phyag ni stong pa'i ye shes yin / rgya ni 'khor ba'i chos las grol / chen po zung du 'jug pa'o*.

[228] Takpo 2005, 135: *rang gis rang rig ye shes ni / legs mthong gang yin 'dir phyag yin / rgya ni 'khor ba'i chos gzung 'dzin las grol zhing des chos thams cad la rgyas btab pa'am 'debs pa'i don*.

[229] Takpo 2005, 134: *phyag rgya che zhes bya ba ni / 'das pa dang ma byon pa dang da ltar byung ba'i de bzhin gshegs pa thams cad bskyed par mdzad pa shes rab kyi pha rol*

(cont'd)

> *Mahāmudrā* is the perfection of wisdom that has produced all the tathāgatas that arise in the past, present and future. *Mudrā* is that which seals non-abiding nirvāṇa or unchanging bliss. It is great because it surpasses the *karmamudrā* and the *jñānamudrā* and is completely free of saṁsāric traces.

For the most part, the explanations read into the terms Mahāmudrā and *phyag rgya chen po* are concerned with explaining the Great Seal as the basis for reality and as the fruition of full awakening. These elaborations are consistent with Saraha's deployment of the term in his *Adamantine Treasury*, although it is clear—as will be explored below—that he had familiarity with other contexts, both Buddhist and non-Buddhist.

The Great Seal: Three and Four Seals Systems[230]

Apart from the Great Seal as the highest view or result, it also has a place within a context that locates it in a system of multiple seals. There are sometimes said to be three seals, and more often four. In the system of three seals it is inevitably the third, and in the system of four seals it can be either the third or the fourth seal. Saraha has placed it third in the system of four, but I will outline the constellation of possibilities. The table drawn below is designed as a summary of possible schemas. These possibilities are particularly relevant to explore here as it is abundantly clear from the *Adamantine Songs* that Saraha was well-versed in this system, as will be detailed below.

---

tu phyin pa yin la / rab tu mi gnas pa'i mya ngan las 'das pa'am mi 'pho ba'i bde bas bde ba la rgyas btab pas na phyag rgya ste / las kyi phyag rgya dang ye shes kyi phyag rgya las khyad par du gyur pa dang / 'khor ba'i bag chags dang bral bar gyur pas na chen po'o.

[230] Much of this material is treated in my "The Extraordinary Path: Saraha's *Adamantine Songs* and the Bka' brgyud Great Seal" (2011). With thanks to the International Institute for Tibetan and Buddhist Studies GmbH (Andiast, Switzerland) for permitting me to use portions of my article.

Three Seals (*Guhyasiddhi, Kālacakra*)	**Four Seals** (*Vajramālā*[231])	**Four Seals** (Saraha)
1. Action Seal: physical consort	1. Action Seal: physical consort	1. Action Seal: physical consort
2. Dharma/Wisdom Seal: visualized or inner consort	2. Dharma Seal: visualized or inner consort	2. Dharma Seal: visualized or inner consort
3. Great Seal: Result	3. Commitment Seal: complete identification with meditation deity	3. Great Seal: result
	4. Great Seal: result	4. Commitment Seal: bodhicitta

The names of the other seals are as follows: the Action Seal (*karmamudrā*, *las kyi phyag rgya*); the Dharma Seal (*dharmamudrā*, *chos kyi phyag rgya*—also sometimes identified as Wisdom Seal, *jñānamudrā*, *ye shes kyi phyag rgya*—principally in the system of three seals); and the Commitment Seal (*samayamudrā*, *dam tshig gyi phyag rgya*). Common to all treatments of the seals, the Action Seal is understood to be both the female consort of a yogin and the practices they undertake as Tantric consorts. Practice with a consort entails the practice of sexual yogas where the sensation of bliss achieved during intercourse and orgasm is cultivated and manipulated by the practitioner as a means to penetrate the bliss of emptiness. Bliss and ultimate awakening are closely linked, and as the source of highest mundane bliss, sexuality is employed *in a strictly ritual context* as a practice to cognize that ultimate bliss.[232] In particular, the

231 Takpo 2005, 143.

232 For a concise, detailed theoretical treatment of the *karmamudrā*, see Guenther (1971, 202–21). For further reading on the subject, I refer readers to Shaw (1994); Simmer–Brown (2001); White (2003); and Snellgrove (1987).

luminosity and freedom from mental elaborations that manifests at the moment of orgasm is seen as a special opportunity to work with the mind.

The Dharma or Wisdom Seal is both the inner—or imagined—consort, and the intense visualization practices associated with her. The inner consort and wisdom/awareness are nearly synonymous here. Relying on the Guru's instructions, the practice that entails visualizing sexual union with an enlightened consort also cultivates that experience of emptiness.[233]

The Commitment Seal has two possible meanings. On one level it describes the altruistic mind of bodhicitta, which entails compassionate engagement with unawakened beings through the bodhisattva vow. This is an especially appropriate understanding when it is ranked as the Fourth Seal, surpassing even the Great Seal. Another level is revealed by an examination of the etymology of the term in both Sanskrit and Tibetan: *samaya* and *dam tshig* both have the connotation of a bond, or something that binds. This is a reference to achieving a level of Tantric practice where the deity one meditates on is bound to one at a profound level, to the degree that one identifies with it constantly instead of one's own ego-centered identity.

In the formulations of three seals, the Great Seal is always the third and highest. The *Kālacakra Tantra* presents the three seals as stages following one after the other:[234]

> By examining the *karmamudrā*,
> One totally abandons the *jñānamudrā*;
> By uniting with the supremely immutable,
> One meditates completely on the Great Seal.

And further:[235]

---

[233] On the association of the female consort with the feminine principal embodying wisdom, see Shaw (1994); Simmer–Brown (2001); and White (2003).

[234] Takpo 2005, 142: *las kyi phyag rgya brtags pa yis / ye shes phyag rgya yongs spangs nas / mchog tu mi 'gyur sbyor ba yis / phyag rgya chen po rnam par sgom.*

[235] Ibid.: *las kyi phyag rgya'i rab sbyor dang / ye shes phyag rgya'i rjes chags dang /phyag rgya chen mo gcig sbyor ba / mi 'gyur ba de 'phel bar 'gyur.*

The union of *karmamudrā*,
The passion of *jñānamudrā*:
Unified in the Great Seal,[236]
The immutable unfolds.

However, many other sources that use the three-seal formulation do not valorize the Action Seal. While this is most likely a device to motivate practitioners to not become complacent and attached to such a presumably pleasurable practice, the accounts can be disturbing. In the *Guhyasiddhi*, Padmavajra writes: "The *karmamudrā* is angry and deceitful, the *jñānamudrā* is exactly the same; abandon this proliferation of conceptualization, and cultivate the Great Seal."[237] Further, a writer identified in Takpo's practice manual (*khrid yig*) as Mañjuśrī writes: in *Asserting the View: A Concise Presentation* (*lta ba'i 'dod pa mdor bstan pa*): "The *karmamudrā* is crooked and vicious, the *jñānamudrā* is the same; having abandoned multiple concepts, follow the Great Seal."[238]

In the formulation of four seals, there is considerable variety in the order. Saraha describes the four as follows in the first of his *Adamantine Songs*: the Action Seal is the map; the Dharma seal is the path; the Great Seal is the result; and the Commitment Seal is the altruistic act:[239]

---

236 In his translation, Lhalungpa (2005, 437–38) translates "phyag rgya chen mo" as Great Mother, with the gloss "'The seal of the great mother' is the literal rendition of a rarely used Tibetan term.... The traditional designation of 'mother' is appropriate for a treatise or a doctrine on ultimate reality, emptiness. In the same way, the term 'great mother' is applied to the doctrine of wisdom gone-beyond (*prajñāparamitā*) and also to the notion of 'expansive emptiness' (*dharmadhātu, choying*)." I am translating it simply as Great Seal, since the term *mudrā* in Sanskrit is feminine, the "mo" is likely both representing that accurately and playing on the references to the *karma* and *jñāna* mudrās as passionate females.

237 Takpo 2005: 142: *las kyi phyag rga khro sgyu can / ye shes phyag rgya yang de bzhin / rnam rtog mang bas spang byas la / phyag rgya chen po rnam bsgom bya*.

238 Ibid.: *las kyi phyag rgya g.yon can gdug / ye shes phyag rgya de bzhin du / rnam rtog mang ba dor byas nas / phyag rgya chen po bsten par byos*. In his *Rgyud sde spyi'i rnam par gzhag pa rgyas par brjod*. Khedrup Je has a formulation of the seals that is completely different from all the others. Because it would entail a lengthy tangent that would not enhance this discussion, I am not summarizing it here. Readers may refer to directly to his text (1998, 229ff.) for details.

239 *Body Treasury*, verse 37.

> The map that is the Action Seal, and the path of the Dharma Seal,
> And the Great Seal that is the result, and the Commitment Seal that is the altruistic act—
> By relying on seals below the Dharma Seal, one will not reach the end;
> One falls into extremes of hope and fear, and becomes damaged by engaging in frivolous activities.

Here it seems clear that it is possible to dispense with the Action Seal altogether, as relying on the bliss of union without the complement of wisdom will produce nothing but attachment.[240] By relying on the Action Seal to guide one, one will not attain the goal and will waste one's time and energy in mental extremes and useless practices. Relying on the Great Seal and the Commitment Seal as bodhicitta is the only way.

Saraha further addresses this system of multiple seals in the *Body Treasury*, and here clearly prioritizes the Great Seal:[241]

> Those ignorant of just that are attached to the Action Seal, Commitment Seal, Dharma Seal, etc.
> These are mere examples that signify just that but cannot capture the meaning.
> Relying on the Great Seal, which is free of subject and object,
> Cognition arises naturally and freshly.

This is consistent with Saraha's critique of anything that enforces a distinction between the practitioner's mind and the goal, the Great Seal. His poetic skill reaches a particularly refined point at this moment in the *Speech Treasury*: "All conventions, the Action Seal, etc. / Are like the

240 In Tibetan traditions, the Action Seal is problematized and the Dharma/Wisdom Seal is emphasized because of the constraints entailed by transmitting these systems of practice in a monastic context. Sexual yoga with a living consort practiced by a monk would constitute a serious infraction of the monastic code. This and other complexities surrounding the difficulties of attempting to maintain monastic, bodhisattva, and Tantric vows simultaneously spawned an entire literature in Tibet (*sdom gsum* or "Three Vows" texts). See Sakya (1968; 2002) and Sobisch (2002) for more on this.

241 Verse 81.

retinue of servants a Universal Monarch."[242] In other words, relying on anything short of the Great Seal itself is like attending to the common subjects of a king while neglecting the king himself.

Saraha and the Great Seal

In the Tibetan context we find the Great Seal discussed clearly as distinct from "Sūtra" or "Tantra," where the Sūtra path—also referred to as the path of the perfections (*pāramitā*)—is defined by the stages, practices, and paths of the Mahāyāna; and "Tantra"—also known as the path of skillful means (*upāya*)—is the path of Tantric practitioners that relies on empowerments as the preliminaries for practice.[243] While it is not entirely obvious that "Great Seal" was sufficiently reified during Saraha's time to be itself subjected to a categorical division into Sūtra and Tantra, certainly Saraha treated practitioners and the practices they engaged in as if they were in fact making such a sharp distinction. Making mention of the chief concepts and practices of each, he continually scoffs at them and posits the Great Seal as the authentic, natural, effortless practice and goal, accessed naturally through the blessings of the Guru. The Guru providing direct instructions on the nature of mind constitutes a particular method of achieving the Great Seal. In the Tibetan context it is referred to as the Direct Path (*gseng lam*), although as Mathes has established this particular appellation was not in use in the South Asian context. Despite this, as Mathes has discerned in the work of Maitrīpa, and as is supported in these songs of Saraha, the Guru as a direct path to cognizing the nature of mind (as distinct from a path that either employs the *pāramitā* path or Tantric empowerments) was clearly known. Saraha identifies this extraordinary path as the authentic Great Seal, identical with the innate. He also soundly critiques both the *parāmita* and Tantric paths. On the shortcomings of Tantra, for example, he writes:[244]

> Cultivating the innate and the blazing of inner fire on an
> object, etc.,
> Commitment, nature of self, and yoga....

[242] Verse 31.

[243] For more on this see Mathes (2006) and Braitstein (2011).

[244] *Body Treasury*, verse 33.

> In the Great Seal, the sameness of all phenomena, how could
> Conceptualization be abandoned and nonconceptualization be practiced?

Here Tantric practices that are intended to cultivate nonconceptualization —blazing of the inner fire on an object, commitment, nature of self—are listed. Saraha then goes on to explain that in the Great Seal all phenomena are equal, thus rendering the abandonment of conceptualization (not to mention engaging in a process that encourages one to distinguish between them and create a duality) contradictory to the very nature of the Great Seal. In a similar vein he writes:[245]

> Primordially free from activities of consciousness, subtle wind, the lower doors, mantra, etc.,
> Free from self and other, accepting and rejecting.
> Don't think of saṁsāra, don't be concerned with nirvāṇa,
> The three times and three worlds are contained in body, speech, and mind.
> No effort in anything, no views, nothing to accept and reject;
> Not differentiating center and perimeter, the middle way is the straight path.

Again, Saraha lists a series of specific Tantric practices from which one must be free in order to find the ever-elusive true middle way, one that must, according to Saraha, be "free of artificiality, the perfect path for the mind."[246] On the other hand, the verse immediately following this reads: "The Perfection of Wisdom path, which is passage, engagement, stages, etc. / Is the cause for the longer cycle by discarding the quick path."[247] The Perfection of Wisdom path, synonymous with the *pāramitā* path, and consisting of the paths, bhūmis, and so forth, is here explained to be slowing down the aspirant's progress towards awakening. Further, when at the end of the same verse Saraha states: "The innate and the

---

245 *Body Treasury*, verses 15–16.

246 *Body Treasury*, verse 16.

247 *Body Treasury*, verse 17.

remedy are without rival,"[248] I suggest that the *pāramitā* path is being identified as being equally an obstacle to the Great Seal.

The incomparable innate is without rival on either the path of *pāramitā* or of *upāya*, indicating that it is beyond any particular method. In a rather evocative set of verses Saraha deprecates scriptural study and Tantric practice, expressing how attaining the Great Seal cannot be accomplished by crystalizing duality in concepts like being learned or not, seeking a goal outside of oneself, or setting out to engage in Tantric practice with specific methods and goals. The very act of searching for the Great Seal ruins it by setting it apart from the innate, as we read in the *Speech Treasury*:[249]

> Even hearing the word "Great Seal" just for an instant,
> Whether scriptural learning is present or not,
> Just by this teaching, this single root, it is attained.
> By one who meditates on the innate meaning
> Without wavering from pure recognition, it is attained.
> It is just that itself; do not seek the Dharma of others.
> Because of searching like a fox in a charnel ground, etc., what is sought after is ruined
> Hey! Just as a Brahmin desires and asks for one who is low-born,
> When they mix together—lowly and good—they cause harm to one another;
> The yoga with signs will not touch the signless goal.
> That which is signless can never be examined.
>
> Signs come into being when you attend to number and time;
> The stages of generation and completion are distinct, so don't think about them.
> Whoever possesses the highest yoga has the convergence of nonduality.

---

248 *Body Treasury*, verse 17.

249 *Speech Treasury*, verses 25–28.

Here we may appeal to some metaphors to clarify this further: being attached to a method or engaging in practices that reinforce the experience of duality is like carrying a raft on one's back *after* having crossed a river, or like taking medication for a disease that is not present.

Lending what I read as a comic touch to his critique of Tantric methods practiced inauthentically (without being grounded in the nondual goal of the Great Seal), Saraha describes practices using the subtle body as a "worldly treasure," and writes in the *Mind Treasury*:[250]

> Drawing energies up and down in the turning centers,
> Guided by those methods, the truth cannot found,
> Although you may grasp and eject and unite and ignite,
> There is no difference between these breath-control practices and a fool suffering from asthma.

In his continuing critique of anything that reifies the Great Seal as a goal, Saraha tell us of the *pāramitā* methods in the *Body Treasury*:[251]

> Hey! In the Great Seal are present body, speech, and mind, the nature of fruition.
> The fruition of the Great Seal is only suitable for the essential meaning, but not for provisional and definitive.

The mentions of provisional and definitive meaning are clearly a reference to the refined workings of Buddhist philosophical thought.[252] According to Saraha, these categories are entirely unsuitable when we are talking about the essential meaning Great Seal, that which is pointed out directly

[250] Verse 24. The complete passage is: Those who discover worldly treasure are ignorant of the benefit of both self and other: / The heart amulet that is the central lotus flower, / Union possessing skillful means, then emanation / To wherever channels abide as aspect of the cakras. / Even those who are free of attachment in the sky of desirelessness. / Drawing energies up and down in the turning *cakras*, / Guided by those methods, the treasure of benefit cannot found.

[251] *Body Treasury*, verse 35.

[252] Saraha again emphasizes going beyond duality when he dismisses the utility of the two truths doctrine in order to approach the goal in the *Body Treasury*, verse 114: "Free of the two truths, meditation on equanimity is nondual."

by the Guru rather than approached intellectually. In the second half of the same verse he describes the attainment:[253]

> All the essentials of path and fruition are distilled there,
> The authentic highest Mahāyāna and the distinctness of the vehicles.

In other words, Saraha acknowledges the "path-and-fruition" scheme of classification while again undermining the duality implied by the formal distinction between the two levels of interpreting the Buddha's teachings (i.e., provisional and definitive). He describes the whole as the Great Seal, where the essential meaning is gathered. In a warning against reifying the distinction between path and fruition, he writes:[254]

> The Great Seal is unchangeable great bliss and,
> Not dependent on a cause, the result is beyond the scope of the intellect.
> The Great Seal is the complete result.
> Conventionally it is illustrated as the goal of the path.

As a summary of his critique of both methods, we read: "Without the use of 'tip of the nose,' etc., shape and space, channel and contact, abide in the primordial nature."[255] In other words, anything from meditation practices that focus on the breath at the tip of the nose (a form of calm abiding meditation [*śamatha*, *zhi gnas*]),[256] to practices generating

---

[253] *Body Treasury*, verse 35 (cont'd).

[254] *Body Treasury*, verse 7.

[255] *Body Treasury*, verse 26.

[256] Calm abiding meditation was mentioned at the outset of verse 26, and thus it seems likely that the reference here to "tip of the nose" (*sna rtse*) is a reference to that type of meditation. However, given the Tantric nature of the remaining items listed in this verse (deities, energies, etc.), it seems equally plausible that the reference here might be to the three points in the subtle body called "nose tips" (*sna rtse*) that are focused on during Tantric perfection stage practices. For a discussion of the latter, see Thurman 2010, 63, 167, 173–74, 187–88, 223, 224, 231–32, 278–80, 283–84, 287–89, 293, 298, 309, 328, 389, etc. (thanks to our editor, Thomas Yarnall, for pointing out this latter possibility).

deities or their maṇḍalas, to practices working with energies in the subtle body, must be abandoned in order to experience the primordial nature.[257]

A question then arises: if all methods should be abandoned, on what basis can one practice *pāramitā* or Tantra methods authentically? How does one gain access to the authentic middle way? The key according to Saraha is the Guru:[258]

> In your reverence to the Guru, the discipline of the secret vehicle is complete.
> The very expression of the outer, inner, and secret initiations, and
> The vase, secret, wisdom,
> Essential direct word initiations, etc.—
> The mundane *siddhis* arising from all these things cannot touch the Great Seal.

The Guru provides all the requisite blessings and instructions, based on the devotion of the disciple. It appears from this verse that accomplishing the Great Seal does not require Tantric initiation, something that will only bring about worldly *siddhis*. Saraha is emphatic that without the Guru there is no awakening, no Great Seal. He explains in the *Body Treasury*, "Precious devotion is the wish-granting jewel of instruction / Place it so that you are free of mental engagement and non-engagement."[259] Further, in the *Speech Treasury* he writes:[260]

> From the Guru, teachings, transmissions, commentaries, and pith instructions are taught.
> With the right transmission and reasoning, and desiring to realize the intrinsic identity,
> Realization comes from the pure possession of the pith instructions, relying on the Guru,

257 "Must" is a strong word. It is also possible that he is saying these practices must be put aside once they are no longer necessary.

258 *Body Treasury*, verse 34.

259 *Body Treasury*, verse 82.

260 *Speech Treasury*, verse 5.

If the Guru is worshiped, innate highest bliss will be
accomplished.
Bow at the Guru's feet, because the Guru's actions are free
of defilement.
"If you worship the Guru, great blessings will arise,"
declared the Conqueror.

Devotion itself constitutes the correct behavior and attitude, above and beyond the codes and conventions of either the *pāramitā* or *upāya* paths. In the final stanza of the *Speech Treasury* Saraha tells us:[261]

Hey! Whoever possesses the Great Seal, the supreme
qualities,
Has the basis of all *siddhi*s because of delighting the Guru.
Not abandoning the most precious Guru, the qualities
arise.
May whatever rare being has confidence
Realize this text of the yogis!

The greatest attribute a practitioner may have, it seems, is the capacity for profound devotion to the guru. Clearly demonstrating this, Saraha closes the last of the three *Adamantine Songs*, the *Mind Treasury*, with the following two stanzas:[262]

Those desiring realization always look to just that;
Those with sincere devotion rely on the precious Guru,
And from the highest Guru the secret qualities will arise.
Possessing the meaning, the essential sign will be
victorious in the battle against the defilements.
With the transmission of the Guru
Who possesses the secret meaning itself,
May whoever goes through this nondual door arrive at
liberation!

---

261 Verse 48.

262 Verses 26–27.

Key Theme 2: The Innate

The next theme that requires special attention is what I translate as "the innate" or "innate nature" (*sahaja, lhan cig skye pa*). Although *sahaja* has been substantially treated as a key principal to siddha movements in general in the first chapter, a discussion of its particular use in Saraha's *Adamantine Songs* is now in order. The term "innate" appears frequently in the *Adamantine Songs* (just over a dozen times in the *Body Treasury*, and three times in each of the *Speech* and *Mind* treasuries), and it pervades his famous *Dohā Trilogy*.

It is often deployed in the *Adamantine Songs* as synonymous with various other terms, including pristine wisdom, the Great Seal, clear light, bodhicitta, and the nondual state that is the goal. What appears to be key to understanding Saraha's use of the term is that it indicates the nature of the goal, the Great Seal, etc. as being, in essence, identical with whatever arises. If *sahaja* pervades the realized mind, whatever arises in dependence on that mind is experienced as awakening itself. Awakening, in effect, is simultaneous with the experience of phenomena and is therefore *sahaja*, innate to it, arising simultaneously with it, not separate from it. There cannot, therefore, be a specific setting, environment, or cultivation that is particularly conducive to realization of the Great Seal. This is consistent with his refusal of the known systems of cultivation and philosophy. A delightful ambiguity results as to whether *sahaja* describes the nature of mind, the nature of phenomena, or their mutually conditioned arising. In verse 14 of the *Body Treasury* we read:

> Like the faultless lotus expands from one root,
> It abides as the innate nature within sentient beings.
> Even when one is tainted by the power of wrongly seeing
> the existence of "other,"
> Just like the lotus flower,
> By the power of seeing rightly, it is the immutable Great
> Seal.

Verse 75 of the same Treasury tells us:

> Unborn and ultimate, it illuminates completely,
> Therefore, everything appears beyond the intellect.
> That wisdom which is beyond the intellect in the three
> realms,

> Is the innate nature itself.
> Determine this to be the root of all recognition without exception.

Its relationship to the pristine wisdom that cognizes nonduality is emphasized both above and in the following exclamation from the *Mind Treasury*: "Hey! The pristine wisdom is the innate nature."[263] Its illuminating power is stressed in the following verse that draws out the metaphor of the innate as an illuminating lamp:[264]

> The lamp of the innate that is hard to surpass
> Is the principle that is the union of means and wisdom:
> Unborn, empty, impartial, radiant.

It is important to mention that the term *gnyug ma* (*nija*) is also used in the *Adamantine Songs*. Commonly translated as "innate" or "innate nature," its meaning and connotation overlaps significantly with that of *lhan skye*, though they are not seamless synonyms. Where the latter has the "born together" or "born simultaneous with" sense embedded in it (which makes it particularly conducive to being used as an instruction as well as a description), the former describes less of a process than a state. Only appearing in the *Body Treasury*, I have translated *gnyug ma* differently depending on its context: as "natural state" in verses 26 and 61 (*gnyug ma*); as "primordial goal" in verse 22 (*gnyug ma'i don*); and finally as "authentic nature" in verses 64, 86, and 96 (*gnyug ma'i ngo bo*).

Key Theme 3: Symbolic Terms

Overview of Symbolic Terms

This section treats the four symbolic terms (*brda*) recognition (*dran pa*), decognition (*dran med*), unborn (*skye med*), and beyond the intellect (*blo las 'das*). They warrant discussion in their own section as they are strongly emphasized in the commentarial tradition as central to interpreting Saraha's *Dohā Trilogy* and they appear frequently throughout the *Adamantine Songs*. Symbolic terms are ordinary words that

---

[263] Verse 1.

[264] Verse 6.

acquire extraordinary connotation when deployed in particular contexts. On how to understand symbolic terms, Guenther writes:[265]

> These are...key terms used in the elucidation of the progressive deepening of mystic insight and the felt knowledge of existence. As symbol terms they must not be confused with the connotations these words have in ordinary language.

Brda can be translated as a "sign" or a "symbol," and indeed refers to something that communicates a meaning to someone. That is the broadest definition of *brda* and in this sense it can be any word, sound, or gesture that intentionally communicates anything. For that reason I feel it is necessary to explore the ordinary uses the terms in order to fully grasp how Saraha uses them. I discuss recognition and decognition together, beginning by determining what the terms could reasonably signify to a Tibetan audience and transitioning into what they mean in the context of the *Adamantine Songs*. This is followed by a discussion of the terms unborn and beyond the intellect that is also best understood when treated together. I will similarly examine the range of meanings they may have held for a Tibetan audience and then examine how Saraha uses them. The final portion of this section on the symbolic terms looks at how Saraha uses the four terms together throughout the *Adamantine Songs*. First, a brief introduction to the commentarial tradition on the symbolic terms is necessary.

While it is not possible to definitively establish the date of the earliest commentary that emphasizes the terms recognition (*dran pa*), decognition (*dran med*), unborn (*skye med*) and beyond the intellect (*blo las 'das*), we can tentatively place this tradition in South Asia during the early eleventh century. The commentary by the author known in Tibetan as Nyime (*gnyis med*) Avadhūtipa, known to us as Maitrīpa, is likely the earliest. If we accept that Maitrīpa was one of Marpa's (1012–1097) direct teachers while the latter was in India, then that commentary, entitled *An Elucidation of the Essential Meaning of the Treasury of Dohā*,[266] dates to somewhere approximately in the very late tenth or very

---

[265] Guenther 1969, 6 n5.

[266] *dohākośa hṛdayārthagītitikanāma, do ha mdzod kyi snying po don gyi glu'i 'grel pa.*

early eleventh century CE. This is followed closely by Kyeme Dechen's (*skye med bde chen*) commentary on the *King Dohā* entitled *Lamp of Meaning: A Commentary on the Treasury of Dohā*.[267] This may also be dated tentatively to the late eleventh century if we accept Karma Trinlepa's assertion in his fifteenth century commentary that Kyeme Dechen and the famous Nepali master Balpo Asu are the same person.[268] Both these commentaries read Saraha's *King Dohā* intensely through the lens of these four symbolic (*brda*) terms.

As mentioned above, the words identified as symbolic terms are not unusual or special in themselves, but their context as symbolic terms alters how one should understand them and the specific meaning they connote in a particular context. Their special connotation transmits meaning beyond the letter of the word itself, and in esoteric contexts —such as this one—they are said to be infused with that meaning from an awakened source. That source could be the *dharmakāya* itself or, more likely, an awakening messenger such as a ḍāka.[269]

The particular uses of these terms pose a number of problems for any translator. In the first wave of translating Saraha's poems from their South Asian source language to Tibetan, the lineage of translators was carefully defined and controlled, as was the lineage of the receiving audience. A multivalent Sanskrit or Apabhraṁśa term could be translated with an equally multivalent Tibetan term, since the translation was very unlikely to be read by an inappropriately prepared or educated reader. The person who was transmitting the text could situate key terms, and if an inappropriately prepared person were to hear or read the work, not knowing the meaning of the symbolic terms would serve as layer of code impenetrable to the wrong audience. In this current wave of translation of Saraha, however, the context is radically different. His songs are not being passed from master to disciple in a controlled soteriological context. They are translated, published, and read widely. This is a challenge for a translator—what to do with the heavily coded symbolic terms? This

---

267 *dohākośa nāmacaryāgīti ārthapradīpanāmaṭika, do ha mdzod ces bya ba spyod pa'i glu'i 'grel ba don kyi sgron ma zhes bya ba.*

268 Karma Trinlepa, 3b.

269 The four terms discussed here are said in Tibetan sources to be in the ḍaka language (Karma Trinlepa, 10a).

translation attempts to find as precise language as possible to translate the symbolic terms. Since I am not heir to a Mahāmudrā transmission, and understand that these poems are read predominantly, in their English translations, as literature (albeit often by Buddhists with the intention of acquiring some inspiration), it is my conviction that precision is appropriate to the current function of the text. After all, the commentaries are themselves drawing on Saraha's own emphasis. As the *Queen Dohā* tells us explicitly: "The path itself is illustrated by the *brda*."[270]

Recognition and Decognition

There is a wide range of terms that Tibetan translators translated as *dran pa*, though the Sanskrit, *smṛti*, is by far the most common. As a translation of *smṛti*, *dran pa* can mean mindfulness,[271] the act of concentrating in a focused and alert manner. Mindfulness appears in the list of four close mindfulnesses (*catvāri smṛtyupasthāna*, *dran pa nye bar bzhag pa gzhi*), meditative techniques taught in the early Buddhist scriptures.[272] They are the mindfulnesses of body/form (*kāya*), feelings (*vedanā*), mind (*citta*) and dharma/phenomena (*dharma*). Detailed in a variety of Buddhist scriptures as the mindfulnesses, they are also the same that appear as the seventh element of the eight-fold path. These mindfulnesses, of course, are the very foundation of Buddhist praxis and are substantially discussed in countless Buddhist commentaries. Here it will suffice to cite Cox: "The practice of mindfulness is tantamount to the central praxis of Buddhism: namely, as the single path leading to the ultimate soteriological goal of enlightenment and nirvāṇa."[273]

Dran pa is also *smṛti*, third of the five object-determining mental events in Asaṅga's *Abhidharmasamuccaya*.[274] In this very particular context it can be best defined as inspection, recollection, or adherence. Here

---

[270] "*lam nyid brdas ston pa*," 20a.

[271] I refer readers to Cox (1992) for a detailed discussion of *smrti* as it employed in early Indian Buddhist literature.

[272] See, for example, the *Mahāsatipaṭṭhānasutta* (DN 22), the *Satipaṭṭhānasutta* (MN 10), the *Satipaṭṭhānasamyutta* (SN 47), or the *Anapanasamyutta* (SN 54).

[273] Cox 1992, 70.

[274] See Jaini (1992) for a more detailed discussion of *smṛti* in Abhidharma literature.

it is in a series of stages of examination of an object that eventually allow one to define it individually.[275] It can be understood as inspection, recollection, or adherence to the object. Here *dran pa* is further elaborated as a type of inspection that arises only with respect to something familiar that has not been forgotten.[276] This particular feature is interesting because it entails the faculty of memory. Asaṅga defines *dran pa* thus: "What is [*dran pa*]? It is not to let what one knows slip away from one's mind. Its function is not to be distracted."[277]

Dran pa also translates the important term *saṁjñā* (perception), the third skandha.[278] Described in the *Khandha Sutta* in this way: "Whatever kind of perception there is [whether past, future, or present, internal or external, gross or subtle, inferior or superior, far or near:] this is called the aggregate of perception";[279] it is the mental act of grasping the distinguishing qualities of an object. Taking note of an object's features and identifying it, perception is divided into six categories according to the sense objects that it takes note of: forms, sounds, smells, tastes, tactile objects, and mental objects.

It is also worthwhile looking at what dictionaries may tell us about uses and translations of the term. Beginning with the range of Sanskrit terms translated by Tibetans as *dran pa,* Chandra Das cites *avalamba*, the dependence of a thing upon another, support; *smṛti* which he translates as remembrance, recollection, memory, thinking of, calling to mind, discrimination, understanding; and finally *saṁjñā***,** which is the third skandha:

---

[275] In Tibetan these five are called the *yul nges byed lnga,* literally the five object determining mental events. The first is interest, intention, or inclination (*chanda*, *'dun pa*), the very movement of mind towards an object. The second is an intensified interest where mind stays with its object (*sadhimokṣa*, *mos pa*). The fourth is intense concentration, where mind focuses one-pointedly on the object (*samādhi*, *ting nge 'dzin*;); and the fifth object-determining event is appreciative discrimination or discriminating wisdom, where the characteristics of the object are determined, enabling mind to *know* what it is (*prajñā*, *shes rab*).

[276] Guenther and Kawamura 1975, 32.

[277] Ibid.

[278] See discussions of the aggregates (*skandhas, khandhas*) in the Mahāhatthipadopama Sutta (MN 28), the Mahāpuññama Sutta (MN 109), and the Khemaka Sutta (SN 22.89).

[279] Bhikkhu Bodhi 2000, 886.

recognition or perception, and also refers to consciousness, knowledge, understanding, intellect, mind, hint, sign, name, designation, footstep, track, and intelligible.[280] The *Sambhota Dictionary*[281] and the *Nitārtha Online Dictionary*[282] cite only *smṛti* and *anusmṛti* (recollection or remembering). Lokesh Chandra's *Tibetan-Sanskrit Dictionary*[283] provides a much more substantial list. In addition to the above four Sanskrit terms, he adds: *avabhāsa*, splendor, luster, light, knowledge, perception, appearance, manifestation, inspiration; *smara*, recollection, remembrance; *smaraṇa*, remembering, remembrance, recollection, memory, tradition, regretting, rhetorical recollection; and *smṛta*, remembered, recollected, called to mind, regarded, laid down. J.S. Negi's *Tibetan-Sanskrit Dictionary* includes many of the above translations and does not suggest anything not found in the above list.[284] In short, an overwhelming number of important Sanskrit terms have been translated into Tibetan by the word *dran pa*.

Furthermore, we also should keep in mind how the Tibetan term previously has been translated into English to draw out the nuances. *Dran pa* appears to be most commonly translated as mindfulness. This occurs, for example, in a teaching entitled "The Four Foundations of Mindfulness" given by Dzogchen Ponlop Rinpoche, who explains that it means "mindfulness" in the sense of how one relates to an object of concentration in the course of meditation.[285] Traleg Kyabgon Rinpoche uses it with a similar meaning in his recent book, *The Practice of Lojong*, where he explains that *dran pa,* mindfulness, "is the ability to focus and pay attention to the object of meditation in an unwavering fashion."[286] In both these contexts, the definition is drawn from early scriptural sources (the *Mahāsatipaṭṭhānasutta*, for example) or from Asaṅga's discussion in the

[280] s.v. *dran pa*.

[281] s.v. *dran pa*.

[282] s.v. *dran pa*.

[283] s.v. *dran pa*.

[284] s.v. *dran pa*.

[285] Dzogchen Ponlop Rinpoche, http://nalandabodhi.org/mindfulness.html.

[286] Traleg 2007, 39.

Abhidharmasamuccaya where *dran pa* is clearly part of vocabulary relating to language pertaining to meditation.

Turning now to the many ways that *dran pa* has been translated into English in dictionaries, Chandra Das provides us with the following possibilities: recollection, remembrance, memory, self-recollection, consideration, to think, ponder, remember, recollect, become conscious, to think with love or affection, the dependence of a thing upon another.[287] The *Tibetan & Himalayan Library Translation Tool* dictionary[288] keeps the same as above but also increases the range: mindfulness, presence, awareness, inspection, keep thinking about, be concerned about, recall, non-slipping of mind, thinking of, meditate, sensibility, dependence of a thing upon another, become conscious, long for, be attached to, mindful presence, and to remind oneself.[289] Tony Duff's *Illuminator* dictionary[290] provides the following possible translations: to remember, to recall, to miss, to think of, mindfulness, recollection, remembrance, memory, recall, thought, rumination, and bringing to mind.[291] Duff further points to the existence of a specialized usage in Tantric contexts, explaining that "by definition, mindfulness is a part of *sems* dualistic mind" and explaining further, "normally when discussing the path of meditation, mindfulness is something that eventually has to be abandoned."[292] The specialized use he points to is mindfulness of the *dharmatā* (*chos nyid kyi dran pa*), defined as follows:[293]

> This mindfulness is not the mindfulness belonging to dualistic mind as defined above. It is the innate quality of the wisdom mind that experiences the dharmatā of keeping with itself, without needed an external, watching, dualistic factor.

---

[287] s.v. *dran pa*.

[288] Pellegrini, Andrés M. http://www.thlib.org/reference/dictionaries/tibetan-dictionary/translate.php

[289] s.v. *dran pa*.

[290] Duff 2007.

[291] s.v. *dran pa*.

[292] Ibid.

[293] Ibid.

This then leads to a very reasonable question: can we therefore say that it is appropriate to translate *dran pa* as "mindfulness" in Saraha's context? Although some have chosen to do so,[294] most do not, and an examination of where and how it is used in his songs demonstrates that something else going on. The first quite obvious difference is that in all the above contexts, *dran pa* has a connotation of being intentional, deliberate, and **positive**, that is to say, conducive to awakening. For Saraha, it means something quite different. In fact, when used as a symbolic term, *dran pa* is the basis of bewildered perception. Considering all this, and thinking about the context of translating Saraha, I have chosen to use **recognition** for the symbolic term *dran pa*, so that the term includes the "re" implied by memory, and the "cognition" entailed in mindfulness.[295]

So far we have seen *dran pa* as cultivated, intentional, intense awareness and as a tool for the aspiring Buddhist practitioner. There are moments in the text where Saraha's use of the term is consistent with this. In the *Speech Treasury*, for example, we read: "Whoever meditates on the innate meaning / Without wavering from pure mindfulness (*dran pa*), obtains [the goal]."[296] In the *Body Treasury* there is another example:[297]

> The practice of meditation and recitation of mantras are
> but your mind,
> Even meditational deities are your own mind.
> Due to that, ḍākinīs, making prophecies, etc., are your own
> mind:
> Mind displays itself in the arising of whatever it recollects
> (*dran pa*).

When it is deployed as a symbolic term, however, *dran pa* takes on the meaning of incorrect conventional perception, which will be detailed

---

294 For example, Khenchen Thrangu Rinpoche's (2006) commentary on the *King Dohā* places special emphasis on the term in its *abhidharmic* sense.

295 I was pointed this way to some degree by Nyanaponika Thera's (1992) discussion of *sañña* (*saṁjñā*). This aligns Saraha's use of the term *dran pa* more clearly with *saṁjñā* than with *smṛti* or *anusmṛti*.

296 *Speech Treasury*, verse 25.

297 *Body Treasury*, verse 55.

below. Since we cannot read the *Adamantine Songs* with the help of a commentary, determining when *dran pa* means mindfulness, recollection, etc., and when it has a specialized use has required careful, close reading. I have noted that *dran pa*'s use as a symbolic term is regularly signaled by the presence of its complementary (or opposite?) term, *dran med*, in a position of prominence and privilege close by. While I hesitate to draw an exaggerated conclusion from this, it is worth keeping in mind that *dran pa* being embedded in a constellation of other symbolic terms —either in the same verse or one immediately adjoining—may signal a specialized use. This will be discussed in more detail below, but first we will turn our attention to *dran med*.

An examination of the same reference sources yields some interesting results. Importantly, *dran med* is simply not a common or widely used term in the Sūtras and Abhidharma texts reviewed above in the discussion of recognition (*dran pa*). As the opposite of *dran pa*, it is the condition remedied by *dran pa*. For this reason, I will turn immediately to the dictionary sources. Many of the dictionary sources that identify the greatest range of meanings for *dran pa* have the fewest possibilities for *dran med*. Turning first to possible Sanskrit words translated as *dran med*, Lokesh Chandra's *Tibetan-Sanskrit Dictionary* allows for only one possibility: *visaṁjñā*. *Visaṁjñā* is defined as insensible, unconscious, and confused. In short, it is to be without *saṁjñā*.[298] Negi adds *niḥsaṁjñā* (unconscious) to the range of possibilities.[299] In Apte's *Sanskrit-English Dictionary*, we find *vismṛti* (forgetfulness, oblivion, loss of memory),[300] *asmṛti* (forgotten, inconsistent with *smṛti*),[301] and *vismaraṇa* (forgetting, forgetfulness, oblivion)[302] as the possible opposites of *smṛti*.[303]

---

[298] s.v. *dran med*.

[299] s.v. *dran pa med*.

[300] s.v. *vismṛt*.

[301] s.v. *asmṛti*.

[302] s.v. *vismaraṇa*.

[303] Intriguingly, Waldron (2003, 198 n69) suggests *vijñāna* in a note on *saṁjñā* as apperception. He writes: "*Saṃjñā* is formally the opposite of *vijñāna* (P. *viññāna*), which is composed of *vi-*, "dis," plus the same root *jñā*. While *vijñāna* stresses disjunctive discernment, *saṃjñā* emphasizes a conjunctive construction of an image or idea that brings disparate sensations together into a whole, often connected with a name or concept."

Suggestions for how to translate *dran med* (or its "long hand" version: *dran pa med pa*) into English are also illuminating. Tony Duff's *Illuminator* dictionary, offering such breadth on *dran pa*, doesn't have *dran med* listed in the dictionary at all. Chandra Das' *Tibetan-English Dictionary* suggests to swoon, become unconscious, to lose one's memory or senses.[304] In a similar vein, the *Sambhota Dictionary* offers unconsciousness, to be in a coma, oblivious, and absent-minded.[305] Needless to say, these are not terms that are generally associated with the rituals and practices of *mahāmudrā*. Other uses of the term are "without conscious recollection or ordinary attention," "without thinking," "no thought," and "mindlessly."

Returning to our discussion of *dran pa* and *dran med* as symbolic terms, while all of this may be plausible in certain circumstance, in Saraha's poems *dran med* is consistently used to describe a state that is advanced beyond *dran pa*, one where appearances are purified. It is always positive, always one of the goals of *mahāmudrā* practice. In the *Body Treasury Adamantine Song* we find the following definition of the two terms in Saraha's own words: "*Dran med* is the nature of nonconceptuality, and *dran pa* is dependently arisen and adventitious."[306] In another example, we find the following verse in his *Body Treasury*:[307]

> In the sphere of *dran med*, meditative equipoise is great bliss;
> In the sphere of great bliss, one abides in continuous nonconceptuality.
> Not engaging the mind, appearance is purified spontaneously.
> The condition is unobstructed *dran pa*, illuminating awareness.

Here, where *dran med* characterizes a sphere or realm of experience where meditative equipoise (*samāhita*, *mnyam bzhag*) is great bliss, and where

---

304 s.v. *dran pa med pa*.

305 s.v. *dran med*.

306 *Body Treasury*, verse 62.

307 *Body Treasury*, verse 13.

appearances continue to arise, we are clearly not talking about having fallen into a coma or a long-lasting swoon. In that experience of *dran med*, in which the mind is not engaged, *dran pa* is experienced in an unobstructed manner as illuminating awareness. This is very similar to a passage from the *King Dohā*, though rather than the emphasis on *mnyam bzhag* we saw above, here it is on meditative concentration (*samādhi*, *ting nge 'dzin*):[308]

> Mind united with concentration is *dran med,*
> The afflictions are completely purified, it is just that.

Nonetheless, whether it is being set in the context of the practice of concentration or its fruition, the state referred to as *dran med* is not a swoon. Further in the *Body Treasury Adamantine Song* we read:[309]

> Whoever is free from hope and fear of nirvāṇa and
> saṁsāra,
> Not finding body and mind, rests freely in *dran med.*
> Suchness is not found by the intellect; it is self-arising.

One, therefore, who is free from hoping for nirvāṇa and from fearing saṁsāra is free of distinguishing pure and impure, starting point and goal, free we may say, of subject-object duality entirely. In other words, this is a desirable state.

Further, I offer that "Not finding body and mind" may be Saraha's direct critique of the four mindfulnesses of body, feeling, mind, and phenomena, the *dran pa* (as *smṛti*) so dear to the path discussed briefly above. Furthermore, by abandoning training concentration by focusing on the body or mind, it seems that Saraha discards Asaṅga's well-known sense of mindfulness as well. Recall the definition in the *Abhidharma-samuccaya*: "It is not to let what one knows slip away from one's mind. Its function is not to be distracted." Instead of an exercise in object-definition, or in intentionally and one-pointedly focusing on the four objects designated as objects of mindfulness (body, feelings, mind, and

---

308 *dran med ting nge 'dzin du sbyor / nyon mongs yongs su dag pa'ang de nyid do* (15b).

309 *Body Treasury*, verse 25.

phenomena), one must overcome that object-defining process entirely and rest freely in *dran med*.

In the *Queen Dohā*, I find some suggestion that Saraha is also explicitly critiquing *dran pa* as *saṁjñā*, the third aggregate of perception. Perception, of course, depends on the meeting of sense organs and sense objects, and is understood to have occurred when the object's features have been noted and it has been identified. Turning that on its head, in the *Queen Dohā* Saraha tells us that in order to understand the symbolic terms as the path itself, "You should rely on form, sound, smell, taste, contact/sensation, and mental objects as the highest Guru."[310] Perhaps we should not be surprised to find that Saraha, renowned for *not* adhering to any system of cultivation, appears to be not so much a proponent of mindfulness as he is of mind*less*ness. I do not mean to suggest that Saraha identifies insight with foolish, careless behavior. Rather, he discards traditional methods of cultivation in favor of a path he redefines according to his own methods. This reorientation is reflected in his deployment of these specific terms as symbolic. Again, in the *Body Treasury Adamantine Song*, Saraha declares:[311]

> From the natural liberation of *dran pa*, *dran med* arises
> freely.
> Recognize whatever is experienced as mere appearances,
> and *dran med* is restored.

Dran med is here again privileged over *dran pa*.[312] Refining our understanding of what Saraha intends with *dran pa*, it is made clear here that *dran med* is what needs to be cultivated or restored, and *dran pa* is what needs to be liberated and in fact undone. Based on the structure of the above verse, we can see that "from the natural liberation of *dran pa*" aligns with "recognize whatever is experienced as mere appearances." This indicates that that the process of learning to recognize phenomena

---

[310] *bla ma mchog dag la gzugs sgra dri ro reg dang chos la brten par bya* (20a).

[311] *Body Treasury*, verse 38.

[312] This is what stops me from using, for example, Kapstein's "mnemic engagement" and "amnesis"—in the Dzogchen context amnesis is negatively valued (Kapstein 1992). For that reason, though the Tibetan terms are still *dran pa* and *dran med*, I do not think it is wise to match these terms in translation since they refer to different things.

and experiences as "mere appearances" is the very process of liberating *dran pa* and restoring or enabling *dran med*. Again, *dran med* is clearly privileged and not akin to being in a coma. For *dran med*, which must not be confused with a swoon, I have chosen to use *de*-cognition as a translation, a term that I find both unsettling and pleasing. A precise manner of referring to the process of cultivating mind*less*ness that Saraha exhorts his readers and listeners to engage in with abandon, decognition forces one to imagine a way of *knowing* and *experiencing* differently.

Unborn and Beyond the Intellect

The term *skye med* (unborn), or a longer version of it—*skye ba med pa*—is used to translate a rather lengthy range of terms from Sanskrit. Among the possibilities suggested by Lokesh Chandra are: *aja* (not born, existing from all eternity), *ajanani* (non-birth, cessation of existence), *ajāti* (without birth, without production) and *ajātika* (something that is without birth or production).[313] Negi lists the following: *anutpāda* (nonproduction not coming into existence; not taking effect), *anutpattiḥ* (nonproduction, not produced), *ajātiḥ* (without birth, without production), *asaṁbhavaḥ* (non-existence, cessation), *asaṁbhūtatā* (that which not produced or arisen), *ajanmā* (unborn), *ajātikaḥ* (something that is without birth or production), and *anutpannaḥ* (unborn, unproduced).[314] In Tibetan-English dictionaries we find *skye med* translated as unborn, unproduced, birthless, unoriginated, not come about, nonarising, uncreated, not produced, without arising/birth, nonliving, without origination, not coming into existence, absence of origination, uncreated, cessation of existence;[315] nonproduction, not coming into existence;[316] and "Nonarising."[317] The *Nitartha* online dictionary[318] explains, "In the aspect of ultimate truth, all phenomena are devoid of an independent, concrete

---

313 s.v. *skye med.*

314 s.v. *skye ba med pa.*

315 *Tibetan & Himalayan Library Translation Tool*, s.v. *skye med.*

316 Ibid. s.v. *skye ba med pa.*

317 curiously, there is no entry under either *skye med* or *skye ba med pa* in Chandra Das.

318 Dzogchen Ponlop 2003. http://www.nitartha.org/dictionary_search04.html

identity and have therefore no basis for such attributes as 'arising, dwelling, or ceasing' i.e. coming into being, remaining in time and place, and ceasing to exist."[319] Most unlike the circumstance I find myself in with the other three *brda* terms, however, in this case I have a good indication of what the term is that Tibetan translators were working with: *aja*. This is because it is used in the title of the *Mind Treasury*, conveniently reproduced "in the Indian language":[320] *citta kośa* ***aja*** *vajra gīti*.

Saraha uses *skye med* to indicate nondiscrimination and nonduality. In a state beyond relating to appearances at all, this term connotes the awareness of an awakened being beyond all conventions. As such, it is beyond the parameters of language to describe it. Referred to as "the secret experience,"[321] it defies explanation and is illustrated either by metaphors or as a mysterious descriptive term coupled with other terms that defy definition, such as the Great Seal, mind itself, etc. Since recognition is the bewildered dualistic perception and experience of arising and cessation, and decognition is the experience of that same arising and cessation free of the reifying, dualistic bewildered mind, *skye med*, the unborn,[322] is beyond the experience of phenomena arising as such altogether. Thrangu Rinpoche writes that it is "the realization that all appearances from the very beginning have been without birth or true arising,"[323] drawing out the term as a description of the experience of one who has cognized emptiness. While recognition and decognition describe two modes of experiencing conventional reality (one bewildered, the other not), unborn is the experience or insight into the illusory nature, or total insubstantiality, of arising. Supporting this, in the *Body Treasury* we find:[324]

---

[319] s.v. *skye ba med pa*.

[320] *gya gar skad du*.

[321] ST 43.

[322] In his translation of the *King Dohā* and two commentaries on it, Guenther (1969) translates it as "unorigination."

[323] Khenchen Thrangu Rinpoche 2006, 104.

[324] *Body Treasury*, verse 62.

> Recognition, decognition and the unborn are united.
> Decognition, which is the nature of nonconceptuality, and
> Recognition, which is dependently arisen and adventitious,
> These two have one taste in the unborn nature.

Most examples of how this symbolic term is used will be presented after the discussion of "beyond the intellect" below, as they are nearly always found together. These two symbolic terms are closely linked, as that which is beyond the intellect is used to describe how the unborn is experienced.

There is not much secondary material to discuss under the heading of *blo las 'das* as it does not appear to exist as anything but a specialized term. I translate it rather literally as "beyond the intellect" as it captures what the term indicates in the context of Saraha's songs.[325] As the term only appears in this very limited context it is particularly challenging to imagine what it translates from "the Indian language." According to Hopkins[326] and Chandra Das,[327] *blo* can be used to translate *buddhi*, *mati,* and *dhī*. *Buddhi* can refer to the power of forming and retaining conceptions and general notions, intelligence, reason, intellect, mind, discernment, and judgment;[328] *mati* to devotion, prayer, worship, hymn, thought, design, intention, resolution, determination, inclination, wish, mind, perception, understanding, intelligence, sense, and judgment;[329] and *dhī* to thought, reflection, meditation, devotion, prayer, understanding, intelligence, knowledge, mind, disposition, and intention.[330] *Las 'das* and *las 'das pa* mean to transcend or go beyond. The only sources where I found *blo las 'das* as a term, the two possible translations are "conceptual mind is transcended" and "beyond mind."[331]

---

325 Guenther's translation (1969) is "transcendence." I have opted not to use transcendence because as the Tibetan term, it is quite specific about what is transcended.

326 s.v. *blo*.

327 s.v. *blo*.

328 Cologne Digital Sanskrit Lexicon s.v. *buddhi*.

329 Ibid. s.v. *mati*.

330 Ibid. s.v. *dhī*.

331 *Tibetan & Himalayan Library Translation Tool* and Nitartha Online Tibetan Dictionary s.v. *blo las 'das*.

The term "beyond the intellect" itself indicates that it defies definition. It is inconceivable. In the *Adamantine Songs* the term is often used to qualify the experience of the unborn or to indicate something beyond it.[332] As symbolic terms that point towards insight into something that is beyond all conventions of expression or experience, both the unborn and beyond the intellect naturally cannot be adequately described by discussion alone. The discussion must be informed by experience. An examination of how the terms *skye med* and *blo las 'das* are used together in the *Adamantine Songs* reveals little beyond their close relationship. The terms are employed to describe an experience of the Great Seal, but merely reading them does not grant access to that experience. Verse 43 of the *Body Treasury* reads:

> The qualities of the unborn are unchanging, like a rock,
> They do not follow after, the way echoes arise.
> Beyond the intellect and not an object for the senses,
> The qualities of the Great Seal are like the sky.

Verse 57 of the *Body Treasury* points to there not being a distinct reality or realm described by the unborn and beyond the intellect, rather a transformed experience of conventional reality:

> If there are no distinctions, the unborn is liberated in its own place;
> If you transcend the intellect, then there is no action or non-action.
> Although the manner of illustrating Buddhas and sentient beings is different,
> They arise simultaneously—it is a question of knowledge and ignorance.

Explanations in Commentaries on the Dohā Trilogy

Both Nyime Avadhūtipa's and Kyeme Dechen's commentaries on Saraha's *Dohā Trilogy* use the four symbolic terms as a consistent interpretive lens though which to read the *dohās*. This is curious, to say the

332 Khenchen Thrangu Rinpoche writes, "At the level of the fourth symbol, one realizes that the nature of the mind is not only beyond existence but also beyond nonexistence" (2006, 106).

least, given the paucity of appearances of the terms in the *dohā*s themselves. Only two verses in the *King Dohā* employ the symbolic terms *dran pa* and *dran med*, and they appear in the *Queen Dohā* once. They do not appear in the *People Dohā* at all. *Skye med* and *blo las 'das* do not appear in the *dohā*s at all. Despite this, the commentaries focus obsessively on these terms. Saraha's trilogy of *Adamantine Songs* on the other hand, invoke these four terms with startling regularity. *Dran pa* and *dran med* appear over 120 times; *skye med* over 50 times; and *blo las 'das* more than 25 times. Since there unfortunately do not exist (to my knowledge) any commentaries on the *Adamantine Songs*, there are no commentarial signposts to guide one towards the meaning of key concepts and critical terms. Given this state of affairs, the commentaries on Saraha's *dohā* collections are a naturally helpful source of direction. They have enabled me to put these different works in dialogue with each other. The commentaries have clearly made the symbolic terms important and inform how Saraha's *dohā*s are interpreted right down to the present day. This naturally raises the questions: Why was so much ado made of these terms in the *dohā*s, when they appear so infrequently? Why did nobody comment directly on the *Adamantine Songs*, where they figure so prominently? Perhaps in the course of the transmission of an old text, the most popular strata of interpretation became naturalized and therefore invisible. That is to say, perhaps this question has thus far gone unasked because the association of the *dohā*s with the symbolic terms is an example of *dran pa*: a habit of interpretation.

So let us turn briefly to Saraha's *dohā*s, and the one pair of verses in the *King Dohā* where Saraha actually uses some of this terminology:[333]

> Conventional truth is *dran med*;
> And mind that became no-mind;
> Just that, completely transformed, is the best of the best,
> This supreme among the best, friends, should be known by
> you!

[333] *kun rdzob bden pa dran pa med pa ste // sems dang sems ni med par gyur pa'o // de nyid yongs su gyur pa mchog gi mchog // mchog gi dam pa grogs dag shes par gyis // sems ni dran med ting nge 'dzin du sbyor // nyon mongs yongs su dag pa'ang de nyid do // ji ltar 'dam skyes 'dam gyis mi tshugs bzhin // srid 'byung nyes pas rgyal chos mi gos so //* (15b)

> Mind united with concentration is *dran med*,
> The afflictions are completely purified, it is just that.
> As a lotus is not affected by the mud from which it rises,
> By worldly good and bad, you will not be sullied.

Here, the commentary by Kyeme Dechen is extremely helpful. Commenting on the first of the above verses, he puts *dran med* in the larger context of the four *brda* terms. It is worth noting that in the above verses, *dran pa* is not explicitly mentioned. Kyeme Dechen explains that in the sphere of conventional truth, there is incorrect conventional perception (*log pa'i kun rdzob*) and correct conventional perception (*yang dag pa'i kun rdzob*).[334] *Dran pa* is the basis of the incorrect, or bewildered, perception. *Dran med,* however, is the basis for correct conventional perception. Where *dran pa* provides continuity it leads directly to a perception of objects that appear to persist and to have some kind of concrete existence. This deluded experience of objects is the cause of bewilderment. *Dran med* on the other hand, undoes that false experience of continuity and stability by identifying *dran pa*, recognition, with experience and perception rather than as a quality inhering in an external object. With *dran pa* thus "undone," one can still apprehend objects but does not reify them. In this way *dran med* constitutes correct conventional truth, while perception based on *dran pa* is bewildered, or incorrect as it is premised on the experience of continuous, persisting objects. In his commentary on the following verse, Kyeme Dechen continues by explaining that "mind which is *dran pa* is adventitious and arises due to specific conditions, just like a bubble in water,"[335] while *dran med* "is a meditative absorption that is the play of a lion."[336]

Dran pa, then, is a kind of object identification based on repeated experience that gets conflated with continuity, and expresses the activity of a dualistic mind and its experience of all phenomena. *Dran med* on the

---

334 Kyeme Dechen, 49b.

335 These words precisely echo Saraha's own definition of *dran pa* in verse 62 of the *Body Treasury*: "*dran pa* is dependently arisen and adventitious" (*rten 'brel glo bur skye ba'i dran pa*). The passage from Kyeme Dechen reads, "*dran pa'i sems de ni glo bur ba rkyen las skyes pa / chu nang gi sbur ma lta bu'am*" (50a).

336 *dran med seng ge rnam par rtse ba'i ting nge 'dzin* (ibid.)

other hand, the undoing of that illusion, does not send one into a swoon or a coma from which state nothing arises. From the sphere of decognition, phenomena arise and desist as phenomena are wont to do, but without the false overlay of object-making continuity, the illusion projected by a mind taking its recognition too seriously. After all, Saraha as the model Mahāmudrā siddha is specifically engaging with appearances; he rejects distinguishing between appearances and emptiness, meditation and nonmeditation, saṁsāra and nirvāṇa. This goes some distance to explaining why Tibetan translators used such multivalent terms to express this concept of Saraha's, as it certainly entails all these notions of memory, repeated experience, attachment, and object construction.

Application in the Adamantine Songs

Now let us return to some key moments in Saraha's songs with this much more precise understanding of the terms *dran pa, dran med*, *skye med*, and *blo las 'das* in mind. In the *Body Treasury Adamantine Song*, the term *dran pa,* recognition, appears for the first time in the fourth verse:[337]

> Self-grasping mind causes a constellation of recognition;
> In this nature, diverse appearances dawn.
> Although all beings abide in a state like darkness
> The lamp of *yoga* blazes when it finds just that.
>
> The essential meaning is beyond the scope of reason;
> It is not evident and is obscured by recognition's power.
> It is the path of bliss, nonconceptual, unconditioned
> decognition.
> Beyond any path, how does a result appear beyond the
> intellect?

As discussed above, recognition is the basis of the incorrect, or bewildered, perception. As a kind of object identification based on repeated experience that gets conflated with continuity, recognition expresses the ordinary activity of mind and its experience of all phenomena. Wherever the term "recognition" appears in the *Adamantine Songs*, readers should

---

[337] *Body Treasury*, verses 4–5.

thereby understand continuity falsely imputed upon appearances that leads to their reification, and thus to a bewildered, dualistic experience of phenomena. *Dran med*, or decognition, sets up a contrast between conventional designation and true insight in verses 7 and 8:[338]

> The Great Seal is unchangeable great bliss and,
> Not dependent on a cause, the result is beyond the scope of
>   the intellect.
> The Great Seal is the complete result.
> Conventionally, it is illustrated as the goal of the path.
>
> The essential meaning is without expressed and
>   expressing,
> The sphere of awareness is decognition, the expression of
>   everything.

In contrast to recognition, which is the basis of bewildered perception, decognition is the basis for correct conventional perception. Decognition undoes the false experience of continuity and stability by identifying recognition with experience and perception, rather than as a quality inhering in an external object. With recognition thus "undone," one still apprehends objects but does not reify them. In this way, decognition constitutes correct conventional truth, while perception based on recognition is bewildered, or incorrect as it is premised on the experience of continuous, persisting objects. Recall that in the *King Dohā* Saraha states explicitly that "decognition *is* conventional truth."[339]

Continuing with our close reading of the *Body Treasury*:[340]

> Although recognition originates conditioned by
>   appearances,
> It does not transcend the condition which is the
>   decognition of emptiness.
> In this nonconceptual goal there is no activity and no view.
> How deluded! To search for oneself in others!

---

[338] *Body Treasury*, verses 7–8.

[339] *kun rdzob bden pa dran pa med pa ste*. (15b)

[340] *Body Treasury*, verses 10 and 13.

> In the sphere of decognition, meditative equipoise is great bliss;
> In the sphere of great bliss, one abides in continuous nonconceptuality.
> Not engaging the mind, appearance is purified spontaneously.
> The condition is unobstructed recognition, illuminating awareness.

These two stanzas take us in a full circle, from appearances to appearances. Abiding in the state of decognition, where one doesn't impute an essence onto objects, is blissful. Abiding in that bliss brought about by decognition is abiding in a state completely free of conceptuality. Free of conceptuality, appearances are completely, naturally pure. One ascends, therefore, through the stages laid out by Saraha in order to return to the ordinary world of appearances, but in a purified state.

A later verse sates:[341]

> Not understanding direct contact, conceptual compassion
> Is a cause for pollution, leading you to undergo the experience of saṁsāra,
> Emptiness and compassion are inseparable and devoid of arising.
> Whoever is free from hope and fear of nirvāṇa and saṁsāra,
> Not finding body and mind, rests freely in decognition.
> Just that is not found by the intellect; it is self-arising.

In this stanza we find some of the clearest evidence of the status of decognition. "Direct contact" is of course the contact between sense organ and sense object. If that experience is conceptualized, it quickly enforces the reification of subject and object, self and other. Contact with another sentient being, for example, may lead to the arising of compassion. If that compassion is grounded in the belief in discrete entities, "self" and "other," however, it is polluted by duality and leads to deeper entanglement in saṁsāra. If that which is experienced is informed by emptiness,

---

[341] *Body Treasury*, verse 25.

however, compassion can manifest in a non-samsaric way. Thus freed of duality by insight into emptiness, one is even freed of the duality of saṁsāra and nirvāṇa. That freedom is here described as resting freely in *dran med*.

Later we read:[342]

> In just that, there is no distinction of antidotes, one leaves it in its natural place.
> Whatever concepts arise, they arise in true freedom.
> From the natural liberation of recognition, decognition arises freely.
> Recognize whatever is experienced as mere appearances, and decognition is restored.

These instructions on radically training nonduality ask the listener/reader to not judge experiences as good or bad, pure or defiled. In other words, phenomena and experiences do not need to be evaluated as conducive to awakening or in need of an antidote. Without the overlay of dualistic discursive thought, whatever arises does so in freedom and thereby manifests just that. The ability to do this is referred to by Saraha here as the "natural liberation of recognition (*dran pa*)"—or decognition (*dran med*).

Another important passage from the *Body Treasury* reads:[343]

> As for the expression, "cessation of dualistic appearances,"
> It refers to the sweeping away of recognition and the gathering of decognition as nourishment.
>
> In just that, which is unborn, beyond the intellect,
> Subject and object are burned and purified
> By the fire of decognition and unborn wisdom.
> By offering that which is beyond the intellect and
> By the power of wishing prayers, subsequent births do not continue.

This begins with a reconfirmation of the same message found stanza 38, cited above. Stanzas 50 and 51 are of particular interest as they make

[342] *Body Treasury*, verse 38.

[343] *Body Treasury*, verses 50–51.

explicit mention of all four of the symbolic terms so central to the commentaries on the *dohās*. Here, the Great Seal is identified as unborn (*skye med*) and beyond the intellect (*blo las 'das*). Duality, subject and object, are destroyed in the fire of decognition, thus enabling the experience of the Great Seal. Note that the only mention of *dran pa*, recognition, is it being swept away. This is rather strong language. The four symbolic terms again appear together later, emphasizing a similar point:[344]

> Therefore, the Great Seal is the highest union:
> Recognition, decognition, and the unborn are united.
> Decognition, which is the nature of nonconceptuality, and
> Recognition, which is dependently arisen and adventitious,
> These two have one taste in the unborn nature.
> The arisen and arising are beyond the intellect.

The establishment of decognition as the very basis of accomplishing the Great Seal is confirmed again in strong terms:[345]

> Hey! The uncontrived Seal is great bliss.
> In the expanse of decognition, it is self-illuminating.
> It is unborn and pervasive like space.
> It abides in the realm which is beyond the intellect.

No fewer than seventeen more stanzas drawn from the *Body Treasury* alone can be considered relevant to this discussion. There is one grouping of seven stanzas together that warrant being cited in their entirety before we move on to the *Speech* and *Mind Treasuries*:[346]

> Hey! Thus the wise who are accomplished in skillful
> methods,
> Will seal decognition with the unborn.
> Because it is free of recognition, it is sealed by
> decognition.
> With appearance, emptiness is sealed.
> With emptiness, appearance is sealed.

---

[344] *Body Treasury*, verse 62.

[345] *Body Treasury*, verse 72.

[346] *Body Treasury*, verses 110–116.

When recognition and appearance arise as the taste of
  bliss,
They are sealed by emptiness and decognition.
When appearance and recognition and the seal of
  emptiness
Are sealed by abiding in decognition,
Appearance and recognition, dawning as the taste of bliss
Will not be analyzed by the contemplation of signs, and
  will remain beyond the characterizing intellect.

Recognition and appearance are sealed by the unborn;
The unborn is sealed by the beyond the intellect.
Because recognition is the seal of the bliss that is
  decognition,
It has not become nothing, and has not fallen into the
  extreme of nihilism.

As the abiding and arising are sealed,
They are not reified and do not fall into the extreme of
  eternalism.
Everything is unborn and beyond the intellect;
Everything possesses the continuum of great bliss;
Knowing this, one does not fall into the extreme of
  indifference.

Recognition is the substance of saṁsāra, and
In the realization of decognition,
Take equanimity as the path:
Probed by awareness, emptiness is equanimity, and
Reflexive awareness, free of subject and object, is
  equanimity.
Free of the two truths, meditation on equanimity is
  nondual.
Meditative absorption without thoughts of anything
  whatsoever is the best equanimity.
Equanimity which is neutral is not meditation.

Cognition in its natural place emanates from the
experience of decognition.
Characteristics of recognition are taken as the path of
decognition.

Carried on the path of bliss, it is unobservable, it is beyond
the intellect.
Not conceptualized as dual, the bliss is uninterrupted.

It is not in the *Body Treasury* alone that we find substantial use of the symbolic terms. The concepts here remain very important in the significantly shorter *Speech* and *Mind Treasuries*, despite the fact such references are less common than in the *Body Treasury*. In the *Body Treasury*, thirty of the 117 verses use some combination of the symbolic terms. That means that in just over 25% of the verses the terms are used. In the *Speech Treasury*, out of forty-eight stanzas, the symbolic terms appear in seven (approximately 14%), and in the *Mind Treasury*, out of twenty-seven they appear in three (approximately 11%).

In the *Speech Treasury*, the power of decognition to burn up duality entirely appears in the second stanza:[347]

As soon as decognition illuminates, the benefit of self and
others is not two:
The aspects of the Great Seal are innumerable and
unutterable.
When real and unreal are discarded completely, there is no
saṁsāra and nirvāṇa.

The emphasis on decognition as correct conventional truth reappears later, where the locus of the experience of entities without a mistakenly imputed own-nature (*svabhāva*, *rang bzhin*;) is identified both with decognition and the unborn. The indivisibility of everything from entities to meditative equipoise is experienced in that sphere:[348]

---

347 *Speech Treasury*, verse 2.

348 *Speech Treasury*, verse 19.

Although the own-nature of entities appear due to the
conditions for arising,
They are not experienced beyond the sphere of the non-
arisen.
Entities, non-entities, meditative equipoise, etc.; all are
indivisible.
That is the sphere of decognition and the unborn.

Then, right at the end of the *Speech Treasury* come four significant verses. They begin by drawing a distinction between cognition that depends on signs (*mtshan ma*) and decognition, which as a *brda* term connotes meaning free from signs, in an entirely new way. Training in decognition as a mode of experiencing phenomena is the very antidote to the experience of duality, that is to say, to objects that arise with own-nature. After purifying the experience of saṁsāra with decognition, the Great Seal is accomplished:[349]

Recognition that relies on signs is the cause of wandering.
When the objective world is not seen in that itself
The experience of signs will dissolve into decognition.

The yoga with signs is the path of the three realms of
saṁsāra,
Conceptual things contain the seeds for carelessness.
[But] the yoga of decognition is like the center of space.

If one does not make distinctions, self-essence does not
arise,
The minds of other sentient beings are not experienced.
When they see just that, the wise will become practiced.

Abiding in recognition, conceptuality, and form,
Is abandoned in abiding that is decognition, the three
realms purified.
Nonarising, just that, is the abode of all the *siddhi*s.
Not seeing outer and inner is the accomplishment of all.

---

[349] *Speech Treasury*, verses 44–47.

Finally, in the condensed *Mind Treasury* we find the symbolic terms appearing only three times, among which two instances only refer to decognition. Unsurprisingly at this point, decognition is used to express the experience of phenomena and experiences arising free of clinging and duality. Someone who is abiding in the world free of dualistic concepts is depicted by the metaphor of a forest animal roaming in solitude and freedom:[350]

> Dwelling in the deep forest, deer roam alone;
> Not attached to the cause is the result itself.
> Illuminating appearance and non-appearance, devoid of
> object, devoid of attachment,
> Not thinking "real" and "empty," it is inexpressible
> decognition,
> There is bliss in the three aspects of the innate.

The purity of appearances and experiences is attained through training in decognition, breaking the habit of duality (recognition). The paradoxes found below in verse 8 may be interpreted as exploring the tension between understanding that awakening is both innate, and yet still needs to be cultivated:[351]

> Although a distinction between sentient beings and
> Buddhas is inconceivable,
> When there is pure conduct, [that is] continuous Great
> Yoga.
> Although the nature of recognition is not encompassed by
> thought,
> Primordial purity is absorbed in the realm of decognition.

The last reference to the symbolic terms comes in this pair of stanzas that emphasize all four:[352]

---

[350] *Mind Treasury*, verse 3.

[351] *Mind Treasury*, verse 8.

[352] *Mind Treasury*, verses 16–17.

If seen one-pointedly, one possesses the ultimate qualities.
Although by acting one-pointedly there is not the slightest
object of meditation.

Mental elaboration immolates itself; decognition is
pacifying healing.
Decognition and nonarising are like reflections in a mirror.
Through freedom from conventions, the path is unborn,
beyond the intellect.
Unsullied recognition with signs is habitually taught;
It is free from beginning and its past and future
unimaginable.

One-pointed focus indicates intense meditative absorption. Since meditation is described in conventional terms as having an *object*, here Saraha is making it clear that liberation only results from one-pointed focus that is free of any object. Despite the fact that habitually one is taught recognition (*dran pa* with all its many referents) with signs, in fact one needs to be freed of those conventions and liberated into the space of decognition, the unborn and that which is beyond the intellect. Mental elaborations, the results of recognition, are pacified and healed in the blazing of decognition.

I conclude this discussion of the four symbolic terms with the following verse from the *Body Treasury*:[353]

Through attention, conceptual thought cognizes difference.
There can be no falsity in this decognition!

Through diligence on the path, distinct results arise.
There can be no truth in this recognition!

*Through the power of equanimity, rest—at times—in
meditation.*
There can be no duality in this unborn nature!

*Apply the labels "bring to mind" and "don't bring to
mind."*
There is no effort in this beyond the intellect!

---

[353] *Body Treasury*, verse 9.

Conclusions

While overall I have treated the three *Adamantine Songs* as parts of a single work, it must be kept in mind that as a literary term a "treasury" (*kośa*) is by definition a category that more accurately could be translated into English as "miscellany." For that reason, the songs may not—either severally or together—be read with the expectation of an underlying narrative or didactic structure. It has therefore been more useful to allow them to speak to me through the coherent themes that are developed throughout them and the key terms that must—in light of both the commentarial tradition and the poems themselves—be treated as important concepts. Having begun with a structural evaluation of the three songs as a unit, my choice to treat as key the themes of the Great Seal (*phyag chen*), the innate (*lhan cig skyes pa / lhan skyes*), and the four symbolic (*brda*) terms, including recognition (*dran pa*), decognition (*dran med*), the unborn (*skye med*), and beyond the intellect (*blo las 'das / blo 'das*), was guided principally by the content of the poems themselves. I sincerely hope that the result has been more helpful than tedious, and that this will be the first of many such attempts to understand Saraha's adamantine suchness.

Introduction to the Translation and Critical Edition

Initially using the Derge Tengyur (*sde dge bstan 'gyur*) edition as a skeleton, I compared and studied the five versions of the poems making my own editorial decisions where there were textual variants. Where alternatives exist (whether in spelling, punctuation, grammatical particles, vocabulary, or entire lines of poetry), they have been marked with footnotes.

While four of the five sources may be identified as "canonical," this ought not give readers the impression that they are therefore unproblematic or consistent with each other. The numerous versions of the Tibetan canon—their composition, patronage, reproduction, and appellation—have been the subject of rather a lot of discussion. Paul Harrison provides a useful and illuminating exploration of the various incarnations of the Kangyur (*bka' 'gyur)* in his 1996 essay, "A Brief History of the Tibetan bKa' 'gyur," and the editor's introduction to *Tibetan Literature: Studies in Genre*[354] teases out some the complexities belonging to Kangyur, Tengyur as well as other large "authoritative" collections of Tibetan literature.

I have identified the four canonical sources as the Derge (*sde dge*) (D), Chone (*co ne*) (C), Narthang (*snar thang*) (N) and "Peking" (P) Tengyurs. All were compiled over time, sometimes being revised with enormous time gaps in between (as in the case of the Narthang, which has versions from the fourteenth and eighteenth centuries). The Peking edition, for example, which is one of the most frequently referred to versions, doesn't properly exist as such. What is most commonly referred to as "the" Peking canon is in fact a series of editions made from woodblocks, beginning in circa 1411 with the Yongle edition, but which inevitably wore out and needed to be recarved. Each new woodblock carving naturally entailed some changes, errors, and small alterations, and as a result there also exists (as "the Peking edition") the Wanli impression (1605), the two Kangxi impressions of 1684/92 and 1700, 1717–1720, the Qianlong of 1737, and at least one more impression.[355]

---

[354] Cabezon and Jackson 1996, 11–37.

[355] Harrison 1996, 81.

From this brief discussion, it should be clear that there is a certain amount of fluidity inherent in the so-called "canon" of Tibetan Buddhism.

The fifth version of the *Adamantine Songs* (M) is taken from the collection *'phags yul grub dbang dam pa rnams kyi zab mo'i do ha rnams las kho la byung mu tig phreng ba bzhugs so*, or "Pearl Garland of the Profound *Dohās* of the Noble Great *Siddhas* of India," which was ordered, put together, and carved into woodblocks overseen by the great Jamgön Ju Mipham Gyatso ('jam mgon 'ju mi pham rgya mtsho; 1846–1912). While in theory this is supposed to be an edited volume, it is in fact very lightly edited, containing numerous small corrections (and errors), clearly principally drawn from the same source as the Derge and Chone editions of the Tengyur. In fact, the M, D, and C editions differ little from each other, with only minor exceptions. Additionally, the P and N editions also differ little from each other, though are quite distinct from the M, D, and C group. Throughout my comparison of the five recensions, I began and continue to think of them as two groups, one consisting of M, D, and C and other consisting of P and N. I believe this reflects the provenance of the various versions of the Tengyur.

Another issue that must be mentioned here is versification. In Apabhraṁśa and Sanskrit verse, each stanza tends to be explicitly numbered and when not so are nonetheless easily discerned by either 2- or 4-line stanza construction. The structure of these *Adamantine Songs* is really rather loose and there are no clear indications of how long each stanza should be. I have marked and numbered the stanzas where it appears to be appropriate. In addition, I have numbered the lines which will allow readers to easily find corresponding passages in any given edition available to them. The stanza and line numbering are consistent between the English translation and the Tibetan critical edition that follow.

PART TWO

❧

Translation

❧

A Body Treasury Called the Immortal Adamantine Song

Homage to Mañjuśrī!

1. Hey! Wearing matted-locks, grasping at self and agent,
Brahmins, Jains, hedonists,[356]
Materialists accepting a real basis for things
Claim omniscience but don't even know themselves.
They are deluded and far from the path of liberation.

2. Vaibhāṣikas and Sautrāntikas,
Yogācārins and Mādhyamikas, etc.
Criticize each other and argue;
Ignorant of the space-like equality of appearance and
emptiness itself,
They turn their backs on the innate.[357]

---

[356] This is an attempt to translation the Tibetan term "Dagapa." While it could be a corruption of a *Carvaka*, the materialist school referred to on the next line, it could be a reference to people who believe in and for the moment (*da ga* means "this very moment") —in other words, hedonists. P and N provide the alternative reading "*sang ga pa*," but that has no meanings at all.

[357] In the same vein as the opening stanzas of his *People Dohā,* Saraha begins the *Body Treasury* with a thorough dismissal of the practices and beliefs of all those who surrounded him in his circa ninth century CE context. Not limiting his critique to followers of non-Buddhist schools, he is equally harsh on the four schools of Buddhist thought laid out in Siddhānta literature: Vaibhāṣikas and Sautrāntikas who, described in broad strokes, believe in the existence of *dharmas* as the basic building blocks of phenomena and in the existence of objects outside of and relation to the experiencing self; and the Yogācārins and Mādhyamikas, whose principal debates revolve around what, if anything, can be said to exist, how it appears, how it is perceived, and the nature of emptiness. See, for example, Napper 1989.

3. Body, speech, and mind are resplendent like cotton and oil in a lamp,
Endowed with just that, they are radiant like a lamp that is self-illuminating.
Because illuminating reflexive awareness pervades all beings
Indivisibly, that is the unborn nature.

4. Self-grasping mind causes a constellation of recognition;
In this nature, diverse appearances dawn.
Although all beings abide in a state like darkness
The lamp of yoga blazes when it finds just that.

5. The essential meaning is beyond the scope of reason;
It is not evident and is obscured by recognition's power.
It is the path of bliss, nonconceptual, unconditioned decognition.
Beyond any path, how does a result appear beyond the intellect?

6. From the treasury of innate mind
Pure and impure arise as saṁsāra and nirvāna.
Although arising, in the unborn nature they are one,
Free of self-nature, that itself is labeled "immutable."

7. The Great Seal is unchangeable great bliss and,
Not dependent on a cause, the result is beyond the scope of the intellect.
The Great Seal is the complete result.
Conventionally, it is illustrated as the goal of the path.

8. The essential meaning is without expressed and expressing,
The sphere of awareness is decognition, the expression of everything.

9. *Through attention, conceptual thought cognizes difference.*
There can be no falsity in this decognition!
Through diligence on the path, distinct results arise.
There can be no truth in this recognition!

Through the power of equanimity, rest—at times—in meditation.
There can be no duality in this unborn nature!
Apply the labels "bring to mind" and "don't bring to mind."[358]
There is no effort in this beyond-the-intellect!

10. Although recognition originates conditioned by appearances,
It does not transcend the condition which is the decognition of emptiness.
In this nonconceptual goal there is no activity and no view.
How deluded! To search for oneself in others!

11. Hey! That itself is difficult to realize as adamantine,
Not understanding this, mind chases after words.
It is difficult to meet that goal which is free of activity.
When the nature of activity, which is nonaction, is understood,
You will have found the sole intention of the Buddhas, beyond all objects.

12. The Conqueror's body is the unchanging, noncorporeal *dharmatā*.[359]
It does not reside in the body and is free from action and agency.
On a contaminated path, a result cannot be seen,
In the sphere of the unborn nature, his mind does not discriminate.

13. In the sphere of decognition, meditative equipoise is great bliss;
In the sphere of great bliss, one abides in continuous nonconceptuality.[360]

---

[358] In this verse Saraha is either in conversation with himself, or responding to four statements that he considers inaccurate. I have indicated this process by italicizing the statements he is responding to.

[359] The truth nature, the true nature of things as they are.

[360] P and N have an alternative rendering of this line that translates as: Abide in the self, in the blissful continuity of nonconceptuality.

Not engaging the mind, appearance is purified spontaneously.
The condition is unobstructed recognition, illuminating awareness.

14. As the faultless lotus expands from one root,
It abides as the innate nature within sentient beings.
Even when one is tainted by the power of wrongly seeing the existence of "other,"
Just like the lotus flower,
By the power of seeing rightly, it is the immutable Great Seal.

15. Even tainted by the mud of subject and object,
The root is the great selfhood, unchangeable in the three times.
Primordially free from activities of consciousness, subtle wind,[361] the lower doors,[362] mantra, etc.,
Free from self and other, accepting and rejecting.

16. Don't think of saṁsāra, don't be concerned with nirvāna,
The three times and three worlds[363] are contained in body, speech, and mind.
No effort in anything, no views, nothing to accept and reject,
Not differentiating center and perimeter, the middle way is the straight path.

17. When free of artificiality, it is the supreme path for the mind.
The Perfection of Wisdom path, which is passage, engagement, stages,[364] etc.

---

[361] That is, *vāyu*, the energy that moves through the subtle body in Tantric practice.

[362] The "lower doors" is a reference to practices that entail using the generative organs (i.e. union practice) or substances that emerge from them.

[363] The three times are past, present, and future; the three worlds usually refer to the human world, nāga world (located below the human world), and world of the gods (located above the human world).

[364] This a reference to the Mahāyāna path that entails the five paths and ten (or fourteen) *bhūmis*, etc.

Is the cause for the duration of saṁsāra by discarding the quick path.
The innate and the remedy are without rival.

18. In just that, the four *kāyas*, the five wisdoms, the afflictions, etc. are gathered.
Therefore, on the path which is saṁsāra,
Do not engage with whatever arises as the object, the object is not seen.
There is no joy or non-joy in the true nature.

19. Grasping and conceptualization are the uncontrived truth body,
The sense faculties do not apprehend on their own, they abide in emptiness.
Inexpressible experience is uninterrupted.
You should understand how to apply it to your own mental continuum.

20. In this faultless point, the Great Seal
Will be experienced like ocean and space.
When the senses are free of objects, there is no abyss to fall into;
One becomes attached by reifying recognition.

21. By leaving objects in their natural place, elaborations are again cast away.
Without rising and setting, the darkness of conceptuality will cease.
Dharmatā has one taste, the same as flowers for bees;
The faults and virtues are equal in the indivisible nature.
Amazing though it is, the experience cannot be expressed.

22. *Indivisible bliss,*[365] *like water into water,*
The innate and that yoga are inseparable.
One discerns a single essence in many thoughts,
Decognition is one, decognition is manifold.
Whoever wishes to engage in the primordial goal, the path of desire,
Practice the yoga—the simultaneous arising of bliss
And emptiness—in a manner beyond the intellect.

23. There is no inner or outer, self or other.
Knowing the object as it is, is taught as natural liberation.
Although in the truth body the three *kāyas* are inseparable,
If one practices, distinct results arise.

24. Hey! When inseparability is realized, wrong views are quickly destroyed.
When it is understood that unborn emptiness is indivisible from the goal of direct contact,
The forest and leaves have no basis.

25. Not understanding direct contact, conceptual compassion
Is a cause for pollution, leading to the experience of saṁsāra,
Emptiness and compassion are inseparable and devoid of arising.
Whoever is free from hope and fear of nirvāṇa and saṁsāra,
Not finding body and mind, rests freely in decognition.
That itself is not found by the intellect; it is self-arising.

26. That defined calm abiding, meditative equipoise and post-meditation,
Is not ultimate, it is not practiced by a mind in meditation.
Form, etc.,[366] is illumined effortlessly by body, speech, and mind.

---

[365] If we follow the P and N versions, this would read "Indivisible truth…."

[366] This indicates that the list of the aggregates follows. Awareness consisting of merely these five aggregates is part of the intended outcome of "regular" calm-abiding meditation.

Without the use of "tip of the nose," etc., shape and space,
Channel and contact, abide in the natural state.

27. All appearances are indestructible bliss,
Simply understanding the appearance of mere thoughts as illusion illuminates.
The reflection of the moon is devoid of parts and objectivity;
Even when searched for, it does not exist. Even when looked at, it is not seen.

28. Call to mind that recognition which appeared as illusion,
Nothing is seen apart from this decognition.
Although appearing as recognition, there is no grasping.
Although touched by recognition, it is free from the thought of contact.

29. Since, being beyond conceptualization, it is free, it is devoid of arising.
Although recognition arises, there is no engagement with the object.
Leave it in its original empty state where nothing is established.
Whatever you may do, the Seal is uninterrupted.

30. The four Great Seals have four branches:
The branch of realization of the unborn meaning; and
The branch of nondistinction of the two truths, and
Realization of contact of the unborn nature and appearance
Is the branch of nongrasping recognition and
Emptiness devoid of conditions and thought, beyond the intellect
Is the branch of not accepting or rejecting things.

31. With just that as the basis, "freedom from attachment," and
"Possessing investigation and analysis,"
"Joy and bliss," and "residing in the wilderness," etc.
Are taught as the objects illustrating this convention.[367]

---

[367] i.e. the four branches.

32. It is said that beings have high, middling, and low capacities.
For the benefit of the weak-minded, the learned ones thoroughly explained:
"The Great Seal does not abide anywhere at all."
It is explained like this in order to be free from moral structures.
Whatever appears, don't separate pure and impure, accept it all as *siddhi*s.[368]

33. Cultivating the innate and the blazing of inner fire on an object, etc.
Commitment, nature of self, and yoga…
In the Great Seal, the sameness of all phenomena, how could
Conceptualization be abandoned and nonconceptualization be practiced?

34. In your reverence to the Guru, the discipline of the secret vehicle is complete.
The very expression of the outer, inner, and secret initiations, and
The vase, secret, wisdom,
Essential direct word initiations, etc.
The mundane *siddhi*s arising from all these things cannot touch the Great Seal.

35. Hey! In the Great Seal are present body, speech, and mind, the nature of fruition.
The fruition of the Great Seal is only suitable for the essential meaning, but not for provisional and definitive.
It is the unsurpassed secret vehicle, the essence of all.
The essentials of path and fruition are distilled there,
The authentic highest Mahāyāna and the distinctness of the vehicles.

[368] i.e. accomplishments, evidence of attainment or awakening.

36. The characteristics by which one ascertains the Great Seal are:
Recognition and decognition are unborn, nondual,
Why would it not remain like space, beyond the intellect?

37. The map that is the action seal, and the path of the Dharma seal,
And the Great Seal that is the result, and the Commitment Seal that is the altruistic act—
By relying on seals below the Dharma Seal, one will not reach the end,
One falls into extremes of hope and fear, and becomes damaged by engaging in frivolous activities.

38. In that itself, there is no distinction of antidotes, one leaves it in its natural place.
Whatever concepts arise, they arise in true freedom.
From the natural liberation of recognition, decognition arises freely.
Recognize whatever is experienced as mere appearances, and decognition is restored.

39. Possessing the natural state itself, unborn and pure,
Pervading all, it abides like moisture in water,
Uninterrupted, it flows like a stream of water,
Like a lamp, it illuminates: reflexive awareness, bodhicitta,[369]
While not ceasing, mindful awareness is naturally empty.

40. What is this perfect reality?
If it exists elsewhere, it should be seen by all.
Even though you possess it yourself, it is concealed like the face of a guru.
Mind itself is Buddha,
But contaminated by recognition, suchness is imputed to be something else.

---

[369] The mind of awakening, generated on the basis of great compassion.

41. *Since it is the Buddha, what are its qualities?*
The qualities are like the whiteness and the cotton cloth.
The qualities that are just that *are* the Great Seal;
The nature and its qualities are not distinct and various.

42. The Great Seal and the fourth, etc.,
The qualities are not distinct, are not various.
In the qualities of decognition, the unstirring ocean,
There is no recognition, just as there are no waves in still water.

43. The qualities of the unborn are unchanging, like a rock,
They do not follow after, the way echoes arise.
Beyond the intellect and not an object for the senses,
The qualities of the Great Seal are like the sky.

44. Recognition arises from the minds of beings,
Therefore, emptiness need not be sought elsewhere.
Although appearing as four, it is of one quality:
So why is it expressed as appearing as four seals?

45. The aforementioned attributes arose as four.
The Great Seal should not be conceived as three.
Do not abide in anything and practice without attachment,
Like a bee drinking nectar from a flower.

46. The wisdom of discriminating awareness is skillful means.
When one encounters a flavor, there is no clinging to it.
This, however, will not be known by all.
Although the essential point pervades all six realms of beings in an instant,
Sentient beings are fettered by recognition like the threads of an endless knot.

47. Since recognition arises from mind, it is the cause of delusion,
But *knowing* without mental engagement is Buddhahood.
In that delusion there is not wisdom and methods.
Hey! When you know their inseparability, that alone is the supreme method.

48. All Buddhas, sentient beings and phenomena,
Arise simultaneously with mind itself—
When the absence of engagement is merely born in your mind,
Appearance as recognition disappears, there is no truth and falsehood;
Therefore it is not the object of just that alone.

49. Just as sound does not manifest as an object to the eye,
Nonconceptuality is not an object of investigation.
When, due to emptiness, recognition is merely illuminated,
From the disappearance of appearance as recognition, nothing to be seen.

50. Pristine cognition cannot become deaf, blind, and mute;
In that which is devoid of recognition, there is no ground for
deafness, blindness, or muteness.
It is free of all such conventions as "matter."
As for the expression, "cessation of dualistic appearances,"
It refers to the sweeping away of recognition and the gathering of decognition as nourishment.

51. In just that, unborn, beyond the intellect,
Subject and object are burned and purified
By the fire of decognition and unborn wisdom.
By offering that which is beyond the intellect and
By the power of wishing prayers, subsequent births do not continue.

52. Because of that, the Great Seal is primary,
It is not dependent on someone, it does not rely on anything,
Most unlike entering into water, joining an assembly, sharing a feast,
The Vedas, or disturbing a town.

53. Since the Great Seal is nothing other than oneself,
By receiving offerings, thoughts, guests, and objects of veneration as oneself,

Make the offering to one's own freedom from thought
[And] partake in the unborn assembly that is beyond the intellect.

54. Since the Great Seal is not dependent on an "other,"
The object of meditation is oneself and the meditator one's own mind.
Beyond the intellect, it is devoid of focusing on oneself.
Because just that is the fruition, it is not dependent on other factors.

55. The practice of meditation and recitation of mantras are but one's mind,
Even meditational deities are one's own mind.
Due to that, ḍākinīs, making prophecies, etc., are one's own mind:
Mind displays itself in whatever thoughts appear.

56. Where there is no recognition, no-thing can be observed.
Since the Great Seal is from nothing other than oneself,
Offering to and relying upon Buddha, Dharma, Sangha, etc.
Parents, precious ones, own-nature and bodhicitta
Is the cause of recognition.

57. If there are no distinctions, the unborn is liberated in its own place;
If you transcend the intellect, then there is no action or non-action.
Although the manner of illustrating Buddhas and sentient beings is different,
They arise simultaneously—it is a question of knowledge and ignorance.

58. Even though something appears, if it is not conceptualized with recognition,
Sentient beings themselves are the unborn result.
If something does not appear, but it is conceptualized in recognition,
Even the Buddhas themselves cause the cycle of three realms.

59. What can be upheld in the mind free of recognition?
Sentient beings may appear, they are the same as Buddhas.
If one desires to cognize recognition as Buddha,
Even though Buddhas appear, they are not distinct from sentient beings.

60. Therefore the duality of appearance and examination should be discarded as it is beyond analysis,
Once discarded, [since] it is not other than self, the continuum of being is severed.
It is tainted by the conceptual thought, "It comes from something other than self."
In luminous appearances, mind is nonconceptual and non-grasping.

61. Therefore, freed of dualistic notions of existence and non-existence,
When you abide in this natural state, whatever you do is blissful.
One who sustains the essence, apprehending the clear light of recognition,
[And] free of the two clingings,[370] will always abide in the authentic state.

62. Therefore, the Great Seal is the highest union:[371]
Recognition, decognition and the unborn are united.
Decognition, which is the nature of nonconceptuality, and
Recognition, which is dependently arisen and adventitious,
These two have one taste in the unborn nature.
The arisen and arising are beyond the intellect.

63. The union of emptiness and clear light etc.,
Uncontrived, uncreated, unborn and naturally self-liberated,

---

[370] Existence (eternalism) and non-existence (nihilism).

[371] As opposed to the action seal (union practice).

That is explained as the three *kāyas*: truth body, enjoyment body and
The diverse appearances of the transformation body;
The authentic nature is the essence body,
Compassion and emptiness, indivisible and unborn.

64. The experience based on the action seal is contrived.
As such, it arises through the power of conditions;
Since it depends on something else, it is not suchness.

65. Although the Dharma Seal is uncontrived,
Even if experienced, its non-establishment will not be seen.
If the Great Seal is experienced,
The diversity of thoughts will be recognized as the unborn nature.

66. That which appears as an entity is empty of own-nature,
Sentient beings and the unborn are the indivisible meaning,
Characterized by compassion and means and presented by metaphors.

67. Though appearances are diverse, do not swerve from the object that is beyond the intellect,
Constantly observe the essential yoga,
Abide in the Great Seal in all activities,
Leave the mode of being of things in the unborn sphere.

68. With the condition of wind, from a clear ocean
Ripples of water and waves temporarily arise.
However, they are indivisible from the ocean.
Conditioned by recognition, conceptualization temporarily arises,
Decognition of the above is suchness.
Unborn and beyond the intellect, these they are equally wondrous.

69. Thus, just as there is no origination in the Great Seal in the past,
It is absent in the future, too.
Although origination may occur due to the force of conditions,
They are indivisible from the unborn nature.
Formless, it pervades everything,
Is unchanging, and present at all times.

70. Like space, it is devoid of origination and cessation.
Just as the rope that is grasped as a snake is devoid of snake,
The truth body, enjoyment body and the transformation body are indivisible.
The essential nature is beyond the sphere of the intellect.

71. The Great Seal is instantaneous full awakening,
Just that arises as the form body[372] for the sake of sentient beings.
Results correspond to their cause, and results ripen,
And the pure result is that you will engage in altruistic acts.
The state is said to be especially beyond expression.

72. Hey! The uncontrived Seal is great bliss.
In the expanse of decognition, it is self-illuminating.
It is unborn and pervasive like space.
It abides in the realm beyond the intellect.

73. Appearance free of elaboration is great bliss,
Decognition does not conceptualize anything.
The variety of recognition appears as mind,
But when examined and sought, it cannot be found.

74. The unborn nature is free from grasping.
As it is free of grasping, it is without activity.

---

[372] When the *kāyas* are simply divided into two categories, they are form body (*rūpakāya*, which could be said to include both the transformation body and the enjoyment body) and truth body (*dharmakāya*).

Recognition is illusory, a mere reflexive event.
It shines free of illusion, free of liberation and free of recognition.

75. Unborn and ultimate, it illuminates completely,
Therefore, everything appears beyond the intellect.
That wisdom which is beyond the intellect in the three realms,
Is the innate nature itself.
Determine this to be the root of all recognition without exception.

76. Place decognition in the realm of the unborn nature.
Uncontrived, just that is beyond the domain of the intellect,
It arises as the self-blazing of wakefulness.
Through this arising, concepts, as complements of saṁsāra, arise.

77. Having understood that the path of liberation is suchness,
As though self-arisen, one abides in the sphere which is free from thought.
Recognition, which is self-illuminating, is not established as entities.

78. This unborn great bliss is the uncontrived awakened intention.
Since it appears directly to the senses, there is nothing to be grasped.
In the domain of decognition there is nothing to be seen.
Since it is devoid of basis, there is nothing to train in.

79. In one whose mind is free from occupation, that is the Great Seal;
Whatever diverse wakeful cognitions are there, are of signs.
In just that, the Great Seal, there are no distinctions.
Realization and nonrealization—the two are not distinct.

80. Not abiding in the extremes of eternalism and nihilism, it is free of faults.
When one's own nature is realized, it is not from elsewhere.

When dependent origination, the path of nirvāṇa, is taught and realized as unborn, that is the Great Seal.

81. Those ignorant of just that are attached to the Action Seal, Commitment Seal, Dharma Seal, etc.[373]
These are mere examples that signify that but cannot capture the meaning.
Relying on the Great Seal, which is free of subject and object,
Cognition arises naturally and freshly.

82. Free of desire, it abides in the authentic nature settled into itself.
The cognition of ordinary appearances is itself the intellect,
Its natural state in the thoughts that recollect "is" and "is not."
Precious devotion is the wish-granting jewel of instruction,
Place it free of mental engagement and non-engagement.

83. Since reflexive awareness is itself the Great Seal,
It is taught in and by the Great Seal itself.
Do not allow mind to engage in the diverse objects of recognition.

84. Free of "inner" and "outer," the seal is undisputed, and
One who is endowed with the life of the Great Seal is free of desire—
For when desire arises, this too is the cause of recognition.

85. In the Great Seal which is one's own mind,
Distinctions between "recognition" and "absence of recognition" do not arise.

---

[373] Here, Saraha is altering the order of the four seals—previously (verse 38) he has the commitment seal following the great seal as the altruistic re-engagement with the world. In this case, he reverts to the ordering of the seals with the Great as the fourth. This is consistent with the ordering of the seals in the *Cakrasaṁvara Tantra* (Gray 2007) and the *Hevajra Tantra* (Farrow 1992).

Delusion and nondelusion are beyond the domain of the intellect.
Proliferation of fixed concepts about recognition is the cause of saṁsāra.

86. Clear light, which is the Great Seal, is the authentic nature.
Unchanging in any way, it is one in the mind of awakening.
In just that, subject and object are free of essence.
Meaningful appearance is seen in wisdom itself.

87. The arising of appearances is seen by the power of distortion,
Because in the assembly of recognition, they are examined by thoughts.
The engagement of mind in the domain of recognition and decognition
Is free of thought, even when body, speech, and mind are exerted.

88. When there is no duality, there is no nature of saṁsāra.
This is the nature of ever-fluctuating various recognitions.
It does not exist at all in the tip of the nose seal,
Therefore, settle into the thought-free ethics of the Great Seal.

89. Hey! The stages of generation—inner and outer, deep and not deep, and
The nature of ultimate reality, inhalation and exhalation,
Sealing by action and dharma seals,
Are the whole yoga of the completion stage.

90. The Great Seal is the stage of the essential nature,
The Commitment Seal is the stage of complete accomplishment,
The stage of the thorough accomplishment of all,
The Action Seal is the essence of empowerment, and

That which is endowed with the four joys,[374] and has the nature of method,
The Dharma Seal is diverse appearance;
Among the four joys, it is "the innate."

91. As for the Great Seal, the unborn nature,
It is free of dualistic thought, and its nature is beyond the intellect.
The unstained result is complete Buddhahood.

92. The Commitment Seal is a yoga of characteristics.
The result—gods, meditational deities and the maṇḍala—is for the benefit of sentient beings,
The noble parents[375] symbolize skillful means and wisdom.

93. Endowed with the four joys, the Commitment Seal is great.
Accordingly, although the application of skillful means may be harnessed,
The profound is established by means of the Dharma Seal,
And mind itself is revealed on its own as the Great Seal.

94. By singling out thoughts that are flavored by joy, and
By distinguishing thoughts flavored by great joy, and
By singling out thoughts that are the innate joy,
The appearance of no-joy reveals thoughts as the unborn.
Thus the profound Dharma seal is shown.

95. Where knowledge which is the four joys arises,
Is undifferentiated and abides in the manner of total absorption,

---

374 The four joys are: joy (*ānanda—dga' ba*); great joy (*paramānanda—mchog dga'*); joylessness (*vilaksana—dga' bral*); and innate joy (*sahajānanda—lhan cig skyes pa'i dga' ba*). They describe stages of bliss experienced in Tantric practice.

375 *pha ma*: this refers to the union of awakened Buddha aspects, and symbolizes every possible form of (awakened) union: wisdom and compassion, wisdom and means, left and right channels, etc. The union of all these elements indicates full awakening.

It abides in the pure experience of conceptualization, and
Within the mind, non-recognition and cognition are undifferentiated.
Examples and the path are taught in order to tame designations.

96. The arising of the Great Seal, the mind itself,
Manifests everything: the miraculous display, the arising of the unborn.
Since it is beyond the intellect, it is shown to be the unborn nature.
Both the unborn and entities which are born,
Are not different when they are left in the authentic nature.

97. Wherever this movement of diverse recognition takes place,
By engaging decognition, conceptualization will be unobstructed.
If the cognition is left in its own place, it will abide.
The cause of birth is grasping at appearance and emptiness as two;
But when it is understood that they are not distinct, that is the great bliss.

98. Because the experience has dawned, one will be free of discordant grasping.
There is no recognition; there are no such objects.
Decognition and the unity of appearance and emptiness are not different.

99. In the unborn yoga of signlessness,[376]
In the daily yoga, where there is no meditative equipoise and subsequent states,
Whatever thoughts of appearance and arising come into being,

---

[376] For an excellent detailed discussion of the generation and completion stages, I refer readers to Powers (1995) and Beyer (1978).

Because you abide free of recognition, which is empty, just
that,
Appearance and emptiness are indivisible; there are no
thoughts to be taken into the mind.

100. In the direct encounter with just that, the experience of the
unborn,
The empty nature of appearance dawns as great bliss.
Just as melted ice can be drunk as water,[377]
So, whatever appears, does so richly as unborn great bliss.

---

[377] Water in its diverse states appears often in the *Body Treasury*: verse 22 describes the experience of the innate as: "Bliss indivisible, like water [mixing] into water"; and verse 40 tells us that the innate, pervading all sentient beings, "abides like moisture in water, / In continuity which is like the uninterruptedness of the water of a flowing stream." The image of waves and the ocean as the demonstration of thoughts as neither separate from nor identical to mind was discussed above in verse 69. Here it is appropriate to mention that water appears as the principal metaphor in his *King Dohā* (*Dohākośa nāma Caryā gīti / do ha mdzod ces bya ba spyod pa'i glu*), fulfilling the same multiple functions as it does in the *Adamantine Songs*. From the opening verse, water is key: "Just as when unmoving water struck by the wind, / Becomes stirred by waves, / So Saraha appears to the King / In many ways, although he is one man." (*ji ltar rlung gis brgyab pas mi g.yo ba'i / chu la g.yo pas rba rlabs rnam su 'gyur / de ltar rgyal pos mda' snun snang ba yang / gcig nyid na yang rnam pa sna tshogs byed*). Continuing with analogies like, "Although there are many rivers they become one in the ocean / And though there are many lies, [they will be] conquered by one truth" (*chu bo sna tshogs pa yang rgya mtsho gcig nyid dang / brdzun pa dum dag kyang bden pa gcig gis 'joms*; verse 4). The *King Dohā* has another "water" verse worth quoting in full: "Just as a cloud comes from the ocean, and / However much rain the earth accepts, / They stay the same, like the sky, / Without increasing or decreasing." (*ji ltar chu 'dzin gyis ni rgya mtsho las / chu blangs nas ni sa gzhi gang byas kyang / de ni mnyams nam mkha' dag dang mnyam / 'phel ba med cing 'grib pa dag kyang med*; verse 5) That the same chemical composition can appear as a solid, a liquid and as vapor (clouds, for example), demonstrates how one cannot trust form to indicate the nature of something; in fact, it points to the absence of one natural form of anything. Saraha uses water to demonstrate how flowing, existing as waves, rain, or stillness are not characteristics of water but instead products of the conditions surrounding it. The analogous states of peace and agitation experienced as mind should therefore similarly be understood as products of ambient conditions and not indicative of the nature of mind itself.

101. Equanimity is free of recognition although conceptualization is not obstructed;
By being beyond the intellect, it is free of deluded meditation.
When one rests in that, the experience of great bliss occurs.
First the experience of appearance and emptiness occurs,
Like recognizing water even when it appears as ice.

102. Second, without obstructing the appearance of recognition,
Emptiness and bliss arise undifferentiated.
Just as ice melts into water,
Recognition and decognition dissolve in the unborn.

103. Since everything is undifferentiated, it is one in the great bliss.
This is like ice melting into water.
If one knows whatever is encountered to be the nature of everything,
One will not be held by bondage and freedom and will not chase after recognition.

104. The mind will not be obstructed as though tightly tied,
When the knot is undone, one is freed and mind itself is directed at will.
As the crow returns to the ship,[378]
When just that is known, appearance is enjoyment.

105. Just like an elephant tamed by using the hook,
Remaining free of action, it is like an elephant mastered.[379]
Acquaintance with recognition and decognition is harmless.
By knowing appearance and emptiness, one is free of conceptualization.

---

[378] This is a reference to the practice of bringing a crow on board a seafaring ship: when searching for land (for the purposes of our metaphor, this implies searching for something solid to grasp) the crow is released. If it finds land, it will not return; if there is no land, however, the crow will return to the ship. The same metaphor appears in *Dohākośa*, verse 70.

[379] The elephant and the hook is a metaphor for methods that need only be used to train the mind, but not to maintain discipline afterwards; although the elephant may be tamed with a hook (the ankus, an ancient implement for assisting in training elephants that certainly predates Saraha), once it is tame the hook is unnecessary.

106. By resting in origination, without differentiation, recognition is not caused.
That itself, the all-pervasive Lord, is like knowing all enemies.[380]
Dissolving of appearance into emptiness is like dissolving salt into water;
Dissolving recognition and decognition is just that.

107. In the two types of arising there is no cause for arising.
When the wisdom that is the encounter with the unborn dawns,
Recognition manifests wisdom without bias and without mental objects,
It blazes like fire spreads through tinder,
Or like the experience of the unutterable bliss of a youth.[381]

108. Though diversity appears, it does not become recognition;
A gently flowing stream does not become waves.
Since it illuminates its own nature, recognition is a lamp.

109. Just as the Great Seal is not revealed anywhere,
It is like a *sarkone* bird abiding in the sky.
The conduct of realization is not determined by discrimination,
Like *patari* animals, you will be free from longing and attachment.
When the result that is beyond the intellect is desired, it is not attained.
Among the best medicines, it is the *beta* itself.[382]

---

[380] Just as the Lord who presides over a maṇḍala has a full view of all enemies who may with to disrupt the sacred kingdom, suchness is wakefulness, vigilance, and skill.

[381] The unutterable bliss of a youth is presumably the exquisite desire and passion experienced by one who has fallen in love for the first time—a desire that pervades each thought and action.

[382] The *sarkone* bird and *patari* animals defy explanation. I consulted numerous experts whose skills in Tibetan greatly exceed my own, and these remain a mystery. Birds, nonetheless, are a pervasive metaphor for non-abiding, as they move through the sky without leaving any traces. The "ri" in *patari* may be—if the word is Tibetan—indicating that this is a reference to animals that live in isolation on mountains. Animals who roam mountain

(cont'd)

110. Hey! Thus the wise who are accomplished in skillful methods
Will seal decognition with the unborn:
Because it is free of recognition, it is sealed by decognition;
With appearance, emptiness is sealed;
With emptiness, appearance is sealed.

111. When recognition and appearance arise as the taste of bliss,
They are sealed by emptiness and decognition.
When appearance and recognition and the seal of emptiness
Are sealed by abiding in decognition,
Appearance and recognition, dawning as the taste of bliss
Will not be analyzed by the contemplation of signs, and will remain beyond the characterizing intellect.

112. Recognition and appearance are sealed by the unborn;
The unborn is sealed by the beyond the intellect.
Because recognition is the seal of the bliss that is decognition,
It has not become nothing, and has not fallen into the extreme of nihilism.

113. As the abiding and arising are sealed,
They are not reified and do not fall into the extreme of eternalism.
Everything is unborn and beyond the intellect;
Everything possesses the continuum of great bliss;
Knowing this, one does not fall into the extreme of indifference.

114. Recognition is the substance of saṁsāra;
In the realization of decognition,
Take equanimity as the path:
Probed by awareness, emptiness is equanimity, and
Reflexive awareness, free of subject and object, is equanimity.
Free of the two truths, meditation on equanimity is nondual.

---

wildernesses are symbols of detachment from worldly life. The *beta* is a type of evergreen that bears fruit, a supremely rare and effective medicinal plant.

Meditative absorption without recognition of anything whatsoever is the best equanimity.
Equanimity which is neutral is not meditation.

115. Cognition in its natural place emanates from the experience of decognition;
Characteristics of recognition are taken as the path of decognition.

116. Carried on the path of bliss, it is unobservable, it is beyond the intellect;
Not conceptualized as dual, the bliss is uninterrupted.

117. Hey! Free of experience, one is released from subject and object,
Then that itself will be seen, the meaning of the Great Seal.
In the great treasury of jewels which is the ultimate result,
May whoever desires to abide in the Great Seal,
Realize the unsullied result!

This was sung by Saraha.
The *Body Treasury called the Immortal Adamantine Song* is complete!

A Speech Treasury Called the Gentle Voiced Adamantine Song

Homage to Mañjughoṣa!

1. Hey! The one-pointed *samādhi* pervades all conduct with one taste:
Realization of the reality and nonreality of thoughts will cause the abandonment of saṁsāra!
The union of appearance and emptiness is inseparability itself;
Once everything has arisen as the nature of the dharmadhātu, it abides in dissolution.

2. As soon as decognition illuminates, the benefit of self and others is not two:
the aspects of the Great Seal are innumerable and unutterable.
When real and unreal are discarded completely, there is no saṁsāra and nirvāṇa
If the pool has no cover, the wheels in the four directions are abandoned.[383]

3. Childish ignorance brings about entering saṁsāric causation;
With weak knowledge—grasping—the benefit of self and others cannot be accomplished.
Just as a burning lamp cannot possibly appear to the blind,
Even wishing to benefit self and others, grasping only leads to grasping.

---

[383] The reference to the covered pool—a common element of a pleasure garden—is rather cryptic, to say the least. It has been suggested that the wheels of the four directions are also part of the structure of such a pool, which would allow me to interpret this line as an illustration of how when you remove one part of something, the whole structure ceases to exist (in this case referring to how once duality is discarded, everything is experienced equally as the Great Seal).

4. Since there is thought, abandoning and not abandoning are imputed;
But reflexive awareness, free of appearances, is devoid of all conceptual designations.
Without skillful means, even one's own benefit is not accomplished; there is only convention.

5. Abiding in the indivisible goal is itself the teacher,[384] and
The essential sign, which is entering into the *Dharmadhātu*, is the teaching.
From the Guru, teachings, transmissions, commentaries, and pith instructions are taught.
With the right transmission and reasoning, and desiring to realize the intrinsic identity,
Realization comes from the pure possession of the pith instructions, relying on the Guru,
If the Guru is worshipped, innate highest bliss will be accomplished.

6. Bow at the Guru's feet, because the Guru's actions are free of defilement;
"If you worship the Guru, great blessings will arise," declared the Conqueror.

7. Hey! Even though one may move through the sky, it's nothing more than an illusory city,
If one perseveres with liberation, the level of the Conqueror will undoubtedly be reached.

8. [For] the increase of the arising and expansion of empowerments, blessings, expressed and expression,
First the student should supplicate with mudrās, offerings, and praise;

---

[384] The Guru is identified as "abiding in the indivisible goal," located the a critical aspect of the teacher as the inner Guru rather than the outer Guru. For a detailed explanation of the many roles and definitions of the Guru, see Rig 'dzin Dorje (2001).

Afterwards, the master will in stages grant the profound empowerment.
Requested with words of praise, the Empowerment of Awareness Display is given.

9. The vow of the secret empowerment[385] that relies on the Seal will be given;
Permission is given, then afterwards the teachings spread out.
The student will make offerings afterwards: the profound empowerment and vows.

10. The teachings are the stages of development, etc.,
The stage of the essential nature is taught, and
The expression of the experience of meditation, etc., everything.[386]

11. One who does not abide in anything whatsoever is like the *sarkone* bird, not constructing a support in anything.
In the pure bliss of freedom from desire there is no abiding.
Free of singularity or duality, it is not based in or a basis for anything.
The nondual yoga is the blissful experience arising in itself.
When the entity conceptualized as "self" is abandoned, one is as vast as the boundaries of space.

12. If one wishes to enter the pure city beyond suffering,[387]
Apply the great yoga as a rain-like continuum to everything that arises from contact with the six senses,[388]

---

[385] *gsang dbang*.

[386] Verses 8–10 characterize the view of of an imaginary interlocutor whom Saraha is challenging with his subitist view.

[387] i.e., nirvāṇa. This appears to be contrasting the illusory city of verse 7. Saraha here emphasizes that the methods must be used on everything that arises in contact with the sense consciousnesses, as phenomena, properly understood, all have the single taste of the innate.

[388] i.e., visual, auditory, gustatory, olfactory, tactile, mental.

Without exception, whatever arises from contact dependent on conditions is unborn emptiness.
Through nondual meditation the path is quickly and irreversibly entered.

13. When the true nature of sentient beings and Buddhas is known, there is no more striving.
Based on the training in the one taste of everything, the result is attained.
If they train, beings will doubtlessly be liberated from saṁsāra.
Demons and discord will be completely vanquished.

14. Don't practice the yoga with signs, equanimity is not a yoga.
Swiftly accomplishing the pristine cognition of the wise, obstacles come to an end.
By practicing with signs, even those skilled in provisional meaning—fools!—are bound;
But those who rely on the single taste of the Great Seal, move in the sky.[389]

15. If one relies on the path of continually practicing nonduality, [the goal] will be accomplished in this very life.
Don't abide in the sphere of illusory appearance, there is no object of thought.
The fetter of the Eight Worldy Dharmas[390] is without power [against] the most excellent conduct,[391]
Accomplishing compassion and skillful means, your desirelessness will become as vast as the sky.

---

[389] As far as I can tell, this is something of a *double* (or even *triple*) *entendre*: it both contrasts those who are no longer are limited by ordinary concepts (those who are *mkhar 'gro*) with the provisionally endowed sages (*mkhas*), and is a reference to becoming a *ḍāka* or *ḍākinī*, or "sky-goer" (*mkha' 'dro ma*). Being one who goes in the sky (like a bird) is also to be one who does not leave or rely on traces (signs).

[390] (*'jig rten chos brgyad*) they are: gain, loss, reputation, infamy, praise, degradation, pleasure, and misery.

[391] The conduct of the yogi is continually implementing the yoga of nonduality.

16. Supreme is the skillful method that possesses the four branches of the Great Seal.[392]
In the realm of the single miracle of the single seal that has four aspects,
In the realm of nonduality, relax into the Great Seal and settle there.

17. When one possesses awakening mind free of abandoning or accepting, one is like an elephant.
Depending on the nature of the cognition, a cow, if desired, can appear as a horse;
Striving for the goal that is free of cognition and appearances is the practice of yoga.

18. The result that is the accomplishment of the four *kāyas* is the realm of great bliss.
Bodies that are the path of appearances arise;
But possessing the power of the three *kāyas*, one is completely free of conceptualization.
Knowledge and what is knowable are the pure sphere of one's own mindstream.

19. Although the own-nature of entities appear due to the conditions for arising,
They are not experienced beyond the sphere of the non-arisen.
Entities, non-entities, meditative equipoise, etc.
Their indivisibility is the sphere of decognition and the unborn.

---

[392] This is a reference back to the four branches listed in the *Body Treasury*: 1) the branch of realization of the unborn nature (*skye med don rtogs pa*); 2) the branch of not distinguishing/inseparability of the two truths (*bden gnyis tha mi dad*) and realization of contact of unborn nature and appearance (*snang ba skye med thug phrad nyid du rtogs*); 3) the branch of nongrasping of thought (*dran pa gzung du med pa*) and emptiness devoid of conditions and thought (memory) and which is beyond the intellect (*stong pa rkyen dang dran med blo las 'das*); 4) the branch of not accepting or rejecting things (*dngos po dgag sgrub med pa*). (*Body Treasury*, verses 30–32)

20. The Great Seal is always free of essential characteristics;
Because the aggregates are purified, [it] is beyond the secret sphere.
The essential characteristic of the four joys is the sphere of the Great Seal,
It is not your own mindstream; it is free of wisdom and means.

21. Since that itself is not attained by tip of the nose meditation, etc.,
Even practicing for pure thatness is not the ultimate.
Abide in adamantine reflexive awareness; the hero's yoga
Is not like the nature of omniscience.

22. The ocean's waves have the same nature as echoes,
Just by counting them, one will not arrive anywhere.[393]
Associating attributes with the accomplishment of vows and results,
Is the conventional path of signified, signifier, and words.

23. Where is the thought "vows," or the thought "skillful means," etc.?
It can't be learned in the sphere that is beyond the intellect.
Practicing Tantric austerities, outer and inner will be transformed,
Possessing just that, one is extraordinary;
In not possessing that itself, one is the same as beasts.[394]

24. Meditate on the innate nature with just that, secretly.
Although a vow without skillful means is a mistake, it is not evil.
Not yearning for this or that,
The Great Seal manifests instantly;
But when that itself is abandoned, contact will never occur.

---

[393] "Counting" presumably refers to counting the breaths, typical calm abiding (*śamatha*, *zhi gnas*) meditation practice. Here, concentrating on counting breaths is akin to focusing on waves instead of the ocean, or echoes instead of the original sound.

[394] i.e., ignorant: experience still characterized by dualistic mind.

25. Even hearing the word, "Great Seal," just for an instant,
Whether scriptural learning is present or not,
Just by this teaching, this single root, it is attained.
By one who meditates on the innate meaning
Without wavering from pure recognition, it is attained.

26. It is just that; do not seek the Dharma of others.
Because of searching like a fox in a charnel ground, etc. what is sought after is ruined.

27. Hey! Just as when a Brahmin desires and asks for one who is low-born,
When they mix together—lowly and good—they cause harm to one another,[395]
The yoga with signs will not touch the signless goal.
That which is signless can never be examined;
Signs come into being when one attends to number and time.

28. The teachings are the stages of development, etc.
The stages of generation and completion are distinct, so don't think about them.
Whoever possesses the highest yoga has the convergence of nonduality.
[For] whoever is ignorant, decognition is an object of distraction
Meditate on the flowing continuity of recognition.

29. The uncommon, extraordinary secret mantra:
From the beginning one abides in the true nature.
When the accomplishments are gathered, the innate nature is encountered.
Just that, specifically, is beyond the sphere of reflexive awareness.

---

395 They cause harm to one another only within the confines of ordinary thought. According to an oral commentary by the Fourteenth Shamar Rinpoche, the Brahmin here can also represent the deity generated in meditation, which by extension means that Tantric practice engaged in by "ordinary" dualistic mind (the dualistic yoga referred to in the following line) can be at best useless and at worst, even harmful.

30. Just that is the abode of bliss and empty of entities;
Because all phenomena are pure, the blissful own-nature is the goal.
Not abiding in anything whatsoever, beyond the sphere of the intellect,
It is empty: without objects, without abiding, and without basis.

31. *EVAM*[396] is the cause of accomplishing the essential nature.
The convergence of Vajradhara and the sacred instructions of the Lama that is one's own awareness, is the unsullied
Great Seal lineage.
All conventions, the Action Seal, etc.,
Are like the retinue of servants of a Universal Monarch.

32. All the stages of Generation—outer, inner, and profound—
Are to the Seal of Completion like little stars to the sun and moon.
In that way transcendent bliss, bliss, supreme bliss, etc.
The very root of the cakra of innate bliss
Are illumined in the meditation that is the purifier, the unsullied.

33. Possessing just that, pristine cognition is perpetually enjoyed.
Emptiness, which is the undifferentiated mind, is the vast state;
Meditate relying on the skillful means possessing the means of body and speech.
Generation of recognition is the cause and condition of the ripening result.

---

[396] *EVAM* is a complex and multivalent term in the Tantric context. As the first word of all works ascribed to the Buddha (*evam mayā śrutam*, "thus have I heard") it has taken on an enormous range of meanings. *E* and *VAM* are separated as syllables held to represent everything from the left and right channels, to the *yogin* and his consort, to compassion (means) and wisdom, to (though solely in the context of the *Hevajra Tantra*) the navel and heart energy centers (*cakras*). In all these cases, *E* and *VAM* must be united for complete awakening and the great bliss. Thus, *EVAM* can stand for that union. In this case, he is using it to describe the union of Vajradhara—the primordial Tantric Buddha—with the pure awareness that is one's Guru's instructions. In comparison to that highest union that is originally nondual, conventions like the Action Seal (consort practice), or Generation and Completion phases of deity yoga meditations, are insignificant.

34. Possessing righteous actions, one can apply the skillful means of liberation,
Experiencing the Action Seal, pride arises.
Experiencing the meditation possessing just that is the path of liberation.

35. Though you desire to see the *vajra* in the *padma,*
That itself will not be liberated by the path of desire.
But if you rely on the experiences of the Action Seal,
In your own ordinary body, the Great Seal will be kindled.
The Great Seal pervades everything,
Like a Precious Jewel or a Sky Prince.

36. The five aggregates, etc. become the highest secret.
Saṁsāra and nirvāṇa abide innately in each other.
In that itself, which is due to the kindness of the Guru,
One discovers that signs and accomplishments are unnecessary.

37. The Supreme Great Seal itself is stainless;
Because it is the state to be obtained, it should be practiced:
Through the nondual union of permanence and annihilation, oneness is established,
By understanding the transmission and essential instructions, it should be known.

38. When that itself is accomplished, there will be no doubt.
The Great Seal illuminates; when in meditation it is recognized,
That itself will without question be realized.
When just that is known, practice by the power of habituation.

39. When that itself isn't recognized and one relies on the three vital points,
Upper doors, lower doors, and consort,
One is just like a beast, a duck, a fish, etc.

40. Comprehending conventions in one's own continuum of awareness,
Investigating outer and inner, if essencelessness is accepted
Even though there may be worldly clamor, it makes no difference.

41. Desiring to be liberated through the doors of truth and dependent arising, and
Desiring to follow the path to liberation by controlling your senses;
Because of being immature and empty handed, one is beguiled by bliss.
Thus, though wishing to do what needs to be done there is no liberation—one is seduced by falsehood.
One who accepts Sāṁkhya reasoning, Jaina, Vaiśeṣika, etc. views of action and continuity, etc. will wander.[397]

42. Hey! How must saṁsāra be abandoned?
Because there are no causes and conditions, abide in the Great Seal,
Just that, where mind has no object of realization.
By the power of just that, free from signs,
Accomplish the Great Seal in one life.[398]

43. Oh! Wondrous! This is the secret experience!
From the realization of the King of Physicians[399] dawns the unborn.

---

[397] Motivated by desire for an outer goal to be achieved on a *path* or through *doors*, is a fundamentally flawed exercise according to Saraha, because it is dualistic through and through. Such a wish is made only by one who is immature, however noble the intention might be. Here Saraha explicitly names: Jains, Sāmkhyas (a dualistic school of Brahmanical Hinduism) and Vaiśeṣikas (a pluralistic, realist school of Hinduism) as clear examples of paths towards liberation that may appear to be appealing but cause nothing short of continuous wandering in saṁsāra.

[398] Could be read "in one moment."

[399] A common epithet of the Buddha.

Possessing the characteristics of the five wisdoms, etc.
The highest born class sees just that.

44. Recognition that relies on signs is the cause of wandering.
When the objective world is not seen in that itself
The experience of signs will dissolve in the sphere of decognition.

45. The yoga with signs[400] is the path of the three realms of saṁsāra.
Conceptual things contain the seeds for carelessness,
But the yoga of decognition is like the center of space.

46. If one does not make distinctions, self-essence does not arise,
The minds of other sentient beings are not experienced.
When they see just that, the wise will become practiced.

47. Abiding in recognition, conceptuality, and form,
Is abandoned in abiding that is decognition, the three realms purified.
Non-arising, just that, is the abode of all the *siddhi*s;
Not seeing outer and inner is the accomplishment of all.

48. Hey! Whoever possesses the Great Seal, the supreme qualities,
Has the basis of all *siddhi*s because of delighting the Guru.
Not abandoning the most precious Guru, the qualities arise.
May whatever rare being has confidence
Realize this text of the yogis!

Thus ends the *Adamantine Song "Gentle Voiced Speech Treasury"* sung by Saraha.

---

[400] Again, this is a reference to the generation phase of meditation.

Unborn Treasury of Mind Adamantine Song

Homage to Mañjughoṣa!

1. Hey! The pristine wisdom is the innate nature:
It is [none other than] one's own experience of itself,
Just that illuminates awareness, ignorance, and reflexive awareness,
A lamp illuminates the darkness and itself, by itself.

2. The beautifully colored lotus is not attached to the mud;
Without leaving behind the defilement that is dualistic views, illuminate the essence.

3. Dwelling in the deep forest, deer roam alone;
Not being attached to the cause is itself the result.
Illuminating appearance and non-appearance, devoid of object, devoid of attachment,
Without recognition of "real" and "empty," it is inexpressible decognition.
There is bliss in the three aspects of the innate.

4. Because there is freedom from attachment, one is beyond the sphere of dialectics:
Do not follow after fluctuating recognition.
The wisdom of matchless clarity is its[401] essence,
Just as the appearance of the sun's lamp dispels the darkness,
When reflexive awareness blazes, grasping and conceptualization are exhausted.

---

[401] i.e., the essence of the innate.

5. Because of exhausting the obscurations, decognition is unwavering.
Do not generate dualism, existence, non-existence, or conventions;
For the yogin who has grasped adamantine reflexive awareness,
The Great Seal is free of thought, beyond the intellect.

6. The lamp of the innate that is hard to surpass
Is the principle that is the union of means and wisdom:
Unborn, empty, impartial, radiant.

7. Just that is the extraordinary wisdom,
Independent of duality, the continuity of bliss is unbroken;
It is self-arisen, nonconceptual, the rooting out of habits.

8. Although a distinction between sentient beings and Buddhas is inconceivable,
When there is pure conduct, [that is] continuous great yoga.
Although the nature of recognition is not encompassed by thought,
Primordial purity is absorbed in the realm of decognition.

9. The goal is the realization that self-benefit is nondual and unborn,
The pure result is beyond being free of intellect and object.
The skillful means of realization continually pervades all natures.

10. Compassion accomplishing the benefit of beings with skillful means is inconceivable, and
Wisdom is realization without essence, arising, or cessation.
Although the bliss of skillful means arises, grasp it even a bit and it is a fetter,
The natural wisdom of liberation spontaneously arises in oneself.

11. The object of meditation and the meditator are beyond intentionality.
Buddhas and sentient beings are inconceivable,
When the object of realization is unborn, it does not arise in the mind;
When just that is awakened, bliss is indicated by emptiness.

12. The essence of the object of meditation arises from apparent conditions;
Realization free from conceptualization accomplishes relative conventions;
The condition for nondual appearance does not exist.
Natural purity dawns as the arising of magical illusions.

13. Separate and not separate, nonconceptual, and beyond the intellect,
In the nonduality to be realized, the unborn becomes the object.
By saying “empty” you will not realize it!
“Beyond the intellect” is not an object to ponder![402]

14. For one who believes in the three extremes as permanent, it is difficult to obtain,
Even if one apprehends the four joys, just that is difficult.
Because the six sense consciousnesses possess the highest self-arising wisdom,
The appearance of nondual essence will dawn on its own.

15. Hey! The Great Seal, free from conceptuality, is the basis of all.
Because *siddhi*s will arise, it is great, most wondrous.
Having awakened the habit of nonduality, one is freed into self-awareness.

---

[402] The first two lines of this verse appear to be the challenge of an interlocutor, and the second two Saraha’s response.

16. The Great Seal that is free of object and subject:
Śrāvakas,[403] etc., are terrified of essential-characteristic teachings.
If seen one-pointedly, one possesses the consummate qualities,
Although by acting one-pointedly there is not the slightest object of meditation.

17. Mental elaboration immolates itself; decognition is pacifying healing.
Decognition and nonarising are like reflections in a mirror,
Through freedom from conventions, the path is unborn, beyond the intellect.
Unsullied recognition with signs is habitually taught;
It is free from beginning and its past and future unimaginable.

18. Hey! Because of that, the wisdom of insubstantiality is the path of realization.
Just as, if inclined toward the way free of habits,
One is pacified by not grasping at duality and freedom from beginning and end.

19. Free of habits, you are directionless and devoid of wandering.
True union is the very essence of Buddhahood.
"The three kinds of wisdom are both object and skillful means" Buddha said.
Unexemplified, it is beyond the sphere that can be characterized.

20. The sacred essence is not in this arising.
By applying skillful means, the six sense consciousnesses are pacified in their own place.
The five aggregates, etc. are the basis of the pure qualities.
The omniscient one is nondual, free from habituation to apparent objects.

---

403 The "listener" disciples of the Buddha, considered lesser because they are not motivated by great compassion.

21. The highest meaning is not uttered, the conventional is just dialectics.
The path of nirvāṇa is the appearance itself of saṁsāra.
Whatever is encountered is the intention of the Holy Guru,
Realizing that, one will be liberated from the path of saṁsāra.

22. Finding the intended experience of yoga is the perfect Buddha,
On the path of meditation, there is only spontaneity.

23. Hey! In the nondual goal one is liberated by mantras and symbols.
The virtues, like an ocean of jewels, are not exhausted.
When the highest skillful means is reached, one resides in the fourteenth bhūmi.[404]
Wherever one abides, wisdom is obtained from within.

24. Those who discover worldly treasure are ignorant of the benefit of both self and other:
The heart amulet that is the central lotus flower,
Union possessing skillful means, then emanation
To wherever channels abide as aspect of the cakras.
Even those who are free of attachment in the sky of desirelessness,
Drawing energies up and down in the turning cakras,[405]
Guided by those methods, the treasure of benefit cannot found.[406]

---

[404] To the standard list of ten *bhūmi*s add: the level without simile (*dpe med sa*); the level with wisdom (*ye shes ldan sa*); the thoroughly radiant level (*kun tu 'od sa*); and the adamantine level (*rdo rje'i sa*).

[405] Drawing the energies up and down through the channels is again part of Tantric practice.

[406] Literally, "the bottom of truth won't be found."

25. Although one may grasp and eject and unite and ignite,[407]
There is no difference between these breath-control practices[408]
and a fool suffering from asthma.

26. Those desiring realization always look to just that;
Those with sincere devotion rely on the Precious Guru,
And from the highest Guru the secret qualities will arise.
Possessing the meaning, the essential sign will be victorious in
the battle against the defilements.

27. With the transmission of the Guru
Who possesses the secret meaning itself,
May whoever goes through this nondual door arrive at
liberation!

The secret essential meaning, the *Unborn Treasury of Mind Adamantine Song*, composed by the Glorious Saraha, is complete.

---

[407] Presumably a reference to union practice, which is designed to result in the ignition of great bliss.

[408] Controlling the breath is a key element of all the above-mentioned practices.

PART THREE

❧

TIBETAN EDITION

❧

Body Treasury[409]

rgya gar skad du / kāyakośāmṛta badzra gīti[410]
bod skad du / sku'i mdzod 'chi med rdo rje'i glu

'jam dpal gzhon nur gyur ba la phyag 'tshal lo

1. kye ho bdag dang byed par 'dzin pa ral pa can
bram ze gcer bus[411] da[412] ga pa dang ni
kho na nyid gzhi 'dod pa'i[413] rgyang phan[414] pa
thams cad mkhyen zhes zer nas rang ma rig
des ni slu[415] bar 'ong ste thar lam ring

2. bye brag pa dang mdo sde sngags pa dang
rnal 'byor pa dang dbu ma la sogs te
gcig la gcig skyon 'gal zhing rtsod par byed
snang stong mkha' mnyam de nyid mi shes pa
lhan cig skyes la rgyab kyis phyogs par 'gyur

3. sku gsung thugs gsal mar mer ras dang[416] mar nag bzhin
kho na nyid ldan[417] rang snang mar me lta bur gsal
rang rig gsal bas 'gro ba kun la khyab
dbyer med tshul gyis ma skyes pa yi[418] rang bzhin yin

---

[409] In N and P, the *Adamantine Song Cycle* is preceded by a title page reading: *sku gsungs thugs 'chi med rdo rje'i mdzod kyi glu rnal 'byor gyi dbang phyug chen po sa ra ha'i zhabs kyis mdzad pa bzhugs*.

[410] P, N: *kā ya kośāmri dha ba dzra gī tā*.

[411] M: *gcer bu ba*.

[412] P, N: *gcer bu sang ga pa*.

[413] M: *bzhin dod pa'i*; D, C: *bzhi 'dod pa'i*.

[414] P, N: *pan*.

[415] P, N: *bslu*.

[416] P, N: *ras dang* omitted.

[417] P, N: *lhan*.

4. bdag tu 'dzin pa'i sems kyis dran pa sna tshogs rgyu
ngo bo nyid la[419] snang tshul cir yang 'char
mun pa lta bu'i bag la kun gnas kyang
de nyid rnyed pa'i rnal 'byor sgron me 'bar

5. snying po'i don ni rtog ge'i yul las 'das
mngon du mi gsal dran pa'i mthu yis bsgribs
rtog med nges shes[420] dran med bde ba'i lam
ci phyir[421] bgrod med 'bras bu blo las 'das par snang

6. lhan cig skyes pa thugs kyi gter mdzod nas
dag dang ma dag 'khor 'das gzugs su snang
snang yang skye ba med pa'i ngang[422] 'dug cig
de nyid mi g.yo tha snyad rang bzhin med

7. phyag rgya chen po 'gyur med bde chen dang[423]
rgyu la mi ltos[424] 'bras bu blo las 'das
phyag rgya chen po rdzogs pa'i 'bras bu yin
tha snyad lam gyi don la mtshon te sbyar[425]

8. brjod bya rjod byed med pa snying po'i don
kun gyi brjod bya dran med rig pa'i dbyings

9. mos pa'i shes pas rtogs pa tha dad kyang
dran med 'di la brdzun pa yod re skan
lam gyi rtsol bas 'bras bu so so yang

---

418 P, N: *pa'i*.

419 P damaged.

420 P: *rtogs med nges shes*; D: *rtag med des shes*; C, M: *des shes*.

421 D, C, M: omit *ci phyir*.

422 C: *dang*.

423 P: *ngang*.

424 P, N: *bltos*.

425 P, N: *sbyor*.

dran pa 'di la bden pa yod re skan
btang snyoms dbang gis re 'jog tha dad kyang
skye med[426] 'di la gnyis su yod re skan
yid la bya dang mi bya snyad 'dogs kyang
blo 'das 'di la btsal[427] du yod re skan

10. snang pa'i rkyen gyis[428] dran pa skye 'gyur yang
stong pa'i dran med rkyen las 'da' ba med
rtog med don la bya bral blta ru med
rang la gzhan[429] nas tshol ba a[430] re 'khrul

11. kye ho[431] rdo rje lta bur rtogs dka'[432] kho na nyid
ma shes rtsol bas sgra phyir 'brang[433] sems kyis
bya ba med pa'i don dang phrad[434] par dka'[435]
bya ba'i rang bzhin mi bya shes gyur na
rgyal ba'i dgongs pa nyag gcig yul las 'das

12. sku ni mi 'gyur chos nyid khong stong lags
lus la mi gnas bya dang byed pa bral
lam bslad lam gyi[436] 'bras bu mthong mi 'gyur
skye med ngang[437] la mi 'byed rgyal ba'i thugs

---

[426] D: *skye mad*.

[427] P: *bcal*.

[428] *kyis*.

[429] P, N: *bzhag*.

[430] P, N: *e*.

[431] *kye 'o*.

[432] C: *dga'*.

[433] P: *'bangs*.

[434] P: *prad*; N: *phrang*.

[435] C: *dga'*.

[436] P, N: *gyis*.

[437] N: *dang*.

13. dran med ngang la mnyam gzhag bde ba che
bde chen ngang la mi rtog rgyun la gnas[438]
yid la mi byed snang ba rang sar dag
rkyen ni[439] dran pa ma ’gag[440] ye shes gsal

14. rtsa ba gcig rgyas skyon med padma bzhin
’gro ba kun la lhan cig skyes bzhin gnas
gzhan yod log[441] mthong stobs kyis bslad mod kyang
ji bzhin thog ma’i padma me tog bzhin
legs mthong stobs kyis[442] phyag rgya che mi g.yo

15. gzung dang ’dzin pa’i rnyog mas bslad gyur kyang
dus gsum ’gyur med rtsa ba bdag nyid che
rnam shes rlung dang ’og sgo sngags la sogs
ye nas spyod bral rang gzhan btang gzhag bral

16. ’khor bar mi sems[443] mya ngan ’das mi ltos
dus gsum srid gsum sku gsung thugs la ’dus
gang la mi ’bad[444] blang dor lta ba med
mtha’ dbus mi ’byed dbu ma drang po’i[445] lam

17. bcas bcos bral na thugs kyi lam mchog ste
bgrod ’jug rim[446] sogs pha rol phyin pa’i lam
nye lam gzhag[447] nas ring du ’khor ba’i rgyu
lhan cig skyes dang gnyen po ’gran zla bral

---

[438] P, N: *bde chen mi rtogs rgyun tu rang la gnas*.

[439] C: *pi*.

[440] P, N: *’gags*.

[441] C, D, M: *long*.

[442] C, D, M: *kyi*.

[443] D: *sams*.

[444] D: *’bang*; P, N: *ma ’bad*.

[445] D: *pa’i*.

[446] D: *bgrad ’jug ram*; P, N: *rims*.

[447] P, N: *bzhag*.

18. kho na nyid la sku bzhi ye shes lnga
nyon mongs la sogs tshogs pas 'khor ba'i lam
yul du gang skyes mi spyad[448] yul med mthong
ngo bo nyid la dga' dang mi dga' med

19. 'dzin rtog gnyis bcas ma bcos chos kyi sku
dbang po rang yan ma zin stong par gnas
smrar med nyams su myong ba rgyun mi 'chad
rang gi rgyud la sbyar te shes par bya

20. dri ma med pa'i don la phyag rgya che
rgya mtsho nam mkha' lta bu'i nyams myong 'byung
dbang po yul bral ltung ba'i g.yang sa med
dran pas zin pas khyod nyid chags pa ste

21. rang btang gzhag pas spros[449] pa slar la ldog
[450] 'char nub med na rnam rtog mun pa nub
chos nyid ro mnyom bung pa'i[451] me tog mtshungs
skyon dang yon tan dbyer med nyid du mtshungs
ngo mtshar che ste[452] nyams myong smrar ma gtub

22. bde ba[453] dbyer med ji ltar chu gzhag bzhin
lhan cig skyes dang rnal 'byor de mi 'bral
dngos gcig[454] bsam pa du mar dran mthong yang
dran med gcig yin du ma nyid du yin
gang zhig lhan cig skyes dga' bde chen stong

---

[448] C, D, M: *sbyad*.

[449] C, D, M: *sbros*.

[450] The *shad* (/) between lines 88 and 89 does not appear in the D edition, but does in all the others.

[451] D: *bud ba'i*.

[452] P slightly damaged here.

[453] P, N: *bden pa*.

[454] P, N: *cig*.

rnal 'byor spyod pa blo las 'das par sbyod[455]
chags lam gnyug ma'i don la sbyor 'dod na

23. nang dang phyi rol ma dmigs bdag gzhan min
de nyid don[456] shes rang bzhin grol bar[457] bstan
sku gsum chos skur dbye ba med mod kyang
nyams su blangs na 'bras bu so sor[458] 'byung

24. kye ho dbyer med rtogs na lta ngan myur du 'joms
skye med stong pa dbyer med thug phrad don[459]
yin par shes na nags 'dab rten dang bral

25. thug phrad ma shes mtshan ma'i snying rje ni
'khor ba'i gnas su[460] ci spyad zag pa'i rgyu
stong dang snying rje dbyer med skye ba med
gang zhig 'khor dang myang 'das re dogs bral
lus sems ma rnyed dran med rang dgar[461] gzhag
de nyid blo yis ma rnyed rang byung yin

26. mnyam gzhag rjes thob zhi gnas mtshan nyid de
don dam ma yin blo yis bsgom du med
lus ngag sems kyis gzugs sogs rtsol med gsal
sna rtse la sogs dbyibs dang nam mkha' dang
rtsa la reg par ma spyad gnyug mar gnas

27. snang ba thams cad bde ba yod mi[462] byed
dran pa snang tsam sgyu mar shes tsam gsal

---

455 C, P, N: *spyod*.

456 P: *ngong*.

457 N: *brol bar bzhin grol bar*.

458 D, C, M: *so so*.

459 P, N: *do*.

460 N: *gnas su* becomes *gnsu*.

461 P, N: *gar*.

462 P, N: *yid ma*.

zla ba'i gzugs brnyan cha med gzung pas stong
btsal kyang med la bltas kyang mthong ba med

28. sgyu mar snang ba'i dran pa de dran te
dran pa med las cir yang mthong pa med
dran par snang yang de la 'dzin pa med
dran pas reg kyang reg[463] gi bsam bral bas

29. bsam du med pas bral bas skye ba med
dran pa skyes kyang yul la mi spyod par
cir yang ma grub stong pa'i rang sor gzhag
ji ltar byas kyang phyag rgya rgyun mi 'chad

30. yan lag bzhi ldan phyag rgya chen po bzhi
skye med don rtogs pa yi yan lag dang
bden gnyis tha mi dad[464] kyi yan lag dang
snang ba skye med thug phrad nyid du rtogs
dran pa gzung du med pa'i yan lag dang
stong pa rkyen dang dran med blo las 'das
dngos po dgag sgrub med pa'i yan lag go

31. de nyid gzhir ldan 'dod pas dben pa dang
rtog pa dang bcas dpyod par bcas ba dang
dga' dang bde[465] dang dben par gnas la sogs
tha snyad de nyid mtshon pa'i yul du gsungs

32. gzhir ldan rab 'bring tha mar gsungs pa yang
dman pa'i don du mkhas pas rab tu bshad[466]
phyag rgya chen po gang la gnas mi byed
blang dor bral ba'i don du de bzhin bshad

---

463 M: *rag*.

464 D: *mi dar*; P, N: *mid dang*.

465 M: *bed*.

466 The *shad* (/) between lines 142 and 143 does not appear in the D edition, but does in all the others.

gtsang smer[467] mi 'byed gang yang dngos
grub dag[468] tu byed

33. lhan cig skyes dang yul la gtum mo sbar la sogs[469]
dam tshig bdag gi kho na nyid dang rnal 'byor bsgom
dngos po thams cad mnyam nyid phyag rgya[470] chen po la
rtog pa spang zhing mi rtog bsgom pa ci zhig[471] 'gyur

34. bla ma la gus gsang ba'i 'dul sdom de ru rdzogs
phyi nang gsang ba'i dbang bskur so so'i mtshon nyid dang
bum pa gsang ba shes rab ye shes dang
ngo bo nges tshig dbye ba la sogs kun
thun mong mthu skyes phyag rgya che la reg mi nus

35. kye ho[472] phyag rgya che la 'bras bu'i bdag nyid sku gsung thugs ldan pas
'bras bu de yang snying po'i don la 'thad kyis[473] drang dang nges pa'i don la min
lam dang 'bras bu'i snying po thams cad bcud bsdus[474] dang
theg chen bla na med pa'i dngos dang theg[475] pa dag gi khyad par dang
kun gyi snying por gyur nas gsang ba bla na med

---

[467] P, N: *rmer*.

[468] P, N: *dpag*.

[469] D: *sags*.

[470] P, N: *pyag rgya* is absent.

[471] D: *zhag*.

[472] P, N: *kye 'o*.

[473] P, N: *kyi*.

[474] P, N: *'dus*.

[475] N: *thag*

36. phyag rgya chen po[476] nges pa'i mtshan nyid ni
dran dang dran med gnyis su med pas skye med de
blo las 'das shing nam mkha' lta bur cir mi gnas

37. las kyi phyag rgya dpe dang chos kyi phyag rgya'i lam
phyag rgya chen po 'bras bu dam tshig phyag rgya gzhan don te
chos kyi phyag rgya man chad bsten pas mthar mi 'gro
re dogs mthar lhung 'du 'dzi bya ba'i skyon du 'gyur

38. kho na nyid la gnyen po dbyer med rang sor gzhag
rnam rtog ji snyed shar yang lhug pa nyid la shar
dran pa rang sar grol nas dran med lhug pa nyid
gang yang longs spyod snang bar shes shing dran med gsos

39. rang bzhin nyams nyid[477] skye med dag tu ldan
kun la khyab cing 'bab[478] chu lta bur gnas
rgyun mi chad pa'i 'bab chu lta bu dang[479]
mar me ltar gsal rang rig byang chub sems
'gog pa med bzhin dran rig rang gis stong

40. yang dag kho na nyid ni gang zhe na
gzhan na yod na kun gyis mthong bar rigs
rang la yod kyang lkog gyur bla ma'i zhal
sems nyid sangs rgyas kho na nyid yin te
dran pas bslad cing de nyid gzhan du brtags

41. sangs rgyas yin phyir yon tan gang zhe na
yon tan ras dang dkar po lta bu ste
kho na nyid kyi yon tan phyag rgya che
ngo bo yon tan so so tha dad min

---

[476] D: *pa*.

[477] P, N: *rnyed*.

[478] D: *'bang*.

[479] P, N: this line is entirely omitted.

42. phyag rgya che dang bzhi pa la sogs pa[480]
yon tan so so ma yin tha dad min
dran med yon tan rgya mtsho ma 'gul bar
dran par mi 'gyur chu yi dba'[481] rlabs med

43. skye med yon tan mi 'gyur brag dang 'dra
brag ca grag tsam rjes su 'brang ba med
blo las[482] 'das shing yul du ma gyur pa
phyag rgya chen po'i yon tan nam mkha' 'dra

44. dran pa sems can sems las byung ba yin
de phyir stong pa gzhan nas btsal mi dgos
bzhi ru snang yang gcig gi yon tan ni
phyag rgya bzhi ru snang ba ci phyir mtshon

45. gong gi khyad par dag gi bzhi ru byung
phyag rgya chen po gsum du rtog mi byed
gang la mi gnas chags pa med par[483] spyod
me tog sbrang rtsi sbrang mas 'thung dang 'dra

46. so sor rtog pa'i ye shes thabs yin te
ro dang phrad na rol zhen pa med
de ltar kun gyis shes par 'gyur ma yin
snying po'i don gyi 'gro drug khyab mod kyang
'gro ba dran pas bcings te pad tra'i srin

47. sems las dran pa byung phyir 'khrul pa'i rgyu
yid la mi byed shes na sangs rgyas nyid
'khrul pa de la thabs dang shes rab med
kye ho[484] dbyer med shes na thabs mchog de kho na

---

[480] P, N: *la sogs 'og ma kun*.

[481] P, N: *rba*.

[482] D, C, M: *yis*.

[483] P, N: *phyag rgya chen por* (instead of *chags pa*, etc.).

[484] P, N: *kye 'o*.

48. sangs rgyas sems can chos rnam thams cad kun
rang gi sems nyid dag dang lhan cig skyes
yid la mi byed yid la skyes tsam na
dran pa'i snang ba nub ste bden brdzun med
de phyir de nyid kho na'i yul ma yin

49. dper na mig gi yul du sgra mi snang
rnam par mi rtog rtog pa'i[485] yul ma yin
stong pa'i rkyen gyis dran pa gsal tsam na
dran pa'i snang ba nub nas mthong ba med

50. ye shes 'on long lkugs par mi 'gyur te[486]
ma dran pa la 'on long lkugs rgyu med
bems so la sogs tha snyad kun dang bral
snang ba nub ces bya ba'i tha snyad ni
dran pa phyags te dran med gsos su spungs

51. de nyid skye med blo las 'das pa ni
dran pa med[487] dang skye med ye shes mes
gzung[488] 'dzin bsregs sbyangs blo las 'das phul bas
smon lam dbang gis skye ba phyis mi brgyud

52. de phyir phyag rgya chen po sngon song la
su la mi brten gang la rag ma lus
chu[489] la zhugs dang tshogs dang za[490] 'gyed byed
rig[491] byed grong khyer dkrog[492] pa dag dang mtshungs

---

[485] P, N: *dran pa'i* (instead of *rtog pa'i*).

[486] P, N: *ram*.

[487] P, N: *me*.

[488] D: *gzang*.

[489] P, N: *bcu*.

[490] P, N: *zas*.

[491] P: *rigs*.

[492] P: *khrog*.

53. phyag rgya chen po rang las gzhan med phyir
mchod rdzas dran pa mgron[493] dang mchod gnas rang shes pas
mchod pa rang gi dran pa med la mchod
blo las 'das kyi skye med tshogs la rol

54. phyag rgya chen po gzhan la mi ltos phyir
bsgom bya rang la sgom[494] byed rang gi sems
blo 'das rang la dmigs pa nyid dang bral
de nyid 'bras bu yin phyir gzhan la rag ma lus

55. bsgom bsgrub sngags bzlas rang gi sems yin te
yi dam lha yang[495] rang gi sems yi pas
de phyir mkha' 'gro lung ston la sogs rang gi sems
sems ni dran pa cir yang snang bar ston

56. ma dran pa la[496] thams cad dmigs su med
phyag rgya chen po rang las gzhan med phyir
sangs rgyas chos dang dge 'dun la sogs te
pha ma dkon mchog rang bzhin byang chub sems
mchod dang bsnyen bkur byas na dran pa'i rgyu

57. tha dad med na skye med rang sar grol
blo las 'das na[497] bya dang mi bya med
sangs rgyas sems can mtshon tshul so so yang
lhan cig dag tu skyes te rig ma rig

58. gang zhig snang yang dran par mi rtog[498] na
sems can nyid ni 'bras bu skye ba med

---

[493] P, N: *'gron*.

[494] P, N: *bsgom*.

[495] M: *'ang*; C, D: *dang*.

[496] P, N: *ste*.

[497] P, N: *la*.

[498] P, N: *rtogs*.

gang zhig mi snang dran par rtog ce na[499]
sangs rgyas nyid kyang khams gsum 'khor pa'i rgyu

59. gang zhig dran med yid la 'chang byed ci
sems can snang yang sangs rgyas dag dang mtshungs
gang zhig dran pa sangs rgyas rtogs 'dod na
sangs rgyas snang yang sems can[500] khyad par med

60. des na snang brtags gnyis la brtag tu[501] med de bor
bor yang rang las gzhan med 'gro rgyun 'chad
rang las yod snyam rtog gi[502] dran pas bslad
snang ba gsal[503] la mi rtog ma[504] zhen sems

61. de phyir yod dang med pa'i rtog pa gnyis bral te
gnyug mar gnas na gang ltar byas kyang bde
dran pa 'od gsal 'dzin pai' snying po can
zhen pa gnyis dang bral[505] te rang bzhin gnyug mar gzhag

62. des na phyag rgya chen po zung du rab 'jug ste
dran pa dran med skye med zung du 'jug
dran med mi rtog pa yi rang[506] bzhin dang
rten 'brel glo bur skye ba'i dran pa gnyis
skye ba med pa'i ngang[507] du ro gcig phyir
des na skye dang skye ba blo las 'das

---

499 P, N: after this line, extra two lines. The first repeats 254 and the second is similar to but differs from 255: *sems can nyid ni 'bras bu skye ba med / gang zhig mi snang rten pa rtog ge pa//* As it does not change the meaning of the stanza but only adds some redundancy, I have opted to leave it out.

500 N: *sen* (instead of *sems can*).

501 P, N: *du*.

502 P, N, M, C: *ge*.

503 P, N: *bsal*.

504 P, N: *mi*.

505 M: *phral*.

506 C: *rad*.

507 D, C, M: *dang*.

63. ’od gsal stong dang zung du ’jug la sogs
ma bcos ma byas skye med rang sar grol
de la sku gsum chos sku longs sku dang
sna tshogs snang ba sprul sku zhes su bshad
gnyug ma ngo bo nyid kyi sku yin te
snying rje stong dang[508] dbyer med skye ba med

64. las kyi phyag rgya la brten nyams myong ni
bcos[509] ma yin phyir rkyen gyi[510] stobs las byung
gzhan la ltos[511] phyir kho na nyid ma yin

65. chos kyi phyag rgya bcos ma ma yin kyang
nyams su myong bas ma grub nyid mi mthong
phyag rgya chen po nyams su myong ’gyur na
dran pa sna tshogs skye ba med par shes

66. dngos por snang ba ngo bo nyid kyis stong
sems can skye ba med dang dbyer med don
snying rje thabs kyis mtshon bya dpe[512] yis bstan

67. sna tshogs snang yang blo ’das yul mi g.yo
bdag nyid rnal ’byor de nyid rtag tu blta
spyod lam thams cad phyag rgya che la gnas
dngos po’i gnas lugs skye med ngang du gzhag

68. rlung gi rkyen bcas rgya mtsho dang pa las[513]
dba’[514] rlabs chu yi[515] gnyer ma glo bur skye

---

[508] C: *dad*.

[509] D: *btsos*.

[510] P, N: *gyis*.

[511] P, N: *bltos*.

[512] N: *pa*.

[513] D, C: *bral*; M: *pa la*; P, N: *dngas pa la*.

[514] P, N: *rba*.

[515] P, N: *la*.

de nyid rgya mtsho dag dang dbyer med do
dran pas rkyen byas rtog pa glo bur skye
de nyid sngar gyi dran pa med dang ni
skye med blo 'das dag gis[516] ngo mtshar mtshungs

69. de ltar phyag rgya che la skyes pa sngar med bzhin
phyis kyang rkyen gyi[517] stobs kyis[518] skyes srid kyang
skye ba med pa de dag[519] dbyer med do
gzugs can ma yin kun la khyab pa dang
mi 'gyur ba dang dus rnams thams cad[520] pa'o

70. nam mkha lta bur skye 'gag med pa dang
thag[521] pa sbrul bzung sbrul gyi[522] stong pa dang
chos sku longs sku sprul sku dbyer med de
ngo bo nyid ni blo yi yul las 'das

71. phyag rgya chen po skad cig mngon sangs rgyas
de nyid sems can don du gzugs skur byung
rgyu mthun[523] 'bras bu rnam smin 'bras bu dang
dri ma med pa'i 'bras bu gzhan don byed
go 'phang khyad par brjod las 'das par bshad

72. kye ho[524] ma bcos phyag rgya bde ba che
dran med klong du rang shar ba
skye med nam mkha lta bur khyab
blo las 'das pa'i ngang la gnas

---

[516] P, N: *gi*.

[517] P, N: *gyis*.

[518] P, N: *gyis*.

[519] P, N: *dang*.

[520] N: *thad* (instead of *thams cad*).

[521] D: *theg*.

[522] P, N: *de nyid sbrul gyis* (instead of *sbrul bzung sbrul gyi*).

[523] P, N: *'thun*.

[524] P, N: *kyi 'o*.

73. snang[525] ba spros bral bde ba che
dran med cir yang mi rtog pa
dran pa sna tshogs sems su gsal
brtag cing[526] btsal na dmigs su med

74. skye ba med pa ’dzin dang bral
’dzin dang bral ba’i[527] rgyu ba med
dran pa sgyu ma rang rig tsam
sgyu med thar med dran med gsal

75. skye med don dam kun gsal bas
thams cad blo las ’das par snang
khams gsum blo ’das ye shes nyid
lhan cig skyes pa de kho na
dran pa’i rtsa ba ma lus thag bcad do[528]

76. dran med skye ba med pa’i dbyings la dgod
de nyid ma bcos blo yi yul las ’das
dran rig sems kyi rang ’bar nyid du gsal
gsal bas rnam rtog ’khor ba’i grogs su ’gyur

77. thar pa’i lam ni kho na nyid shes nas
rang ’byung ji bzhin bsam bral ngang[529] la gnas
dran pa rang gsal dngos por grub pa med

78. bcos med dgongs pa skye med bde chen ’di
mngon sum snang bas ngos[530] gzung gang yang med
dran med yul du cir yang mthong ba med
rten dang bral bas slob pa gang yang med

---

525 P: *snat*.

526 P, N: *shing*.

527 P, N: *phyir*.

528 P, N: *de*.

529 C: *dad*; P, N: *dang*.

530 D: *ngos* omitted.

79. gang la yid la byar med phyag rgya che
mtshan ma'i dran rig sna tshogs ji snyed pa
de nyid phyag rgya che la dbye ba med
rtogs dang mi rtogs gnyi ga so so min

80. rtag chad mtha' la mi gnas skyon dang bral
rang gi de[531] nyid rtogs na gzhan las min
rten 'brel mya ngan 'das lam bstan pa dang
kye ba med par rtogs na phyag rgya che

81. de nyid mi shes las kyi phyag rgya dang
dam tshig chos la sogs pa rtsol 'dod pa
de nyid mtshon ba'i dpe tsam don mi nus
gzung 'dzin bral ba'i phyag rgya che brten pa
shes pa rang lugs so ma nyid la byung

82. 'dod med rang gzhag[532] gnyug ma'i ngo bor gnas
tha mal snang ba'i shes pa 'di nyid blo
yin min dran pa'i sems la rang gzhag[533] yin
yid ches rin chen gdams ngag yid bzhin gter
yid la bya dang mi bya med par[534] gzhag

83. rang rig phyag rgya chen po nyid yin pas
phyag rgya chen po nyid la nyid kyis bstan
dran pa sna tshogs don la sems ma 'jug

84. phyi nang bral bas rtsod med phyag rgya dang
phyag rgya chen po srog ldan 'dod pa med
'dod pa byung na de yang dran pa'i rgyu

---

531 P: *di*.

532 C, D, M: *gzhan*.

533 P: *bzhag*.

534 P, N: *rang bzhin* (between *par* and *gzhag*).

85. rang sems phyag rgya chen po la
dran dang[535] ma dran tha dad[536] skye ba med
'khrul dang ma 'khrul blo yi yul las 'das
dran pa'i zhen rtog brtas pas 'khor ba'i rgyu

86. 'od gsal phyag rgya chen po gnyug ma'i ngo bo nyid
gang yang 'gyur med byang chub sems su gcig
kho na nyid la gzung 'dzin ngo bo bral
snang ba don ldan ye shes nyid du mthong

87. bsam pas brtags pas dran pa'i tshogs su rgyus
snang ba skye ba log pa'i stobs kyis mthong
dran pa dran med ngang[537] la shes 'jug pa
lus ngag[538] yid kyis 'bad kyang dran rgyu med

88. gnyis su med na 'khor ba'i rang bzhin med
dran pa sna tshogs 'gyu ba'i rang bzhin 'di
sna rtse'i phyag rgya dag la ye nas med
des na phyag rgya chen po bsam med blang dor gzhag

89. kye ho[539] phyi nang zab dang mi zab bskyed rim dang
yongs grub ngo bo nyid dang dbugs dbyung dang
rgyas gdab las dang chos kyi phyag rgya ni
rnal 'byor yongs su rdzogs pa'i rim pa[540] ste

90. phyag rgya chen po ngo bo nyid kyi rim
dam tshig phyag rgya yongs su grub pa'i rim
kun brtags yongs su grub pa'i rgya

---

535 P, N: *pa*.

536 D: *dang*.

537 D, C, P: *dang*.

538 C, M, P, N: *dag*.

539 P, N: *kye 'o*.

540 P: damaged.

las kyi phyag rgya dbang gi ngo bo dang
dga' ba bzhi ldan thabs kyi rang bzhin can
chos kyi phyag rgya sna tshogs snang ba ste
dga' bzhi'i lhan cig skyes pa nyid

91. phyag rgya chen po skye ba med pa la
gzung 'dzin dran bral ngo bo blo las 'das
dri ma med pa'i 'bras bu mngon[541] sangs rgyas

92. dam tshig phyag rgya mtsan ma'i rnal 'byor te
'bras bu lha yid kyil 'khor 'gro ba'i don
rje btsun pha ma thabs dang shes rab mtshon

93. dga' ba bzhi ldan dam tshig phyag rgya che
de ltar thabs kyi sbyor ba kun 'dul yang
zab mo chos kyi phyag rgyas gtan la dbab
sems nyid phyag rgya chen po rang la bstan

94. dga' bas gzung pa'i[542] dran pa bkar[543] pa dang
mchog dgas 'dzin pa'i dran phyed[544] gtang ba dang
lhan cig skyes dgas dran pa bkar bas dang
dga' bral snang ba skye med dran pa gsal
de bzhin zab mo'i chos kyi phyag rgya bstan

95. dga' bzhi ye shes gang du skyes pa dang
tha mi dad cing yongs su thim par gnas
rtog pa'i nyams myong dag la gnas pa dang
yid la ma dran rtog pa tha mi dad
dpe dang lam ste tha snyad 'dul bar bstan

---

[541] P: *mdon*.

[542] P, N: *ba'i*.

[543] P, N: *gar*.

[544] M: *byed*.

96. sems nyid phyag rgya chen po 'char ba ni
skye med skye ba'i cho 'phrul cir yang 'char
blo las 'das pas ma skyes ngo bor bstan
ma[545] skyes pa dang skyes pa'i dngos po gnyis
tha dad med de gnyug ma'i ngo bor gzhag

97. dran pa sna tshogs gang la rgyu ba 'di
dran med 'jug pas rtog pa mi 'gag pa
shes pa[546] rang lugs bzhag na gnas par 'gyur
snang dang stong dang gnyis 'dzin skye ba'i rgyu
tha mi dad par kho na bde ba che

98. nyams myong shar bas mi mthun 'dzin pa bral
dran pa med de 'di 'dra'i yul med pa
dran pa med dang snang stong tha mi dad

99. ma skyes mtshan ma[547] med pa'i rnal 'byor la
mnyam gzhag rjes thob med de rgyun gyi rnal 'byor la
snang dang skye ba dran pa gang skyes kyang
de nyid stong pa dran pa med gnas pas
dran pa yid la byar med snang stong dbyer mi phyed

100. de nyid thug phrad skye med nyams myong la
snang ba'i ngo bo stong pa bde chen shar
cha ba[548] rom chur bzhu btung du btu ba bzhin du
gang snang skye med bde ba chen por chor

101. btang snyoms dran pa med de rtog pa ma bkag kyang
blo las 'das pas rmongs pa sgom[549] dang bral
'di la gnas na bde chen nyams 'byung ste

---

545 C: *me*.

546 P, N: *pas*.

547 N: *mi*.

548 D: *pa*.

549 P, N: *bsgoms*.

dang por snang ba stong pa'i[550] nyams myong 'byung
chab rom snang yang chu ngo shes bzhin du

102. gnyis pa[551] dran pa'i snang ba ma 'gag[552] par
stong pa bde dang tha mi dad par 'byung
chab rom chu ru bzhu ba'i gnas skabs bzhin
dran pa dran med skye ba med la thim

103. thams cad tha mi dad pas bde ba chen por gcig
de nyid chab rom chu ru bzhu ba bzhin
thams cad rang bzhin thug phrad shes gyur na
bcing bkrol dag gis ma bzung[553] dran pa'i rjes ma 'brang

104. 'jur bus bcings pa bzhin du sems mi sgrib[554]
'jur bu klod na grol zhing sems nyid gar[555] dgar btang
ldog pas[556] gzings la 'phur ba'i bya rog bzhin
de nyid shes na snang ba longs spyod yin

105. lcags kyus btab pas glang chen thul ba[557] bzhin
bya bral bzhag pas glang chen lom[558] pa bzhin
dran pa dran med ngo shes gnod pa med
snang dang stong pa shes pas rtog dang bral

106. skye bar gnas pas dbyer med dran mi rgyu
de nyid khyab bdag dgra kun[559] ngo shes bzhin

---

[550] P, N: *par*; *myong ba'i* inserted between *par* and *nyams*.

[551] P, N: *gnyis pa* omitted.

[552] P, N: *'gags*.

[553] P, N: *gzung*.

[554] P, N: *bsgri*.

[555] P, N: *gang*.

[556] P, N: *ldog pas* omitted.

[557] D, C, M: *thim pa*.

[558] M: *lon*.

[559] P, N: *rkun*.

snang pa stong par thim pas lan tshva chur thim bzhin
dran pa dran med thim pa de kho na

107. skye ba rnam pa gnyis la skye rgyu[560] med
thug phrad skye med ye shes shar bas na
dran pa blo yi yul med phyogs med ye shes 'char
spra ba me mched rab[561] 'bar me bzhin du
nyams myong smrar mi[562] btub[563] pa gzhon nu'i bde ba bzhin

108. sna tshogs snang yang dran par mi 'gyur ba[564]
dal ba'i 'bab chus dba'[565] rlabs mi 'gyur bas
rang gi ngo bo gsal bas mar me dran

109. de ltar phyag rgya chen po gang la mi bstan pas
bya sar ko ne mkha' la gnas bzhin du[566]
rtogs pa'i spyod pas blang dor mi byed pa
srog chags pa ta ri bzhin zhen chags med
blo 'das 'bras bu 'dod na med grub pa
sman mchog[567] nang na be[568] ta ji bzhin nyid

110. kye ho[569] de ltar mkhas pa thabs zin dag gis ni
dran pa med la skye med rgyas btab ste
dran pa med pas dran med rgya yis btab

---

[560] P, N: *rgyun*.

[561] D, C, M: *rang*.

[562] P, N: *ma*.

[563] C: *btab*.

[564] D: *pa*.

[565] P, N: *rba*.

[566] P, N: lines 469 and 470 are conflated as: *de ltar phyag rgya chen po mkha' la gnas bzhin du //*

[567] D: *ma chog* (instead of *mchog*).

[568] P, N: *pre*.

[569] P, N: *kye 'o*.

snang bas stong pa la rgyas gdab
stong[570] pas snang ba la rgyas gdab

111. dran dang snang ba bde ba'i ror shar na
stong dang dran med rgya yis[571] thebs pa yin
snang dang dran pa stong ba'i rgya dang ni
dran med gnas pa dag gis[572] rgyas gdab na
snang dang dran pa bde ba'i ror shar nas
mtshan ma'i bsgom pas ma dpyad[573] mtshan ma'i blo las 'das

112. dran dang snang ba dag la skye med rgyas btab[574] pa
skye med dag la blo 'das rgya yis thebs
dran pas dran med bde ba'i rgyas thebs pas
stong par ma song chad pa'i mthar ma lhung

113. gnas pa skye ba dag la rgyas thebs pas
dngos por ma song rtag ba'i mthar ma lhung
thams cad blo las 'das shing skye ba med
thams cad bde ba chen po'i rgyud dang ldan
de ltar shes pas btang snyoms mthar ma lhung

114. dran pa 'khor ba'i dngos po dang
dran pa med pa'i rtogs[575] pa la
btang snyoms lam du khyer bar byed pa dang
rig pas gzhigs nas stong pa btang snyoms dang
gzung 'dzin bral ba'i rang rig btang snyoms pas
bden pa gnyis bral gnyis med btang snyoms bsgom[576]

---

[570] P, N: *stongs*.

[571] P, N: *yi*.

[572] P, N: *gi*.

[573] C: *dbyad*.

[574] N: *gdab*.

[575] P, N: *rtog*.

[576] P, N: *bsgoms*.

gang du ma dran bsam gtan btang snyoms mchog
lung du ma bstan btang snyoms sgom ma yin

115. shes pa sor gzhag dran med nyams 'phro[577] ba
dran pa'i mtshan ma dran med lam du khyer

116. bde ba lam khyer blo 'das ma dmigs pa
gnyis la mi rtog bde ba[578] rgyun mi 'chad

117. kye ho[579] nyams dang bral bas gzung 'dzin gnyis las grol
de nyid phyag rgya chen po'i don mthong 'gyur
'bras bu mthar[580] thug rin chen gter chen la
phyag rgya che la gnas 'dod gang
dri med 'bras bu rtogs par shog

sa ra ha'i zhal snga nas gsungs pa
sku'i mdzod 'chi med rdo rje'i glu zhes bya ba rdzogs so

---

[577] P, N: *'tsho*.

[578] M: *pa*.

[579] P, N: *kye 'o*.

[580] D: *mzar*.

Speech Treasury

rgya gar skad du vāk kośa rucira svara vajra gīti[581]
bod skad du gsung gi mdzod 'jam dbyangs rdo rje'i glu

'jam dpal gzhon nur gyur pa la phyag 'tshal lo

1. kye ho[582] ting 'dzin rtse gcig ro snyoms spyod pa khyad par can
dngos dang dngos med yid rtogs 'khor bar rgyu bas btang bar bya[583]
snang dang stong pa[584] bzung du 'jug pa dbyer med de kho na
chos kyi dbyings kyi rang bzhin thams cad 'byung zhing thim par gnas

2. bdag dang gzhan don gnyis med dran med gsal ba'i dang[585]
phyag rgya chen po'i rnam grangs dpag med brjod las 'das
dngos dang dngos med yongs su btang na 'khor 'das med
rdzing[586] bu gla gab med na phyogs bzhir 'khor lo spangs[587]

3. byis pa ma shes rten 'brel 'khor bar 'jug pa'i rgyu
shes rab zhan pas dngos 'dzin bdag gzhan don mi 'grub
mar me spar[588] yang dmus[589] long dag la snang mi srid
bdag gzhan don 'dod dngos 'dzin rang gis rang la 'dzin

---

[581] P, N: *tsi ta*.

[582] P, N: *kye 'o*.

[583] D, C, M: *bya* is omitted.

[584] D: *stong* (*pa* omitted).

[585] M, P: *ngang*.

[586] M: *rjing*.

[587] D, C: *sbangs*; P, N: *yangs*.

[588] M: *sbar*.

[589] P, N: *dmun*.

4. rtog pa yin phyir btang mi btang la brtag par bya
snang med rang rig rtog pa'i tha snyad kun dang bral
thabs dang bral phyir bdag don mi 'grub mtshan mar 'gyur

5. dbyer med don la gnas pas de nyid ston pa dang
chos kyi dbyings la 'jug pa'i mtshan nyid bstan pa'o
bla ma las[590] bstan lung[591] 'grel[592] gdams ngag rjes su ston
lung dang rigs pas rang gi mtshan nyid rtogs 'dod pa
bla ma la brten[593] gdams ngag ldan pa dag las rnyed
bsnyen bkur byas na lhan cig bde ba mchog thob 'gyur

6. dri ma dang bral bya phyir bla ma'i zhabs la 'dud
mchod na byin rlabs[594] chen po 'byung bar rgyal bas bshad

7. kye ho[595] grong khyer tsam o ngan[596] kus nam[597] mkhar song[598] bzhin du
thar pas 'bad na rgyal ba'i sa la gdon mi za

8. brjod bya rjod byed dbang bskur byin rlabs[599] skye zhing 'phel ba'i gnas
sngon du slob mas bya dang slob dpon bya ba'i rim pa dang
rjes su slob mas bya dang zab mo dbang bskur ba
phyag rgya mchod dang bstod pa dag gis gsol ba gdab
snyan pa'i tshig gis gsol gdab rig pa rtsal dbang[600] dang

---

[590] P, N: *la*.

[591] D: *sung*.

[592] C, D, P, N: *'brel*.

[593] P, N: *bsten*.

[594] P, N: *brlabs*.

[595] P, N: *kye 'o*.

[596] P, N: *sham*.

[597] P, N: *su*.

[598] D: *stong*.

[599] P, N: *brlabs*.

[600] D: *dpang*—abbreviation of: *rig pa'i rtsal dbang*.

9. phyag rgya la brten gsang ba'i dbang bskur[601] sdom sbyin dang
gnang ba sbyin dang rjes su spro[602] ba bstan[603] pa ste
slob mas rjes dbul zab mo'i dbang bskur dam bca' dang

10. bskyed pa'i rim pa la sogs bstan pa ni
ngo bo nyid kyi rim pa bstan pa dang
nyams myong bsgom par bya ba'i brjod bya la sogs kun

11. gang la mi gnas bya sar ko ne gang la rten mi 'cha'
'dod pa med pa'i bde ba dag la mi gnas te
ya zung med phyir gang la rten dang rten byed bral
gnyis med rnal 'byor rang la 'char ba'i nyams myong bde
bdag tu rtog pa'i dngos po btang[604] na nam mkha'i mtha' ltar yangs

12. mya[605] ngan 'das pa'i grong khyer[606] dag tu 'jug 'dod na
tshogs drug thug phrad char pa rgyun gyi rnal 'byor che
snang ba stong pa skye med thug phrad rkyen la rag ma lus
gnyis med goms pas lam myur zung du 'jug mi ldog

13. sems can sangs rgyas rang bzhin yin par shes na rtsol ba med
gang gi ro snyoms sbyong pa dag la brten nas 'bras bu thob
sbyong pa byas na 'gro ba 'khor ba dag las thar bar the tshom med
bdud dang mi mthun phyogs las rnam par rgyal bar 'gyur

14. mtshan ma'i rnal 'byor mi bya btang snyoms rnal 'byor min
mkhas pa'i ye shes myur du thob cing sgrib pa zad

---

[601] C: *bsur*.

[602] C, D, P, N: *sbro*.

[603] P, N: *brtan*.

[604] C: *thtang* (C is damaged – may read *gtang*).

[605] D: *ma*.

[606] D: *khyar*.

mtshan ma'i spyod[607] pas drang don mkhas kyang rmongs rnams 'ching
ro snyoms phyag rgya chen po la brten nam mkhar 'gro

15. gnyis med sbyod lam rgyun du brten[608] na tshe 'dir thob
snang ba sgyu ma'i yul la mi gnas[609] rtog[610] yul med
'jig rten chos brgyad 'ching par mi nus brtul zhugs mchog
snying rje thabs brin[611] sbyod pa chags med mkha' ltar yangs

16. phyag rgya chen po yan lag bzhi ldan thabs kyi mchog
bzhir[612] ldan phyag rgya gcig gi cho 'phrul gcig gi ngang[613]
gnyis med ngang la phyag rgya chen po glod de gzhag

17. byang chub sems ldan btang gzhag med na glang chen 'dra
rtog pa'i ngo bos ba[614] mo rta ltar snang 'dod na
rtog med snang med don la 'bad de rnal 'byor bya

18. sku bzhi mthar phyin 'bras bu bde ba chen po'i ngang
skye bar snang ba lam gyi lus rnams ni
sku gsum mthur[615] ldan rtog pa rnam par bral
shes dang shes bya rang rgyud dag pa'i yul

19. dngos po'i rang bzhin skye ba'i rkyen[616] snang yang
ma skyes pa yi[617] yul las 'das ma myong

---

[607] D, C: *sbyod*.

[608] D, C, M: *bstan*.

[609] P, N: *nub*.

[610] P, N: *btul*.

[611] M: *zin*.

[612] D: *bzhi ra* (instead of *bzhir*).

[613] P, N: *dang*.

[614] P, N: *sab*.

[615] N: *mthar*.

[616] C: *rkyon*.

[617] P, N: *pa'i* (instead of *pa yi*).

dngos po dngos med btang snyoms la sogs kun
’byed pa med de dran med skye med yul

20. phyag rgya che la rtag tu mtshan nyid bral
phung po dag pas gsang ba’i yul las ’das
dga’ ba bzhi yi mtshan nyid phyag rgya’i yul
rang rgyud ma yin shes rab thabs dang bral

21. sna rtse la sogs de nyid ma zin na
de nyid dag la sbyor yang don dam min
rang rig rdo rje gnas te sems dpa’i rnal ’byor ni
thams cad mkhyen pa’i[618] ngo bo ’di ’drar med

22. rgya mtsho’i dba’[619] rlabs brag[620] ca’i ngo bor mtshungs
grangs tsam[621] nyid na gang du’ang slebs pa med
dam tshig bsgrub dang ’bras bu rnam sbyar ba
mtshon bya mtshon byed tshig[622] gi tha snyad lam

23. dam tshig nyams na thabs sogs nyams gang na
blo las ’das pa’i yul du slob pa med
brtul[623] zhugs spyod[624] pas phyi dang nang ’gyur ba
kho na nyid dang ldan na khyad par can
de nyid mi ldan dud ’gro dag dang mtshungs

24. de nyid sbas pas lhan cig[625] skyes bsgoms pa
thabs bral dam tshig ’gal yang nyes pa med

---

618 P, N: *pa*.

619 P, N: *rba*.

620 C: *phrag*.

621 D: *grang sa tsam* (instead of *grangs tsam*); P, N: *grag tsam*.

622 N: *tshi*.

623 M: *brtu la*.

624 D, C: *sbyod*.

625 P, N: *ye shes* (instead of *lhan cig*).

'di dang pha rol grangs la mi ltos[626] par
da lta nyid du mngon gyur phyag rgya che
de nyid spangs na nam yang phrad mi 'gyur

25. phyag rgya chen po skad cig thos pas kyang
snod[627] dang ldan mi ldan la mi ltos par
bstan pa tsam gyis rtsa[628] gcig 'di yis thob
gang zhig dran pa dag la ma yengs pa'i
lhan cig skyes don bsgom dang ldan pas thob

26. de nyid rang yin gzhan gyi chos mi tshol
dur khrod wa sogs tshol phyir 'brangs te phung[629]

27. kye ho[630] bram ze rigs ngan[631] khyim 'dres 'tshol slong bzhin
bzang ngan 'dres pa gcig la gcig gnod de
mtshan ma'i rnal 'byor mtshan med don mi[632] reg
mtshan ma med la bltas pa nam yang med
mtshan ma dus dang grangs la ltos[633] par 'gyur

28. bskyed dang rdzogs ma'i rim pa khyad par bsam[634] mi bya
gnyis med 'dus pa rnal 'byor mchog ldan gang
gang yang ma shes dran med yengs pa'i yul
dran pa'i rgyun sbangs[635] de la goms par bya

---

[626] P, N: *bltos*.

[627] P, N: *smod*.

[628] C, M, P, N: *rtse*.

[629] P, N: *'phung*.

[630] P, N: *kye 'o*.

[631] C: *dan*.

[632] P, N: *mtshan mar reg //* (instead of *mtshan med don mi reg*).

[633] P, N: *bltos*.

[634] D: *bas ma*.

[635] C, M, P, N: *rgyud spangs*.

29. thun mong ma yin gsang sngags khyad par can
thog ma nyid nas bden ba'i ngo bor gnas
dngos grub bsdus pas[636] lhan cig skyes la thug
de nyid khyad par rang rig yul las 'das

30. de nyid bde ba'i gnas dang dngos po stong
chos rnams dag pas rang bzhin bde ba'i don
gang la mi gnas blo yi yul las 'das
yul med gnas med rten dang bral bas stong

31. e wam[637] dngos drub ngo bo nyid kyi rgyu
rdo rje 'chang dang rang rig bla ma'i bka'
'dus pa'i rgyud du dri med phyag rgya che
kun rdzob las kyi phyag rgya la sogs kun
'khor las sgyur rgyal dmangs kyi 'khor dang mtshungs

32. phyi nang zab mo bskyed pa'i rim pa kun[638]
rdzogs pa'i[639] phyag rgya nyi zla'i skar phran bzhin
dga' bral dga' ba mchog tu dga' la sogs
lhan cig skyes dga' 'khor lo'i rtsa ba nyid
dri ma med par dag byed de yi dgongs par gsal

33. de nyid ldan pas rtag tu ye shes myong
dbyer med thugs[640] kyi stong nyid go 'phang[641] yangs
lus ngag thabs ldan thabs la brten bsgom pa
dran pa skyed byed rgyu rkyen 'bras bu smin

---

[636] C: *was*.

[637] P: *bam*; N: *bam* (nasal written as *anusvara*).

[638] P, N: this line is omitted.

[639] P, N: *pa*.

[640] D: *dphyer med thu gas*.

[641] P, N: *'phangs*.

34. las can drang phyir grol ba'i thabs su[642] sbyor
las kyi phyag rgya nyams myong brod pa skyed
de nyid ldan goms nyams myong grol ba'i lam

35. padma rdo rjer sbyor ba mthong 'dod dang
chags can lam gis de nyid grol mi 'gyur
gzhan yang las kyi phyag rgya nyams myong dag brten[643] la
tha mal rang lus[644] phyag rgya chen po[645] sbar[646]
phyag rgya chen po kun du khyab pa'i dpe
rin po che dang nam mkha' lha bur mtshungs

36. phung po lnga sogs gsang ba mchog tu 'gyur
'jig rten 'jig rten 'das pa lhan cig gnas[647]
kho na nyid ni bla ma'i bka' drin gyis
mtshon cing bsgrub mi dgos par rang la rnyed

37. phyag rgya chen po mchog nyid dri ma bral
go 'phang thob par bya phyir spyad[648] par bya
rtag chad gnyis med mnyam sbyor gcig nyid gzhag[649]
lung dang man ngag rig[650] pas shes par bya

38. kho na nyid ni bsgrubs[651] na gdon mi za
phyag rgya chen po gsal te shes goms[652] na

---

[642] P: *su* omitted.

[643] P, N: *bsten*.

[644] P, N: *lus la*.

[645] M: *por*.

[646] N: *sbang*.

[647] P: *'das*.

[648] M: *sbyad*.

[649] P, N: *bzhag*.

[650] P, N: before *rig* insert *dag gis*.

[651] P: *sgrub*; N: *bsgrub*.

[652] P, N: *sgom*.

kho na nyid ni rtogs par the tshom[653] med
de nyid shes na goms pa'i stobs kyis spyod

39. de nyid ma shes steng sgo 'og sgo dang
rig ma la brten gsum po[654] gtsor byed dang
chu bya la sogs nya dang dud 'gror ma mtshungs

40. rang rig rgyud la tha snyad 'jal byed dang
phyi nang gzhigs[655] nas rang bzhin med 'dod na
'jig rten ca co yin mod khyad[656] med mtshungs

41. bden dang rten 'brel sgo nas thar 'dod dang
dbang po bsdams[657] pas thar lam 'dren 'dod dang
byis pa chang[658] pa stong bas 'brid dga' ste
des na bya ba byed 'dod thar med brdzun gyis bslus
grangs can rigs sogs gcer bu bye brag 'dod
byed dang rgyud[659] lta la sogs kyi[660] na 'khyam

42. kye ho[661] de nas 'khor ba ji ltar gtang[662] bar 'gyur
rgyu rkyen med pas rtogs[663] yul ma yin pa'i
sems kyis[664] de nyid phyag rgya che la gnas

---

653 N: *tsom*.

654 M: *bo*.

655 P, N: *gzhig*.

656 C: *byad*.

657 P, N: *gsubs*.

658 C, M: *chad*.

659 D, C, P, N: *rgyur*.

660 M: *kyi*.

661 P, N: *kye 'o*.

662 P, N: *btang*.

663 P, N: *rtags*.

664 D, C, M: *gyi*.

de nyid stobs kyi mtshan ma dang bral zhing
tshe gcig phyag rgya chen po thob par ’gyur

43. kye ho ngo mtshar gsang ba’i sbyod yul ’di
sman pa’i rgyal po rtogs[665] las skye med ’char
ye shes lnga sogs mtshan nyid rang la ldan
dang po’i las can rigs kyis kho na mthong

44. mtshan ma la brten[666] dran pas g.yeng[667] pa’i rgyu
kho na nyid la phyi rol ma dmigs na
mtshan ma’i spyod yul dran med ngang[668] la thim

45. mtshan ma’i rnal ’byor khams gsum ’khor ba’i lam
mtshan ma’i dngos po bag med sa bon bcas
dran med rnal ’byor nam mkha’i dkyil dang mtshungs

46. so sor med na ngo bo ma skyes phyir
skye bo gzhan gyi blo yi spyod yul min
de nyid lta la mkhas pas spyad[669] byar ’byung

47. dran pa rnam rtog[670] gzugs su gnas pa dang
dran med khams gsum dag pa’i gnas su spangs
de nyid ma skyes dngos grub kun gyi gnas
phyi dang nang rol ma dmigs thams cad ’grub

48. kye ho[671] phyag rgya chen po yon tan mchog ldan gang
bla ma mnyes par bya phyir dngos grub kun gyi gzhi

---

[665] P, N: *rtog*.

[666] P, N: *bsten*.

[667] M: *g.yengs*.

[668] C: *dang*.

[669] D: *sbyad*.

[670] M: *rtogs*.

[671] P, N: *’o*.

bla ma dkon mchog mi spang[672] yon tan 'byung [190]
gang zhig dad pa'i sems ldan brgya lam na
rnal 'byor rnams kyis gzhung 'di rtogs par shog[673]

gsung gi mdzod 'jam dbyangs rdo rje'i glu sa ra has gsungs brdzogs so

[672] M: *spods*; D, C: *spongs*.

[673] P, N: significant differences throughout this—*rnal 'byor gzungs kyi gzhung 'di rtog par shog*.

Mind Treasury

rgya gar skad du / tsi tta kośa aja vajra gīti[674]
bod skad du / thugs kyi mdzod skye med rdo rje'i glu[675]

'jam dpal gzhon nur gyur pa la phyag 'tshal lo

1. skye 'o[676] lhan cig skyes pa'i ye shes ni
rang gi[677] nyams su myong ba de kho na
rig dang ma rig rang rig gsal ba de kho na
mar me mun gsal rang gi[678] rang gsal rang la sad[679]

2. 'dam gyi[680] padma 'dam[681] la ma zhen kho dog legs
gzung 'dzin dri ma ma spangs snying po gsal[682]

3. nags khrod gnas pa'i ri dags gcig pur rgyu
rgyu la ma zhen 'bras bu de kho na
snang dang mi snang yul med zhen med[683] gsal
dngos stong ma dran dran med brjod[684] pa med
lhan cig skyes pa rnam[685] gsum nyams[686] su bde

---

[674] P, N: *tse ta*.

[675] Preceeding this poem, the N edition has an entire title page and the P edition has a title "line." Both read as follows: *thugs skye med rdo rje'i glu sa ra has mdzod pa bzhugs so*.

[676] D, C, M: *kye bo*.

[677] P, N: *gyis*.

[678] P, N: *gis*.

[679] N: *sang*.

[680] P: *gyis*.

[681] N: *'daM* (anusvara "*ma*").

[682] P, N: *bsal*.

[683] P, N: *zhen med* is omitted.

[684] D, C, M: *brjed*.

[685] P, N: *rnams*.

[686] N: *nyam*.

4. zhen pa med phyir rtog ge'i yul las 'das
sna tshogs dran phyir rjes su 'brang ba med
gsal dang mi mnyam[687] ye shes snying po nyid
mun sel nyi ma sgron me'i kha dog ltar
rang rig rang la 'bar[688] na 'dzin rtog zad

5. sgrib pa zad phyir dran med yengs ba med
gnyis dang yod dang med dang[689] tha snyad ma skyed cig
phyag rgya chen po bsam med blo las 'das
rang rig rdo rje 'dzin pa rnal 'byor pa

6. 'da' dka' lhan cig skyes pa'i mar me ni
thabs dang shes rab zung du 'jug pa'i don
skye med stong pa 'od gsal[690] ris dang bral

7. khyad par can gyi ye shes kho na nyid
gnyis la mi ltos bde ba rgyun mi 'chad
rang 'byung rtog med bag chags rtsad[691] nas gcod

8. sems can sangs rgyas khyad par bsam yas kyang
spyod lam dag na rgyun gyi rnal 'byor che
dran pa'i rang bzhin bsam kyis mi khyab kyang
gdod nas dag pas dran med dbyings la thim

9. rang don skye med gnyis bral rtogs pa'i don
'bras bu dag pas blo 'das yul med bral
rtogs pa'i thabs rgyun rang[692] bzhin kun la kyab

---

687 P, N: *mnyam pa'i* (instead of *mi mnyam*).

688 M: *'dan*.

689 D, C, M: simply reads *yod med*.

690 M: *gsar* (this is obviously an error); P, N: *…'od gsal stong par ris…*

691 P, N: *brtsad*.

692 M: *babs rgyun ngang bzhin…*

10. thabs kyi 'gro don snying rje bsam yas kyang
ye shes rang bzhin skye 'gag[693] med par rtogs
thabs kyi bde ba skyes kyang de med ma zin 'ching
grol ba'i ye shes rang la lhan cig 'byung

11. bsgom bya sgom[694] byed dmigs pa'i blo las 'das
sangs rgyas sems can bsam gyis mi khyab pa
skye med rtogs pa'i yul na blor mi snang
de nyid sad pas bde ba stong pas mtshon

12. bsgom bya'i ngo bo snang ba'i rkyen las byung
mi rtog rtogs pas kun rdzob tha snyad 'grub
gnyis su med pa'i snang ba rkyen med la
rang bzhin dag pa skye ba'i rnam 'phrul shar

13. bral dang ma bral mi rtog blo las 'das
gnyis med rtogs byar skye med yul du 'gyur
stong par smra bas de nyid rtogs mi 'gyur
blo las 'das pas mno bsam yul ma yin

14. mtha' gsum rtag 'dod dag gis rnyed par bka'[695]
dga' bzhi dag la dmigs kyang de nyid dka'
tshogs drug rang chas ye shes mchog ldan pas
gnyis med bcud kyi snang ba rang la 'char[696]

15. kye ho[697] phyag rgya chen po rtogs[698] bral kun gyi gzhi
dngos grub 'byung[699] pas ngo[700] mtshar rmad du che
gnyis med bag chags sad nas rang rig bral

---

693 D: *'ggra*.

694 P, N: *bsgom*.

695 D, C: *dga'*.

696 D, C, M: *'chad*.

697 P, N: *'o*.

698 M: *rtog*.

699 M: *'gyung*.

700 P: *do*.

16. gzung 'dzin bral[701] ba'i phyag rgya chen po ni
mtshan nyid bstan pas nyan thos la sogs skrag
rtse gcig bltas na yon tan mthar thug ldan
rtse gcig byas kyang cung zad bsgom du med

17. rnam rtog rang 'bar dran med gsos[702] su zhi
dran med snang med me long gzugs brnyan 'dra
tha snyad bral bas skye med blo 'das lam
mtshan ma'i dran pa dri med bag chags bstan
thog mtha'i bral zhing snga[703] phyi'i dus mi dmigs

18. kye ho[704] de phyir dngos med ye shes rtogs pa'i lam
ji ltar bag chags bral ba'i tshul zhen
gnyis su ma gzung gdod mtha' bral bas zhi

19. bag chags bral bas phyogs med rgyu ba stong
zung du 'jug pa sangs rgyas ngo bo nyid
shes rab rnam gsum yul dang thabs[705] su gsungs
dpe dang bral bas mtshon pa'i yul las 'das

20. skye ba 'di la dam pa'i snying po min
thabs kyi sbyor bas tshogs drug rang sar zhi
phung po lnga sogs yon tan dag pa'i zhin
kun mkhyen gnyis med snang yul zhen dang bral

21. don dam smra med kun rdzob rtog ge[706] tsam
mya ngan 'das lam 'khor ba'i snang ba nyid
bla ma dam pa'i dgongs pa thug phrad du
rnyed nas 'khor ba'i lam las grol bar 'gyur

---

[701] M: *bal*.

[702] N: *gso*.

[703] D, C: *sda*.

[704] P, N: *'o*.

[705] N: *thab*.

[706] P, N: *rtse*.

22. rnal 'byor dgongs pa'i nyams rnyed rdzogs sangs rgyas
mnor lam du lhan cig khon yin[707]

23. kye ho[708] gnyis med don du gsang sngags brda yis bkrol
yon tan mi zad rgya mtsho nor bu mtshungs
thabs mchog zin na bcu bzhi'i[709] sa la gnas
gang du gnas kyang ye shes rang las rnyed

24. gter rnyed bdag gzhan gnyis ka'i don la rmongs
snying gi ga'u padma'i[710] me tog dkyil
thabs dang ldan pa sbyor ba de nas 'gyed
'khor lo'i phyogs kyi rtsa gnas gang du yang
'dod dang bral bas chags med nam mkha' la
gyen thur 'dren dang 'khor lo bskor ba yang
thabs kyi 'dren tshul don gyi gting mi rnyed

25. gzung dang 'phang[711] dang sbyar dang sbor ba yang
blun po dbugs mi bde dang khyad med mtshungs

26. rtogs par 'dod pas de nyid rtag tu blta
gus dang dang bas bla ma dkon mchog brten
gsang ba'i yon tan bla ma mchog las 'byung
don ldan mtshan nyid nyon mongs gyul las rgyal

27. gsang ba'i don nyid don dang rab ldan pa'i
bla ma slob dpon lung dang rab ldan nas
mi gnyis sgo nas 'gro ba grol 'gyur shog

thugs kyi mdzod skye med rdo rje'i glu snying po gsang ba'i don
dpal sa ra ha pa'i zhal nas gsungs pa rdzogs so

---

[707] P, N: *yi*.

[708] P, N: *'o*.

[709] P, N: *bzhi*.

[710] P, N: *padma*.

[711] P, N: *gzungs dang 'phangs*.

Bibliographies and Indexes

Bibliographies

Tibetan Sources

Abhayadatta. *grub thob brgyad cu rtsa bzhi'i lo rgyus*. ed. and trans. (into Hindi) Sempa Dorje. Sarnath: Central Institute of Higher Tibetan Studies, 1997.

Chökyi Wangchuk, Shamarpa (6th). *sngon 'dro sadhana*, n.p.

Dondrup Gyel. *bod kyi mgur glu byung 'phel gyi lo rgyus dang khyad chos bsdus par ston pa rig pa'i khye'u rnam par rtsen pa'i skied tshal: mgur glu'i lo rgyus dang khyad chos*. Lhasa: mi rigs dpe skrun khang, 1985.

Gö Lotsawa Shönupel. *bod kyi yul du chos dang chos smra ba ji ltar byung ba'i rim pa deb ther sngon po* (*deb ther sngon po*). 2 volumes. Sri khron Mi rigs Dpe skrun Khang, 2003.

Karma Trinlepa. *do ha skor gsum gyi ti ka 'bring po sems kyi rnam thar ston pa'i me long*. Thimpu: Kunzang Tobgyel, Druk Serig Press, 1984.

Kyeme Dechen. *do ha mdzod ces bya ba sbyod pa'i glu'i 'grel ba don kyi sgron ma zhes bya ba* (*dohākośa nāmacaryāgīti ārthapradīpanāmaṭika*) sde dge bstan gyur, rgyud v. zhi 33b-55b.

Khedrup Je. *Introduction to the Buddhist Tantric Systems* (*rgyud sde spyi'i rnam par gzhag pa rgyas par brjod*). Alex Wayman and F. D. Lessing, trans. Delhi: Motilal Banarsidass, 1998.

Mikyo Dorje, Karmapa. *phyag rgya chen po sgros 'bum*. from *dpal rgyal ba karma pa sku brgyad pa mi bskyod rdo rje'i gsung 'bum*. vol Ya (24). Reprinted by dpal brtsegs bod yig dpe rnyang zhib 'jug khang, 2004.

Mipham Gyatso, Jamgon Ju. *'phags yul grub dbang dam pa rnams kyi zab mo'i do ha rnams las kho la byung mu tig phreng ba bzhugs so*. Gangtok: 1975.

Mipham Chokyi Lodro, Shamarpa (14th). *phyag rgya chen po'i sngon'gro'i nyams len rgyun 'khyer tshogs gnyis zung 'jug*. c. 2000. n.p.

Nyime Avadhūtipa (Maitrīpa). *do ha mdzod kyi snying po don gyi glu'i 'grel pa zhes bya ba (dohākośahpdayārthagītiṭikanāma)*, sde dge bstan gyur, rgyud v. zhi 65b–106b.

Panchen Sönam Drakpa. *rgyud sde spyi'i rnam par bzhag pa skal bsang gi yid 'phrog ces bya ba bzhugs so*.

Pawo Tsukla Trengwa. *chos 'byung mkhas pa'i dga' ston*. Beijing: mi rigs dpe skrun khang, 1986.

Pema Karpo. *Phyag rgya chen po'i man ngag gi bshad sbyar rgyal ba'i gan mdzod*. in *Collected Works (gsung-'bum) of Kun mkhyen Padma dkar po*. Darjeeling: Kargyud Sungrab Nyamso Khang, 1973. vol. 21 pp. 7–370.

Rangjung Dorje, Karmapa. 1991. *nges don phyag rgya chen po'i smon lam zhes bya ba*. reproduced in *Mahamudra: Boundless Joy and Freedom*. Grass Valley: Blue Dolphin.

———. *doha mdzod kyi glu'i don gsal bar byed pa tshig gi rgyan dri ma med pa'i sgron me*. From *Phyag chen rgya gzhung*. Khangra H.P.: Tsondru Senge, Bir Tibet Society, 1985. pp. 567–645.

Sakya Pandita Kunga Gyeltsen. 1968. *sdom pa gsum gyi rab tu dbye ba*. from Complete Works of the Masters of the Sa.skya Sect of Tibetan Buddhism (Sa skya'i bKa' 'bum) vol. 5. Tokyo: Toho Bunkyo. pp. 297–321.

Saraha. *sku'i mdzod 'chi med rdo rje'i glu (kāyakośāmṛta vajragīti)*. sde dge bstan'gyur, rgyud v. zhi ff. 106b–113a

———. *sku'i mdzod 'chi med rdo rje'i glu (kāyakośāmṛta vajragīti)*. co ne bstan'gyur, rgyud v. zhi ff. 107b–114a

———. *sku'i mdzod 'chi med rdo rje'i glu (kāyakośāmṛta vajragīti)*. Peking bstan'gyur, rgyud v. tsi ff. 78a–85a

———. *sku'i mdzod 'chi med rdo rje'i glu (kāyakośāmṛta vajragīti)*. snar thang bstan'gyur, rgyud v. tsi ff. 87b–96a

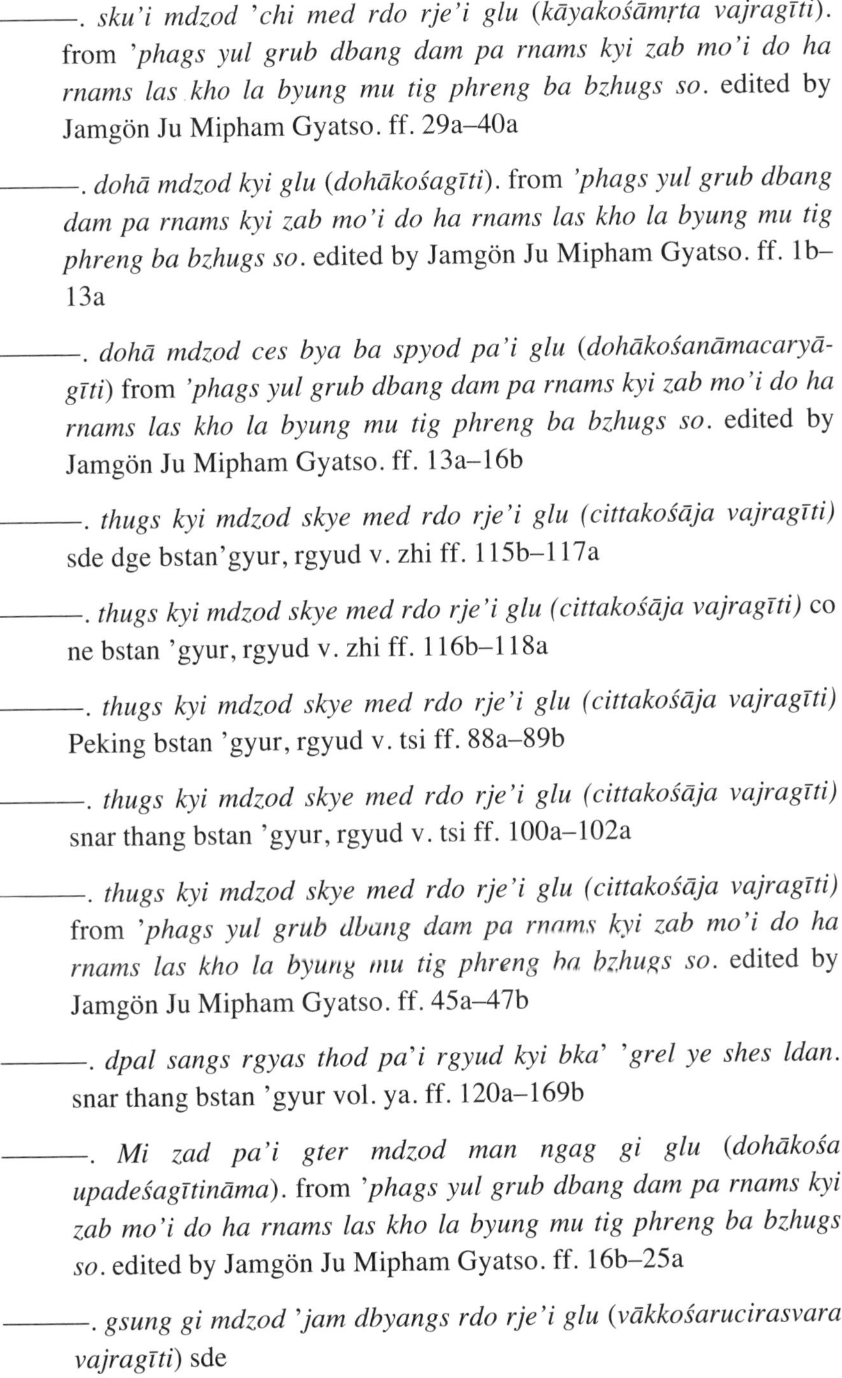

———. *sku'i mdzod 'chi med rdo rje'i glu* (*kāyakośāmṛta vajragīti*). from *'phags yul grub dbang dam pa rnams kyi zab mo'i do ha rnams las kho la byung mu tig phreng ba bzhugs so*. edited by Jamgön Ju Mipham Gyatso. ff. 29a–40a

———. *dohā mdzod kyi glu* (*dohākośagīti*). from *'phags yul grub dbang dam pa rnams kyi zab mo'i do ha rnams las kho la byung mu tig phreng ba bzhugs so*. edited by Jamgön Ju Mipham Gyatso. ff. 1b–13a

———. *dohā mdzod ces bya ba spyod pa'i glu* (*dohākośanāmacaryā-gīti*) from *'phags yul grub dbang dam pa rnams kyi zab mo'i do ha rnams las kho la byung mu tig phreng ba bzhugs so*. edited by Jamgön Ju Mipham Gyatso. ff. 13a–16b

———. *thugs kyi mdzod skye med rdo rje'i glu (cittakośāja vajragīti)* sde dge bstan'gyur, rgyud v. zhi ff. 115b–117a

———. *thugs kyi mdzod skye med rdo rje'i glu (cittakośāja vajragīti)* co ne bstan 'gyur, rgyud v. zhi ff. 116b–118a

———. *thugs kyi mdzod skye med rdo rje'i glu (cittakośāja vajragīti)* Peking bstan 'gyur, rgyud v. tsi ff. 88a–89b

———. *thugs kyi mdzod skye med rdo rje'i glu (cittakośāja vajragīti)* snar thang bstan 'gyur, rgyud v. tsi ff. 100a–102a

———. *thugs kyi mdzod skye med rdo rje'i glu (cittakośāja vajragīti)* from *'phags yul grub dbang dam pa rnams kyi zab mo'i do ha rnams las kho la byung mu tig phreng ba bzhugs so*. edited by Jamgön Ju Mipham Gyatso. ff. 45a–47b

———. *dpal sangs rgyas thod pa'i rgyud kyi bka' 'grel ye shes ldan*. snar thang bstan 'gyur vol. ya. ff. 120a–169b

———. *Mi zad pa'i gter mdzod man ngag gi glu* (*dohākośa upadeśagītināma*). from *'phags yul grub dbang dam pa rnams kyi zab mo'i do ha rnams las kho la byung mu tig phreng ba bzhugs so*. edited by Jamgön Ju Mipham Gyatso. ff. 16b–25a

———. *gsung gi mdzod 'jam dbyangs rdo rje'i glu* (*vākkośarucirasvara vajragīti*) sde dge bstan 'gyur, rgyud v. zhi ff. 113a–115b

———.*gsung gi mdzod 'jam dbyangs rdo rje'i glu* (*vākkośarucirasvara vajragīti*) co-ne

bstan 'gyur, rgyud v. zhi ff. 114a–116b

———. *gsung gi mdzod 'jam dbyangs rdo rje'i glu* (*vākkośarucirasvara vajragīti*) Peking bstan 'gyur, rgyud v. tsi ff. 85a–88a

———. *gsung gi mdzod 'jam dbyangs rdo rje'i glu* (*vākkośarucirasvara vajragīti*) snar thang bstan 'gyur, rgyud v. tsi ff. 96a–99b

———. *gsung gi mdzod 'jam dbyangs rdo rje'i glu* (*vākkośarucirasvara vajragīti*) from *'phags yul grub dbang dam pa rnams kyi zab mo'i do ha rnams las kho la byung mu tig phreng ba bzhugs so*. edited by Jamgön Ju Mipham Gyatso. ff. 40b–45a

Sempa Dorje. Personal interview. 11 February, 2000.

Serdok Panchen Shākya Chokden. *dbu ma'i byung tshul rnam par bshad pa'i gtam yid bzhin lhun po*

Shuchen Tsultrim Rinchen. 1985. *bstan 'gyur dkar chag*. Typeset edition. Xinhua: bod ljongs mi dmangs dpe skrun khang.

Sumpa Yeshe Peljor. 1990. *chos 'byung dpag bsam ljon bzang*. Typeset edition. kan su'u mi rigs dpe skrun khang.

Takpo Tashi Namgyel. 2005. *Phyag chen zla ba'i 'od zer (Nges don phyag rgya chen po'i sgom rim gsal bar byed pa'i legs bshad zla ba 'od zer)*. Sarnath: Vajra Vidya Institute Library.

Taranatha. 1608. *dam pa'i chos rin po che 'phags pa'i yul du ji ltar dir ba'i tshul gsal bar ston pa dgos 'dod kun 'byung*. Chengdu: si khron mi rigs dpe skrun khang, n.d.

———. 1970. *bka babs bdun ldan gyi brgyud pa'i rnam thar ngo mtshar rmad du byung ba rin po che'i lta bu'i rgyan*. Tashijong, H.P.: Sungrab Nyamso Junphel Parkhang. pp. 1–137.

Thuken. 1982. *grub mtha.'* kan su'u mi rigs dpe skrun khang

Non-Tibetan Sources

Apte, V.S. 1998. *Practical Sanskrit-English Dictionary*. Revised and enlarged edition. Kyoto: Rinsen Book Company.

Bagchi, P.C. 1996. "The Cult of the Buddhist Siddhacaryas." In *Studies on the Tantras*. Calcutta: The Ramakrishna Mission Institute of Culture. pp. 101–108.

Bell, Roger T. 1991. *Translation and Translating*. Essex: Longman.

Berzin, Alexander and H. H. the 14th Dalai Lama. 1997. *The Gelug/Kagyu Tradition of Mahamudra*. Ithaca: Snow Lion.

Beyer, Stephan. 1974. *The Buddhist Experience: Sources and Interpretations*. Encino: Dickenson Publishing Company, Inc.

Bhabha, Homi K. 1999. *The Location of Culture*. London: Routledge.

Bhattacharya, Benoytosh. 1996. "Tantrika Culture Among the Buddhists." In *Studies on the Tantras*. Calcutta: The Ramakrishna Mission Institute of Culture. pp. 86–100.

Bhattacharyya, N.N. 1999. *History of the Tantric Religion*. New Delhi: Manohar.

Bhayani, H. C. 1998. *Dohakosagiti of Krnsnapada, Tellopada along with Songs of Vinayasripada, Santipada, and Stray Lyrics and Citations from some Other Siddhas*. Sarnath: Central Institute of Higher Tibetan Studies.

Bhikkhu Bodhi. trans. 2000. "Anapanasamyutta." *Samyutta Nikāya 54*. Boston: Wisdom. pp. 1765–1787.

———. trans. "Khandha Sutta." *Samyutta Nikāya 22.48*. Boston: Wisdom. pp. 886–887.

———. trans. "Khemaka Sutta." *Samyutta Nikāya 22.89*. Boston: Wisdom. pp. 942–ṛ946.

———. trans. "Satipaṭṭhānasamyutta." *Samyutta Nikāya 47*. Boston: Wisdom. pp. 1627–1667.

Braitstein, L. 2008. "Exploring Saraha's Treasury of *Adamantine Songs*," *The Tibet Journal*, vol. 33, no. 1, pp. 40–65.

———. 2011. "The Direct Path: Saraha's *Adamantine Songs* and the Bka' bryud Great Seal." In Matthew Kapstein and Roger R. Jackson ed., *Proceedings of the International Association of Tibetan Studies*. pp. 55–88.

Boord, Martin J. and Losang Norbu Tsonawa. trans. 1996. *Overview of Buddhist Tantra*. Dharamsala: Library of Tibetan Works and Archives.

Burma Pitaka Association. trans. 1984. "Mahāsatipaṭṭhānasutta." *Dīgha Nikāya* 22, Rangoon: Burma Pitaka Association. pp. 307–344.

———. trans. 1990. "Mahāhatthipadopamasutta" *Majjhima Nikāya 28,* Delhi: Sri Satguru. pp. 208–220.

Cabezon, Jose Ignacio. 1994. *Buddhism and Language*. Albany: SUNY Press.

———. 1995. "Comparison as a Principle of Knowledge and its Application to the Translation of Buddhist Texts." In *Buddhist Translations: Problems and Perspectives*. New Delhi: Manohar. pp. 59–74

Cabezon, Jose Ignacio and Roger R. Jackson. 1996. "Editor's Introduction." In *Tibetan Literature: Studies in Genre*. Ithaca: Snow Lion Publications. pp. 11–37.

Cēkkiḻār. 1990. [12th century] *St. Sekkizhar's Periya Purāṇam*. trans. T.N. Ramachandran. Thanjavur: Tamil University.

Chakravarti, Shyamalkanti and Sipra Chakravarti. 1999. "The Concept of Siddhacaryas and their Images." In N.N. Bhattacharyya, ed., *Tantric Buddhism*. New Delhi: Manohar. pp. 232–246.

Chandra Das, Sarat. 2004. *Tibetan English Dictionary*. Reprint. New Delhi: Motilal Banarsidass.

Chang, Garma C.C. trans. 1977. *The Hundred Thousand Songs of Milarepa*. Boulder: Shambhala.

Chogyam Trungpa, Nalanda Translation Committee, trans. 1989. *The Rain of Wisdom: The Vajra Songs of the Kagyu Gurus*. Boston: Shambhala.

Cox, Collett. 1992. "Mindfulness and Memory: The Scope of *Smṛti* from early Buddhism to the Sarvastivadin Abhidharma." In Janet Gyatso, ed., *In the Mirror of Memory: Reflections on Mindfulness and Remembrance in Indian and Tibetan Buddhism*. Albany: SUNY Press. pp. 67–108.

Dasgupta, Shashibhusan 1962. *Obscure Religious Cults*. Calcutta: Firma K. L. Mukhopadhyay.

Davidson, Ronald M. 1990. "Appendix: An Introduction to the Standards of Authenticity in Indian Buddhism." In Robert Buswell, ed., *Chinese Buddhist Apocrypha*. Honolulu: University of Hawaii. pp. 291–326.

———. 2002. *Indian Esoteric Buddhism: A Social History of the Tantric Movement*. New York: Columbia University Press.

———. 2002. "Reframing Sahaja: Genre, Representation, Ritual and Lineage," *Journal of Indian Philosophy*, vol. 30, no. 1, pp. 43–81.

———. 2005. *Tibetan Renaissance: Tantric Buddhism in the Rebirth of Tibetan Culture*. New York: Columbia University Press.

De, Bhakti. 1993. "The Language of the Doha and Caryagiti." In *Aspects of Buddhist Sanskrit*. Sarnath: Central Institute of Higher Tibetan Studies. pp. 307–319.

———. 1999. "The Basic Contents of the Siddhacaryas' Sayings from the Tibetan Translation." In N.N. Bhattacharyya, ed., *Tantric Buddhism*. New Delhi: Manohar. pp. 247–256.

Demieville, Paul. 1952. *Le Concile de Lhasa*. Paris: Imprimerie Nationale de France.

Dimock, Edward C., Jr. 1989. *The Place of the Hidden Moon: Erotic Mysticism in the Vaisnava-sahajiya Cult of Bengal*. Chicago: University of Chicago.

Dorje, Rig 'dzin. 2001. *Dangerous Friend: The Teacher-Student Relationship in Vajrayana Buddhism*. Boston: Shambhala.

Dowman, Keith. 2003. *The Flight of the Garuda: The Dzogchen Tradition of Tibetan Buddhism*. Boston: Wisdom.

Duff, Tony. 2007. *The Illuminator Tibetan-English Encyclopedic Dictionary*. Electronic Edition for Macintosh. 5.15 July 1.

Dundes, Alan and Ved Prakash Vatuk. 1974. "Some Characteristic Meters of Hindi Riddle Prosody," *Asian Folklore Studies*, vol. 33, no. 1, pp. 85–153.

Dzogchen Ponlop. 2003. *Wild Awakening: The Heart of Mahamudra and Dzogchen*. Boston: Shambhala.

———."The Four Foundations of Mindfulness." http://nalandabodhi.org/mindfulness.html (accessed 14 February, 2009).

———. *Nithārtha Online Tibetan-English Dictionary (Rangjung Yeshe)*. http://www.nitartha.org/dictionary_search04.html (accessed 21 October, 2009).

Edgerton, Frankin. 2004. *Buddhist Hybrid Sanskrit Grammar and Dictionary*. Reprint. New Delhi: Munshiram Manoharlal.

Eliade, Mircea. 1958. *Yoga: Immortality and Freedom*. New York: Bollingen Foundation.

English, Elizabeth. 2002. *Vajrayogini: Her Visualizations, Rituals, and Forms*. Boston: Wisdom.

Farrow, G.W. and I. Menon, trans. 1992. *The Concealed Essence of the Hevajra Tantra*. Delhi: Motilal Banarsidass.

Fedotoff, Alexander. 1998. "Versification in Old Tibetan Poetry," *The Tibet Journal*, vol. 23, no. 1, pp. 18–24.

Garfield, Jay. 2002. *Empty Words: Buddhist Philosophy and Cross-Cultural Interpretation*. Oxford: Oxford University Press.

———. 1995. *The Fundamental Wisdom of the Middle Way*. Oxford: Oxford University Press.

Gellner, David N. 1992. *Monk, Householder, and Tantric Priest*. Cambridge: Cambridge University Press.

Gold, Jonathan. 2007. *The Dharma's Gatekeepers: Sakya Pandita on Buddhist Scholarship in Tibet*. Albany: SUNY Press.

Gray, David B. 2007. *The Cakrasamvara Tantra: A Study and Annotated Translation*. New York: American Institute of Buddhist Studies.

Guenther, Herbert. 1969. *The Royal Song of Saraha: A Study in the History of Buddhist Thought*. Seattle: University of Washington.

———, trans. 1971. *The Life and Teaching of Nāropā*. Oxford: Oxford University Press.

———. 1972. *Buddhist Philosophy in Theory and Practice*. Baltimore: Penguin.

———. 1976. *The Tantric View of Life*. Boulder: Shambhala.

———. 1993. *Ecstatic Spontaneity: Saraha's* Three Cycles of Doha. Berkeley: Asian Humanities.

Guenther, Herbert V. and Leslie Kawamura, trans. 1975. *Mind in Buddhist Psychology*. Emeryville, CA: Dharma Publishing.

Gupta, Dharmendra Kumar. 1970. *A Critical Study of Dandin and His Works*. Delhi: Meharchand Lachhmandas.

Gyatso, Janet. 1999. "Healing Burns With Fire: The Facilitations of Experience in Tibetan Buddhism," *Journal of the American Academy of Religion*, vol. 67, no. 1, pp. 113–147.

Harrison, Paul. 1996. "A Brief History of the Tibetan bKa' 'gyur." In *Tibetan Literature: Studies in Genre*. Ithaca: Snow Lion Publications. pp. 70–94.

Heehs, Peter. 2003. "Siddhas, Yogis and Others." In *Indian Religions: A Historical Reader of Spiritual Expression and Experience*. New York: New York University. pp. 281–301.

Hookham, S.K. 1992. *The Buddha Within*. Delhi: Sri Satguru.

Hopkins, Jeffrey. 1995. *Emptiness Yoga: The Tibetan Middle Way*. (1987). Ithaca: Snow Lion.

Hudson, D. Dennis. 1989. "Violent and Fanatical Devotion Among the Nāyaṉārs: A Study in the *Periya Purāṇam* of Cekkilar." In *Criminal Gods and Demon Devotees*. Albany: SUNY Press. pp. 373–404.

Jackson, Roger R. 1982. “Sa skya pandita’s Account of the bSam yas Debate: History as Polemic,” *Journal of the International Association of Buddhist Studies*, vol. 5, no. 1, pp. 89–99.

———. 1996. “‘Poetry’ in Tibet: *Glu*, *mGur*, *sNyan ngag* and ‘Songs of Experience.’” In *Tibetan Literature: Studies in Genre*. Ithaca: Snow Lion. pp. 368–392.

———. 2004. *Tantric Treasures: Three Collections of Mystical Verse from Buddhist India*. Oxford: Oxford University Press.

———. 2012. “Saraha’s Queen Dohās.” In *Yoga in Practice*. Princeton: Princeton University Press. pp. 162–84.

Jaini, Padmanabh S. 1992. “Smṛti in the Abhidharma Literature and the Development of Buddhist Accounts of Memory of the Past.” In Janet Gyatso, ed., *In the Mirror of Memory: Reflections on Mindfulness and Remembrance in Indian and Tibetan Buddhism*. Albany: SUNY Press. pp. 47–59.

Jamgon Kongtrul. 1993. *La Nature du Bouddha*. Huy (Belgium): Editions Kunchab.

———. 1996. *Creation and Completion: Essential Points of Tantric Meditation*. Trans. Sarah Harding. Boston: Wisdom.

Jinpa, Thupten and Jas Elsner, trans. 2000. *Songs of Spiritual Experience: Tibetan Buddhist Poems of Insight and Awakening*. Boston: Shambhala.

Kalu Rinpoche. 1999. *Foundations of Tibetan Buddhism*. Ithaca: Snow Lion.

Kane, P.V. 1971. *History of Sanskrit Poetics*. Delhi: Motilal Banarsidass.

Kapstein, Matthew. 1992. “The Amnesic Monarch and the Five Mnemic Men: ‘Memory’ in Great Perfection (Rdzogs-chen) Thought.” In Janet Gyatso, ed., *In the Mirror of Memory: Reflections on Mindfulness and Remembrance in Indian and Tibetan Buddhism*. Albany: SUNY Press. pp. 239–269.

———. 2000. *The Tibetan Assimilation of Buddhism*. Oxford: Oxford University Press.

———. 2001. (2000). "King Kuñji's Banquet." In David Gordon White, ed., *Tantra in Practice*. New Delhi: Motilal Banarsidass.

———. 2003. "Indian Literary Identity in Tibet." In *Literary Cultures in History: Reconstructions from South Asia*. New Delhi: Oxford University Press. pp. 747–802.

Karma Thinley. 1980. *The History of the Sixteen Karmapas of Tibet*. Boulder: Prajna.

Khenchen Konchog Gyaltshen. 2002. *Garland of Mahamudra Practices*. Ithaca: Snow Lion.

Khenchen Thrangu Rinpoche. 1994. *The Uttara Tantra: A Treatise on Buddha Nature: A Commentary on the Uttara Tantra Sastra of Asanga*. Trans. Ken and Katia Holmes. Delhi: Sri Satguru.

———. 2004. *An Ocean of the Ultimate Meaning: Teachings on Mahamudra*. Boston: Shambhala.

———. 2004. "Songs on Yolmo Snow Mountain from the Songs of Milarepa." In Peter Roberts, trans., *Simhananda: The Lion's Roar*. October 2004 <http://www.simhas.org/teaching6.html>.

———. 2006. *A Song for the King: Saraha on Mahamudra Meditation*. Ed. Michele Martin. Boston: Wisdom.

Kragh, Ulrich. 1998. "Culture and Subculture: A Study of the Mahamudra of sGam po pa." M.A. thesis. University of Copenhagen.

Kunga Rinchen. 2002. "Clarifying the Jewel Rosary of the Fivefold Path." In Khenchen Konshog Gyaltsen, trans., *Garland of Mahamudra Practices*. Ithaca: Snow Lion.

Kvaerne, Per. 1986. *An Anthology of Buddhist Tantric Songs*. Bangkok: White Orchid.

Lama Kunga Rinpoche and Brian Cutillo, trans. 1995. *Drinking the Mountain Stream: Songs of Tibet's Beloved Saint, Milarepa*. Boston: Wisdom.

Lhalungpa, Lobsang P., trans. 1993. *Mahamudra: The Quintessence of Mind and Meditation*. Delhi: Motilal Banarsidass.

Lindtner, Christian. 1987. *Nagarjuniana: Studies in the Writings and Philosophy of Nagarjuna*. Delhi: Motilal Banarsidass.

Little, Layne. 2006. *Bowl Full of Sky: Story-making and the Many Lives of the Siddha Bhōgar*. Diss. University of California, Berkeley.

Lokesh Chandra. 2001. *Tibetan Sanskrit Dictionary*. Reprint. New Delhi: Aditya Prakashan.

Lopez, Donald S. Jr. 1996. "Polemical Literature (dGal lan)." In *Tibetan Literature: Studies in Genre*. Ithaca: Snow Lion. pp. 217–228.

Mar pa Chos kyi bLo gros. 1995. *The Life of the Mahasiddha Tilopa*. Trans. Fabrizio Torricelli and Acharya Sangye T. Naga. Dharamsala: Library of Tibetan Works and Archives.

Martin, Dan. 1992. "A Twelfth-century Tibetan Classic of Mahamudra: *The Path of Ultimate Profundity: The Great Seal Instructions of Zhang*," *Journal of the International Association of Buddhist Studies*, vol. 15, no. 2, pp. 243–319.

Mathes, Klaus-Dieter 2006. "Blending the Sutras with the Tantras: The influence of Maitripa and his circle on the formation of *Sutra Mahamudra* in the Kagyu Schools." In R.M. Davidson and C. Wedemeyer, eds., *Tibetan Buddhist Literature and Praxis: Studies in Its Formative Period*. Leiden: Brill. pp. 201–227.

Nagao, Gadjin. 1991. *Mādhyamika and Yogācāra*. Trans. Leslie Kawamura. Albany: SUNY Press.

Nakamura, Hajime. 1989. *Indian Buddhism: A Survey with Bibliographical Notes*. Delhi: Motilal Banarsidass.

Namkhai Norbu. 1987. *The Crystal and the Way of Light*. Ed. John Shane. New York: Routledge & Kegan Paul.

Napper, Elizabeth. 1989. *Dependent-Arising and Emptiness: A Tibetan Buddhist Interpretation of Mādhyamika Philosophy Emphasizing the Compatibility of Emptiness and Conventional Phenomena*. Boston: Wisdom.

Negi, J.S. 2000. *Tibetan-Sanskrit Dictionary (bod skad dang legs sbyar gyi tshig mdzod chenmo)*. Vol. 6. Sarnath: Central Institute of Higher Tibetan Studies.

Niranjana, Tejaswini. 1992. *Siting Translation: History, Post-Structuralism, and the Colonial Context*. Berkeley: University of California Press.

Novetzke, Christian Lee. 2007. "*Bhakti* and Its Public," *International Journal of Hindu Studies*, vol. 11, no. 3, pp. 255–272.

Nyanaponika Thera. 1992. "The Omission of Memory in the Theravadin List of Dhammas: On the Nature of Sanna." In Janet Gyatso, ed., *In the Mirror of Memory: Reflections on Mindfulness and Remembrance in Indian and Tibetan Buddhism*. Albany: SUNY Press. pp. 61–65.

Nydahl, Ole. 1990. *Ngondro: The Four Foundational Practices of Tibetan Buddhism*. Grass Valley: Blue Dolphin.

———. 1991. *Mahamudra: Boundless Joy and Freedom*. Grass Valley: Blue Dolphin.

Pellegrini, Andrés Montano. *The Tibetan to English Translation Tool*. version 3.3.0. http://www.thlib.org/reference/dictionaries/tibetan-dictionary/translate.php (accessed 21 October, 2009).

Pollock, Sheldon. 2006. *The Language of the Gods in the World of Men: Sanskrit, Culture, and Power in Premodern India*. Berkeley: University of California.

Quintman, Andrew. 2013. *The Yogin and the Madman: Reading the Biographical Corpus of Tibet's Great Saint Milarepa*. New York: Columbia University Press.

Ray, Reginald. 1994. *Buddhist Saints in India*. Oxford: Oxford University Press.

———. 2001. *Secret of the Vajra World: The Tantric Buddhism of Tibet*. Boston: Shambhala.

Rigdzin, Tsepak. 1986. *Tibetan English Dictionary of Buddhist Terminology*. Dharamsala: Library of Tibetan Works and Archives.

Roerich, George N. 1988. trans. *The Blue Annals*. Delhi: Motilal Banarsidass.

Robinson, James, trans. 1979. *Buddha's Lions: The Lives of the Eighty-Four Siddhas*. Berleley: Dharma.

———. 1996. "The Lives of Indian Buddhist Saints: Biography, Hagiography and Myth." In *Tibetan Literature: Studies in Genre*. Ithaca: Snow Lion. pp. 57–69.

Sakya Pandita Kunga Gyaltshen. 2002. *A Clear Differentiation of the Three Codes*. Trans. Jared Douglas Rhoton. Albany: SUNY Press.

Samuel, Geoffrey. 1993. *Civilized Shamans: Buddhism in Tibetan Societies*. Washington DC: Smithsonian Institution.

Sankrtyayan, Rahul. 1984. *Selected Essays of Rahul Sankrityayan*. New Delhi: People's Publishing House.

Sarkar, Rebati Mohan. 1990. *Bauls of Bengal*. New Delhi: Gian Publishing House.

Schaeffer, Kurtis Rice. 2000. *Tales of the Great Brahmin: Creative Traditions of the Buddhist Poet-Saint Saraha*. Diss. Harvard University.

———. 2005. *Dreaming the Great Brahmin: Tibetan Traditions of the Buddhist Poet-Saint Saraha*. London: Oxford University Press.

Shākya Chokden. 2000. *Three Texts on Madhyamaka*. Trans. Komarovski Iaroslav. Dharamsala: Library of Tibetan Works and Archives.

Shahidullah, M. 1928. *Les Chants Mystiques de Kanha et de Saraha*. Paris: Adrien-Maisonneuve.

Shamarpa (H.H. 14th), Mipham Chokyi Lodro Rinpoche. 1997. "View, Meditation and Conduct," *Buddhism Today*, vol 3.

Shaw, Miranda. 1994. *Passionate Enlightenment: Women in Tantric Buddhism*. Princeton: Princeton University Press.

Simmer-Brown, Judith. 2001. *Dakini's Warm Breath*. Boulder: Shambhala Publications.

Smith, E. Gene. 2001. "Golden Rosaries of the Bka' brgyud Schools." In *Among Tibetan Texts*. Boston: Wisdom. pp. 39–51.

———. 2001. "Padma dkar pa and His History of Buddhism." In *Among Tibetan Texts*. Boston: Wisdom. pp. 81–86.

Snellgrove, D.L. 1987. *Indo-Tibetan Buddhism: Indian Buddhists and their Tibetan Successors*. Volume Two. Boston: Shambhala.

Sobisch, Jan-Ulrich. 2002. *Three-vow Theories in Tibetan Buddhism: A Comparative Study of Major Traditions from the Twelfth Through Nineteenth Centuries*. Wiesbaden: Ludwig Reichert Verlag.

Soma Thera, trans. "Satipaṭṭhānasutta." *Majjhima Nikāya* 10, www.accesstoinsight.org/lib/authors/soma/wayof.html#discourse (accessed 14 February 2009).

Spivak, Gayatri. 2000. "The Politics of Translation." In *Translation Studies Reader*. London: Routledge. pp. 397–416.

Stein, R. A. 1971. "Illumination subite ou saisie simultanee: Note sur la terminologie chinoise et tibetaine," *Revue de l'Histoire des Religions*, vol. 179, pp. 3–30.

Sujata, Victoria. 2005. *Tibetan Songs of Realization: Echoes from a Seventeenth-Century Scholar and Siddha in Amdo*. Leiden: Brill.

Takpo Tashi Namgyal. 1993. *Mahamudra: The Quintessence of Mind and Meditation*. Trans. Lobsang P. Lhalungpa. Delhi: Motilal Banarsidass.

Taranatha. 1983. *The Seven Instruction Lineages*. Trans. David Templeman. Dharamsala: Library of Tibetan Works and Archives.

———. 1997. *History of Buddhism in India*. Trans. Lama Chimpa, Alaka Chattopadyaya. Delhi: Motilal Banarsidass.

Templeman, David. 1994. "Dohā, Vajragīti and Caryā Songs." In *Tantra and Popular Religion in Tibet*. New Delhi: Aditya Prakashan.

Thanissaro Bhikkhu. trans. "Mahāpuññāma Sutta" *Majjhima Nikāya 109,* http://www.accesstoinsight.org/tipitaka/mn/mn.109.than.html (accessed 17 October 2009).

Thurman, Robert A.F., trans. 2010. *Brilliant Illumination of the Lamp of the Five Stages (Rim lnga rab tu gsal ba'i sgron me): Practical Instruction in the King of Tantras, The Glorious Esoteric Community*. By Tsong Khapa Losang Drakpa. Introduction and translation by Robert A.F. Thurman. Edited by Thomas F. Yarnall. New York: The American Institute of Buddhist Studies; Columbia University Center for Buddhist Studies; Tibet House US.

Torricelli, Fabrizio. 1997. "Tanjur Text of Tilopa's Dohakosa," *The Tibet Journal*, vol. 22, no. 1, pp. 35–57.

Traleg Kyabgon Rinpoche. 2007. *The Practice of Lojong: Cultivating Compassion Through Training the Mind*. Boston: Shambhala.

Tsang Nyon Heruka. 1995. *The Life of Marpa the Translator*. Trans. Nalanda Translation Committee. (1982). Boston: Shambhala.

Tsele Natsok Rangdrol. 1989. *Lamp of Mahamudra*. Trans. Erik Pema Kunsang. Boston: Shambhala.

Tucci, Giuseppe. 1958. *Minor Buddhist Texts* II. Roma: Instituto Italiano peril Medio ed Estremo Oriente.

Tulku Urgyen Rinpoche. 1995. *Rainbow Painting*. Trans. Erik Pema Kunsang. Boudhanath: Rangjung Yeshe Publications.

Vamadeva, Chandraleka. 1995. *The Concept of* vannanpu "*violent love*" *in Tamil Saivism, with Special Reference to the Periya Purāṇam*. Dissertation, Uppsala University.

van der Kuijp, Leonard. 1996. "Tibetan Historiography." In *Tibetan Literature: Studies in Genre*. Ithaca: Snow Lion. pp. 39–56.

———. 1996. "Tibetan Belles-Lettres: The Influence of Dandin and Ksemendra." In *Tibetan Literature: Studies in Genre*. Ithaca: Snow Lion. pp. 393–410.

Vaudeville, Charlotte. 1974. *Kabir*. London: Oxford University Press.

Waldron, William S. 2003. *The Buddhist Unconscious: The Ālaya-vijñāna in the Context of Indian Buddhist Thought*. London: Routledge Curzon.

Wang-ch'ug Dor-je, Karmapa. 1995. *The Mahamudra: Eliminating the Darkness of Ignorance*. Trans. Alexander Berzin. Dharamsala: Library of Tibetan Works and Archives.

Warder, A. K. 1983. *Indian Kavya Literature*. Volume 4. Delhi: Motilal Banarsidass.

Wayman, Alex, trans. 1977. *Yoga of the Guhyasamājatantra: The Arcane Lore of Forty Verses*. Delhi: Motilal Banarsidass.

———. 1998. *Introduction to the Buddhist Tantric Systems*. Delhi: Motilal Banarsidass.

Wedemeyer, Christian. 2012. *Making Sense of Tantric Buddhism: History, Semiology, and Transgression in the Indian Traditions*. New York: Columbia University Press.

White, D.G. 1996. *The Alchemical Body* Chicago: University of Chicago.

———. 2002. "Le Monde dans le Corps du Siddha: Microcosmologie dans les traditions medievales indiennes." In *Image du Corps dans le Monde Hindou*. Paris: CNRS Editions. pp. 189–212.

———. 2003. *Kiss of the Yogini: "Tantric Sex" in its South Asian Contexts*. Chicago, University of Chicago.

Willis, Janice D. 1995. *Enlightened Beings: Life Stories from the Ganden Oral Tradition*. Boston: Wisdom.

Winternitz, M. 1991. *A History of Indian Literature*. 1933. Trans. S. Ketkar and H. Kohn. 2 volumes. New Delhi: Munshiram Manoharla.

Zwelebil, Kamil V. 1996. *The Siddha Quest for Immortality*. Oxford: Mandrake of Oxford.

Indexes

Cited Personal Names (Sanskrit and Tibetan)

Cited Texts (Sanskrit and Tibetan)

General Index

A

B

C

Ḍ

E

F

G

W

Y